ADVANCE PRAISE FOR

Curriculum Intertext

"Playing at the edges of disciplinary and textual boundaries, Erika Hasebe-Ludt and Wanda Hurren conjoin as well as juxtapose contributors' prose, poetry, visual art, and photography. They thus conjure alchemic spaces where language, pedagogy, and place connect the textures of lived experience and reveal the intersubjectivity inherent in curriculum theorizing, researching, and teaching. *Curriculum Intertext* invokes readers to be aware of their participation in these constructions of meaning. The promise of this timely book is that such awareness might enable us to decalcify solidified spaces between, across, and within the interstices of curriculum as well as social and cultural difference."

Janet L. Miller, Professor, Teachers College, Columbia University

"This book is an extremely important curriculum text and intertext that celebrates Canadian curriculum scholarship with the rich scholarly and artistic discourse of living pedagogy or currere. It is an amazing interpretation and interrogation of a third space, a hybrid space, and a diasporic space of tension between and midst representational and nonrepresentational interplays of performances as intertexts. The contributors lean into Aokian slopes of metonymic writing that evokes a messy text, a middle space of curriculum, the place for a slash, and the persistence of in/stability. It is a text and intertext destined to become a rich resource for curriculum scholars and educators grappling with translating the spaces between curriculum-as-plan and curriculum-as-lived. *Curriculum Intertext: Place/Language/ Pedagogy* exemplifies the foundations and non-foundations of Aoki's living pedagogy and is a 'must read' for those interested in experiencing interplays of knowing seldom found in traditional curriculum texts. It is a remarkable book that will undoubtedly make a significant contribution to curriculum scholarship not only in Canada, but internationally. Curriculum scholarship in Canada is an exciting place/language/pedagogy!"

Rita L. Irwin, Professor and Head, Department of Curriculum Studies, Faculty of Education, University of British Columbia; President, Canadian Association of Curriculum Studies (CACS)

Curriculum

Intertext

Studies in the
Postmodern Theory of Education

Joe L. Kincheloe and Shirley R. Steinberg
General Editors

Vol. 193

PETER LANG
New York • Washington, D.C./Baltimore • Bern
Frankfurt am Main • Berlin • Brussels • Vienna • Oxford

Curriculum
Intertext

Place/Language/Pedagogy

EDITED BY
Erika Hasebe-Ludt and Wanda Hurren

PETER LANG
New York • Washington, D.C./Baltimore • Bern
Frankfurt am Main • Berlin • Brussels • Vienna • Oxford

Library of Congress Cataloging-in-Publication Data

Curriculum intertext: place, language, pedagogy /
edited by Erika Hasebe-Ludt and Wanda Hurren.
p. cm. — (Counterpoints; vol. 193)
Includes bibliographical references.
1. Curriculum planning—Philosophy. 2. Postmodernism and education.
I. Hasebe-Ludt, Erika. II. Hurren, Wanda.
III. Counterpoints (New York, N.Y.); vol. 193.
LB2806.15 .C854   375'.001—dc21   00-067155
ISBN 0-8204-5509-1
ISSN 1058-1634

Die Deutsche Bibliothek-CIP-Einheitsaufnahme

Curriculum intertext: place/language/pedagogy /
ed. by: Erika Hasebe-Ludt and Wanda Hurren.
−New York; Washington, D.C./Baltimore; Bern;
Frankfurt am Main; Berlin; Brussels; Vienna; Oxford: Lang.
(Counterpoints; Vol. 193)
ISBN 0-8204-5509-1

Cover photo by Wanda Hurren
Photo of Erika Hasebe-Ludt by Constance Blomgren
Photo of Wanda Hurren by Don Hall
Cover design by Lisa Barfield

The paper in this book meets the guidelines for permanence and durability
of the Committee on Production Guidelines for Book Longevity
of the Council of Library Resources.

© 2003 Peter Lang Publishing, Inc., New York
275 Seventh Avenue, 28th Floor, New York, NY 10001
www.peterlangusa.com

Printed in the United States of America

Walking in the Cypress Hills: A Poem Found
(With Thanks to Al Purdy)

remember the names
blueberry bagels and autumn blend coffee
lodgepole pines
Swift Current, Maple Creek, Medicine Hat
Gran Wiña Sol wine with Chicken Lickin' entrée
prairie wool (rough fescue) and bluebunch fescue
oat grass, blue gama grass
scrubby cinquefoil, prairie crocus, morning shooting star
prairie cornflower…gaillardia
Bald Butte, Sunburst Lodge, Deer Hollow
trembling aspens
Loch Lomond and Loch Leven
Flicker Trail; Fort Walsh; West Block
evening embers, deer trail, sacred site
not touched by glaciers
Plains Indian tribes
endless prairie
oasis
legends and stories that have become part of the hills
crazy weather, winter chinooks
Warlodge Coulee and Battle Creek
Cree, Blackfoot, Assiniboine, Nakota
Alberta wild rose, prairie lily, prairie crocus
interprovincial park
Saskatchewan and Alberta
meadowlark, ruffed grouse, whitetailed deer, beaver
Whitemud Valley, Ravenscrag
bedrock and cobblestone formations deposited 50 million years ago
Calgary, Saskatoon, Regina
Great Falls, Montana
moose, elk, mule deer, antelope
white spuce, unique orchid species
fox, coyote, porcupine, racoon, bobcat, squirrel
willow groves, meadows, marshlands
ranchlands, valleys and coulees
730 plant species
American wolfers
Gap Road, Cypress Park Café
Magpies
Beaver Creek Ranger Station
remember the names

❱ Table of Contents

❱ Figures

❯ Acknowledgments

All poems and other excerpts that appear in this collection without a source citation are the work of the authors and are printed with their permission. As well, permission was granted for including images and artistic work and lines from poems and passages from the following:

"Anthem," by Leonard Cohen, from *Stranger Music*. Toronto, ON: McClelland & Stewart, 1993. Reprinted by permission of the publisher.

Ted Aoki's handwriting and June Aoki's calligraphy, from the back cover of the *Journal of Curriculum Theorizing, Vol. 11*, No. 4, 1995. Reprinted by permission of the publisher.

Painting by Gerhard Richter, *Wiesental* (1985) reproduced by permission of the artist and The Museum of Modern Art, New York.

Painting by Gerhard Richter, *Mediation* (1986) reproduced by permission of the artist and Musée des Beaux Arts de Montreal/The Montreal Museum of Fine Arts. © Gerhard Richter.

The poems "With Apologies," "Teaching and Learning and Living on the Edge of Pink," "Living a Landscape of Geometrical Progression," and "Statements of Place," by Wanda Hurren, from *Line Dancing: An Atlas of Geography Curriculum and Poetic Possibilities*. New York: Peter Lang, 2000. Reprinted by permission of the publisher.

The poems "My Mother's House" and "Croquet," by Carl Leggo, from *View from my Mother's House*. St. John's, Newfoundland: Killick Press, 1999. Reprinted by permission of the publisher.

The poem "Daisy Griffin," by Carl Leggo, from *Growing Up Perpendicular on the Side of a Hill*. St. John's, Newfoundland: Killick Press, 1994. Reprinted by permission of the publisher.

Poem by Antonio Machada, from W. I. Thompson, *GAIA: A Way of Knowing—Political Implications of the New Biology*, 1987. Hudson, NY: Lindisfarne. Reprinted by permission of the publisher.

Poetry by Renee Norman: "Curriculum as Dream," *Educational Insights, Vol. 3,* No. 1, 1995. "Searching," *Our Schools/Our Selves, Vol. 11*, No. 1, 2001. "A Poet's Symphony," *English Quarterly, Vol. 33*, No. 1&2, 2001. "Mask" has been reprinted, with permission, from *Canadian Woman Studies/Les cahiers de la femme*. It first appeared in the Fall 1997 issue, *Women of Ireland* (*Vol. 17*, No. 3).

Walking in the Cypress Hills: A Poem Found was inspired by Al Purdy's poem "Say the Names," from *Beyond Remembering: The Collected Poems of Al Purdy*. Madeira Park, BC: Harbour Publishing, 2000.

In addition to the contributors, many people in many places helped to bring together the various texts in this book. We extend our sincere thanks to all of them for their encouragement, enthusiasm, and energy. In particular, thank you to Michelle Bertie-Holthe, Carillon Cameron, Paul Dawson, and Kath Remmie at the University of Lethbridge; to Linda Taylor and Chris Taylor at the University of Regina; to Nobuko Nitsu at Hokkai-Gakuen University, and to Gerhard (Gordon) Ludt of Oshino, Japan/Vancouver, BC. We gratefully acknowledge the financial and technical support received from the Faculties of Education at the University of Lethbridge and the University of Regina. To our families, and friends, thank you for your patience and love.

❭ Preface: Some Thoughts on Living In-Between

David Geoffrey Smith

Readers of this book will find themselves engaged by a wide variety of interesting topics, themes, styles of writing, literary genres, and pieces of visual art—all in some ways connected to *curriculum*, once described by Ted Aoki, the inspirational mentor to most of the contributors here, as a "weasel word" that defies easy understanding. This collection of essays well represents, I think, much of the key emergent thinking with respect to curriculum. The studies of narrative, autobiography, place, race, generativity, story, possibility, cultural studies, contingency, pedagogy, and writing, etc., all help us to get a deeper sense of the complex interfaces that are at work whenever curriculum is deliberated and enacted.

The title of the book, however, tells us of the particular way these themes are taken up and held together in a collection. "Intertext" reminds us that between the formal texts of curriculum is another kind of life, the life that mediates, announces, repudiates, or cajoles curriculum formalities. This is the life that lies "in-between" explicit annunciations, and in terms of potential for shaping future directions and alternatives to what is presently at hand, it may be, by far, the more important influence.

Anyone who has had the good fortune of falling under the pedagogical spell of Ted Aoki (and I include myself) knows that Ted was (is) the master of in-between. "Neither this nor that, but this *and* that" is a statement that we not only heard but also witnessed in action. It accounts for the amazing sense of inclusiveness that pervaded all of Ted's classes, the feeling that even though we were all different, with different backgrounds, stories, and experiences, somehow we all belonged together. It is binaries ("this *or* that") that divide us, that force us to choose, to discriminate, that set up the social architecture for categories of insider/outsider, that establish the conditions of conflict over race, class, gender, childhood, and so on, and this was not Ted's way. In a sense, his was the place of no-place, and so his classes were a haven for the dispossessed, the homeless, the bruised, the sufferers of exclusion, and really that includes us all, and that is the point. Dominant culture disallows what it cannot allow, so most of the time, most of us become masterful at hiding our feelings of inadequacy, insecurity, fear, and paranoia. Ted's pedagogical genius was (is) to construct a place safe enough for each of us to explore this Other side of ourselves.

Of course, there were and are difficulties. Living in-between can be exasperating, both for oneself and others, especially in a task-oriented, performance-driven culture like ours. Also, in-betweeness can easily be mistaken for a refusal to assume responsibility for hard decisions, an excuse for avoiding those forks in the road that are part of any person's journey to human maturity. In Ted's case, what was at work was something much more profound. In-betweeness was the deep ethical ground out of which it could be possible to negotiate a conversation between factions, between persons, between traditions. This is the hermeneutic space, the special terrain of Hermes, that allows people to face each other from within their own boundary positions but also across a terrain that seems hospitable to both because of its friendliness and generosity. Most important is the hermeneutic gift of making different sides feel that they may be, at the very least, possibly understandable to each other, not lost in meaningless chaos or a hostile cosmic randomness.

"In-between" is a relational term, and as such it must always have a specific address. That is, in-between cannot be simply another discrete space, one more place hiding behind a mask of identity. In-betweeness always *assumes* an Other, or Others, and such others are always specific and particular in nature, never generic. Ted Aoki lived (lives) specifically between his Japanese origins and his Canadian culture. Each of us can, indeed must, learn to identify the specific Others that define the specific tensions in the middle of which we claim to be living a life, otherwise the result is solipsism, narcissism. This is a cultural and political issue as well as a personal one.

Indeed, an important question for us as teachers today might well be, what specifically are we in-between and in what ways? During the Cold War, the whole world was held in the tension between two competing totalistic ideologies. This condition had strong implications for curriculum and pedagogy. Science curriculum was linked to the race between East and West for the superior technology necessary for military and political superiority. Pedagogical theory in the West gave privilege to the development of autonomous persons with a strong sense of Self, while the Other binary sought loyalty to the collective and the State.

With the Cold War largely dissipated, what and where are the new sources of tension? As teachers and researchers, what specifically are we living in-between? "September 11th" tells us that if the Cold War binary is over, the West, or Euro-American tradition, should not now assume sole authority with respect to defining what is the best "way of life" for all people. Others will have their say too. In fact I would say that the greatest danger of our time lies precisely in the capacity, desire even, to forget the truth of in-betweeness. If Self implies Other, then the "I" that I claim for myself lives in a condition of perpetual non-resolution and incompletion, requiring as a condition of its existence ongoing acts of engagement, conversation, and negotiation with Others whose very identity, too, depends upon "me" for survival. "You" and "I" are the terrains out of which "we" work and shape our shared existence. Such an understanding is, I believe, the necessary foundation for any viable ethics in the new millennium.

Of course at times it all seems so impossible, so difficult. "Are we there yet?" is a question coming not just from the back seat of childhood. It seems to speak most profoundly of our human yearning for a place that we might secure forever and call home. Most of the time it seems just out of reach, just around the corner, a kind of invitation to find our deepest human dignity not in security, but in openness and in generosity, indeed, in-between, in the *now* time between past and future, and in *this* place, which often seems neither here nor there, but which can only be the real place for now.

Curriculum Intertext: Place/Language/Pedagogy. I applaud Erika Hasebe-Ludt and Wanda Hurren for their vision and courage in assembling such a fine collection of papers around such an important theme. It seems prophetic.

David Geoffrey Smith
International Forum on Education and Society
University of Alberta

❯ Invitation to the Intertext

Wanda Hurren and Erika Hasebe-Ludt

It becomes ruthlessly apparent that unless we are able to speak and write in many different voices, using a variety of styles and forms, allowing the work to change and be changed by specific settings, there is no way to converse across borders, to speak to and with diverse communities.
—bell hooks, *Remembered rapture: The writer at work*

It all began with an invitation…

"We invite you to contribute to a new curriculum anthology that aims at addressing the needs of graduate students and instructors of curriculum courses to gain a better understanding of current thinking and research regarding place, language, and pedagogy, and that encourages each of us to venture across and between and into new lines and spaces of curriculum theory, praxis, and research…"

Our idea of initiating this anthology of curriculum intertext originated in places of mutual geographical and philosophical scholarship and in our concerns with teaching curriculum courses at our respective academic institutions. It also found its fertile growing spaces in our shared personal connection with, and admiration of, curriculum scholar and elder Ted T. Aoki. As scholars working in two Canadian universities, our curricular stories have intersected in multiple ways through Ted's influence and his dedication to the interspaces where curriculum theory, research, and teaching meet and are continually negotiated.

Important intersections for our joint and individual travels and for our intertextual imaginings were two conferences: the *Curriculum as Narrative/Narrative as Curriculum* conference held at the University of British Columbia in honor of Ted's scholarship, and a recent Annual Meeting of the American Educational Researchers Association (AERA) held in Montreal. We envisioned a collection of stories, poems, and visual text that would interrupt accepted notions of "textbook." A collection that would celebrate the intertextual nature of curriculum theory, research, and praxis, and that would recognize the impossibility of separating place from language from pedagogy in our curricular endeavours.

When we began to voice our dream of such an anthology of curriculum theory, we were struck by the peculiarity and the physicality of places where we theorize—over telephone lines, underground in metro lines, in the air across flight lines, in large metropolis spaces like Vancouver, Montreal, Seattle, Los Angeles, and in open prairie spaces like Lethbridge, Regina, and the borderlands of the Cypress Hills. In our consideration of both the topographical and scholarly spaces for curriculum theory, practice, and research, we had several questions about our curricular stories: If a story can be placed anywhere and the story does not change, is place a determining factor in the outcome of the story? If we theorize curricula at a large AERA conference in Montreal or a small narrative gathering in Vancouver or on the deck of a hotel swimming pool in Santa Ana, California, or by Monroe Lake in Indiana, does the story change? Is specificity of place important? And what about *how* we tell the story, or the words we choose? How might we read/write curricular stories if our curricular places (both physical and philosophical) overlap or intersect or diverge?

Soon after we issued our invitation, we began to hear from people who dwell in spaces of curricular discourse in ways that question and critique in political, poetic, autobiographical, narrative, hermeneutic ways; people who have been influenced by the spaces of curricular discourse/possibility opened up, most of all, by Ted Aoki. Ted's contribution to this anthology is significant. We see him as the embodiment of Heidegger's human bridge, as the dwelling place of be(com)ing, of generating new visions, of locating other wisdoms. We have come to know him as the place of connectedness between different and diverse perspectives and curricular narratives/discourses.

Various intersections of place, language, and pedagogy are evident in this anthology as the contributors address a multitude of curricular spaces: spaces of theory/practice, old/new, life/death, local/global, translation/relation, coming from/going to, remembering/forgetting, home/not home, individual/collective, stillness/movement, and words/worlds. This anthology began as an invitation to curricular scholars to be at home in displacement, to write their dis/location(s), to imagine the possibilities of a curricular discourse that opens onto meadowland spaces and mountain terrain spaces, borderland spaces, and coulee spaces.

Last November, we met in the in-between space of the Cypress Hills, Canada's first interprovincial park, situated in both the Saskatchewan and Alberta landscapes, a few hours east and west from where the two of us live and work. In between hiking the trails, keeping the fire going, cups of coffee, and glasses of wine, we worked on shaping this collection. Our intent as editors was to achieve a graphically mixed composition with respect to the arrangement of the individual pieces, one that expresses its multiple textualities by juxtaposing writing of various lengths, different fonts, spatial arrangements of the print, headings, etc. This juxtaposing, we felt, was best accomplished through the creative form of an anthology—a gathering of stories, ponderings, poems, art, and so on—rather than a conventional textbook format with numbered chapters and unified sections. The result, after months of editorial and formatting work, is the intertext in front of you. We thank the publishers and series editors of *Counterpoints* for accommodating our approach and for honoring the textual strategies employed by the contributors.

We now extend this invitation to the intertext to you, the reader, to join in the questioning and in the imagining—to venture across and between and into new lines and spaces of curriculum theory, praxis, and research.

Wanda Hurren and Erika Hasebe-Ludt
Regina, Saskatchewan, and Lethbridge, Alberta
May 2002

❭ Locating Living Pedagogy in Teacher "Research": Five Metonymic Moments

Ted T. Aoki

For a teacher researcher, an insistent question is, "Where is living pedagogy located?" Such a question invites a Lacanian anecdote.

Jacques Lacan, a noted but controversial scholar and psychoanalyst, regards the situation of the analyst and analysand as a pedagogical situation, a site of teaching/learning. But for him such a site is not merely a topographical site of the doctor's office as clinic, not merely a social site of doctor and patient, but more so a discursive site—a site of the to and fro flow of language and discourse. For Lacan, the discourse of the master doctor and the patient is inadequate; instead, he opts for the to and fro discourse of teaching/learning. For Lacan, listening to "what" is being said requires listening to "where" the "what" is being said. The "what" can be interpreted in terms of the "where." To help understand the where, allow me to journey through five Metonymic moments.

Moment #1: Living Pedagogy Midst Curriculum-as-Plan/ Curriculum-as-Live(d)

As one interested in curriculum and pedagogy, listening to Lacan's anecdote, I recall Leonard Cohen, a Canadian, who in his poem, "The Anthem," repeated the following refrain:

> Ring the bells that still can ring,
> Forget your perfect offering.
> There is a crack, a crack in everything,
> That's how the light gets in. [1]

---

[1] Leonard Cohen. (1993). *Stranger Music*, p. 373. Toronto: McClelland & Stewart.

Enlightenment? Where? In the middle, in the midst of mediation? Heeding Leonard Cohen, I allow the signifier "curriculum" to appear and then allow a graphic mark to crack the word.

curriculum

curriculum-as-plan/curriculum-as-live(d)

IRPs (Integrated Resource Packages)

plannable/unplannable

predictable/unpredictable

(sayable)......(unsayable)

prescriptive/non-prescriptive

In/through this graphic marking, "curriculum" unfolds into the "curriculum-as-plan" that we typically know as the mandated school subject, and into curricula-as-live(d)—experiences of teachers and students—a multiplicity of curricula, as many as there are teachers and students.

Here, I recall stories of thoughtful teachers who speak of their pedagogic struggles in the midst of the plannable and the unplannable, between the predictable and the unpredictable, between the prescriptible and the non-prescriptible. Their pedagogical where?—between the curriculum-as-plan and the live(d) curricula. Sites of living pedagogy?

Moment #2: Indwelling Midst Presence/Absence

Five years ago, Dennis Sumara and Brent Davis, then co-editors of the *Journal of Curriculum Theorizing (jct)*, asked me to ask June, my wife, for a calligraphic work to be used on the cover of a special issue.[2] After perusing the articles, which referred to scholars such as Foucault,

---

[2] Reference is made to *Journal of Curriculum Theorizing, Vol. 11*, No. 4, 1995.

Lyotard, Derrida, Lacan, bell hooks, and so on, we decided on (yu-mu)—presence/absence. Thinking I would be helping the editors, I scribbled a memo:

> Calligraphed on the cover of this issue is (yu-mu)—yu (有) presence/mu (無) absence. Yu-mu as both "presence" and "absence" marks the space of ambivalence in the midst of which humans dwell. As such, Yu-mu is non-essentialist, denying the privileging of either "presence" or "absence," so deeply inscribed in the binarism of Western epistemology. As the groundless ground in traditions of wisdom, the ambiguity textured in yu-mu is understood as a site pregnant with possibilities. (The calligraphic brushwork is that of June Aoki.)

Surprisingly, this appeared on the back cover.

What I have implied but left unsaid is the way discipline-oriented discourses of curriculum plans are grounded in the metaphysics of presence—privileging presence over absence. So valenced, the discourse assumes the presence of reality or truth hidden in the depth below, calling researchers to search and research, successful engagement resulting in findings that provide insights into the essence of reality. To research, then, is to represent the presence of the essence of reality. This is the language of the discourse of representation which in Western modernity has held hegemonic sway.

It is the hegemony of this discourse that Maxine Greene of Columbia University questions in her powerful article, "Postmodernism and the Crisis of Representation."[3] She calls upon us to move to the edgy edges of representational discourse, and, there, open ourselves to discourses beyond.

There, Elvi Whittaker, an anthropologist at the University of British Columbia, questions the "thingifying" of the presence of culture in her noted article, "Culture: Reification Under Siege."[4]

Both Greene and Whittaker are writing at the edges of Modernist representational discourse, questioning the hegemony of the metaphysics of presence.

---

[3] Maxine Greene. (1994). "Postmodernism and the Crisis of Representation." In *English Education*, Vol. 26, No. 4, December, 206–219.

[4] Elvi Whittaker. (1992). "Culture Reification Under Siege." In *Studies in Symbolic Interaction*, *Vol. 13*, 107–117.

Moment #3: Interplay Midst
Representational Discourse/Non-representational Discourse

Geography, Discipline, and Discourse

I now turn to Dr. Derek Gregory, a professor of geography at the University of British Columbia (UBC), Vancouver, Canada. On his move from Cambridge University in England, he brought with him a manuscript ready for the press. It was titled: *The Geographical Imagination*. The story goes that during his first year of teaching at UBC, he became disenchanted with the manuscript and discarded it. Over the next few years, he rewrote the book, now re-titled *Geographical Imaginations*.[5] In the transformation, he noted the multiplicity of imaginations, and most acutely, the absence of "the," the definite article in which is inscribed the claims of finitude, the presence of the finite. In the new title, the definite article is discarded, and in its place are indefinite articles "a...a...a..."—assuming indefiniteness and infinitude.

In the introduction to his book, Derek Gregory says he is now more interested in the discourse of geography than in the discipline of geography.

Here, I recall Trevor Barnes and James Duncan, colleagues of Derek Gregory, who published a book titled *Writing Worlds: Discourse, Text, and Metaphor in the Representation of Landscape*.[6] Such a focus on discourse and language urges me to recall Lacan in his pedagogical discursive space. Allow me a brief excursion into sign theory.

A Brief Excursion into Sign Theory

Let's begin with de Saussure, structural linguist, who provided us with an image of a sign as a relationship between a signifier (S) and a signified (s), between a word and a concept of reality. For de Saussure the signifier (S) has access to the signified (s) because the bar between them is transparent.

$$\text{Sign} = \frac{\text{(S)} = \quad \text{signifier}}{\text{(s)} = \quad \text{signified}} \quad \text{(transparent bar)}$$

---

[5] Derek Gregory. (1994). *Geographical Imaginations*. Oxford: Blackwell.
[6] Trevor J. Barnes and James S. Duncan (Eds.). (1994). *Writing Worlds: Discourse, Text, and Metaphor in the Representation of Landscape*. London: Routledge.

But de Saussure added that such an understanding of relationships is arbitrary.

Next, let's acknowledge Roman Jacobson, a Russian American linguist, who claims that language has two axes—the vertical (metaphoric) and the horizontal (metonymic).

Lacan with his psychoanalytic interest in language, recognizing the arbitrariness of de Saussure's representational verticality, provided us with a horizontal image, in which signifiers (words) are horizontally arranged in a signifying chain:

$$S...S...S...\qquad \text{(signifying chain)}$$
$$\overline{\qquad}\qquad \text{(opaque bar)}$$
$$(s)\qquad \text{(s) is erased/absent}$$

For Lacan, the bar between signifier and signified is opaque, erasing the signified(s).

Thus, for him, signification is enacted in the spaces of differences between signifiers. Meanings are constituted in the inter-textual play midst signifiers. Here, language participates and performs to constitute effects. It is a discursive world of floating discourse, non-representation, with risks of anarchism and relativism. It is suggestive of the floating world of hypertext with its virtual realities.

Here, we must not forget our key question: Where is living pedagogy located?

Midst the Vertical and the Horizontal

I suggest that the site between representational and non-representational discourses is the site of living pedagogy. This is the site that postcolonial literary scholar Homi Bhabha calls the "Third Space" of ambivalent construction:[7] the site that Trinh Minh-ha, a postcolonial feminist, calls "a hybrid place."[8] It is the site that David Jardine, University of Calgary, calls a site of original difficulty, of ambiguity, ambivalence, and uncertainty, but simultaneously a site of general possibilities and

---

[7] See Jonathan Rutherford (1990). "The Third Space." An interview with Homi Bhabba. In J. Rutherford (Ed.), *Identity: Community, Culture, Difference* (pp. 207–221). London: Lawrence and Wishart.

[8] See Judith Mayne. "From a Hybrid Place." An interview with Trinh Minh-ha. In T. Minh-ha, *Framer Framed* (pp. 137-148). New York: Routledge.

hope—a site challenging us to live well.[9] It is a site that David Smith, University of Alberta, writes about, in his book titled *Pedagon*,[10] pedagogy in the site of agon(y). It is the site Derrida speaks of in his recent book, *Aporias*.[11] It is the site in which Marylin Low and Pat Palulis describe in their article, "Teaching as a Messy Text: Metnonymic Moments in Pedagogic Practice."[12] For Bill Doll, it is the site of chaos in which dwell transformative possibilities. As for me, it is a site of Metonymy—metamorphic writing, metonymic writing.

Moment #4: Midst Self/Other

A few years ago, I was immersed in reading *The Malaise of Modernity* by Charles Taylor of McGill University.[13] He boldly claimed that within Western Modernity, the greatest malaise is "individualism." I was pondering about his remarks when Dr. Jan Walls, of Simon Fraser University in Canada, invited me to a luncheon. I told Jan what Charles Taylor said of "individualism." He told me a story.

When over a century ago, Commodore Perry of the U.S.A. "opened up" Japan, the Japanese linguists were puzzled by the notion of a person as an individual—an individual entity, a self unto itself with its own identity. For the Japanese, a person is graphically textured as 人 (hito), the two strokes saying that it takes at least two to make a person, self and other together. The Japanese linguists were puzzled by the notion of the undivided individual.

Moving into the space of interlanguage and intercultural difference, our Third Space, they allowed intertextual play and coined a new word, 個人 (ko-jin), supposedly meaning "individual." Graphically, the 固 in the first character expresses a past that can be isolated and boxable,

---

[9] David Jardine. (1992). "Reflections on Education, Hermeneutics, and Understanding." In W. Pinar and W. Reynolds (Eds.), *Understanding Curriculum as Phenomenological and Deconstructed Text* (pp. 116–127). New York: Teachers College Press.

[10] David G. Smith. (1999). *Pedagon*. New York: Peter Lang.

[11] Jacques Derrida. (1993). *Aporias*. Stanford, CA: Stanford University Press.

[12] Marilyn Low and Pat Palulis. (2000). "Teaching as a Messy Text: Metonymic Moments in Pedagogical Practice." In *Journal of Curriculum Theorizing, Vol. 16*, No. 2, Summer, 79–80.

[13] Charles Taylor. (1991). *The Malaise of Modernity*. Concord, Ontario: House of Anansi Press.

reflecting the isolated self of the individual. But, on the left, they placed 亻 (a radical of 人) and they added 人 (hito), combining to constitute 亻固人 (ko-jin).

To us 亻固人 (ko-jin) looks Japanese but it is not strictly Japanese. There are elements in it of both English and Japanese; indeed, this is a hybrid constituted in the Third Space.

Such an interpretation suggests that absolute translation is an impossibility, that translation is always incomplete and partial, and further that ongoing translation is always ongoing transformation, generating newness in life's movement.

Moment #5: A Double Reading of a Zen Parable

A few years ago, I was invited to teach at McGill University a course titled "Curriculum Foundations." I replied accepting the invitation, providing I could change the title to "Curriculum Foundations Without Foundations." They agreed.

In the course, we included an article titled "Haiku: Metaphor Without Metaphor,"[14] by German philosopher Günter Wohlfart, who interprets Basho's haiku with the help of a well-known Zen parable:

For those who know nothing about Zen, mountains are but mountains, trees are but trees, and people are but people. When one has studied Zen for a short time, one becomes aware of the invalidity and of the transitoriness of all forms, and mountains are no longer mountains, trees are no longer trees, and people are no longer people. For while the ignorant believe in the reality of material things, those who are even partly enlightened can see that they are mere apparitions, that they have no lasting reality, and that they disappear like fleeting clouds. Whereas—as the parable concludes—(he) [sic] who has gained full understanding of Zen knows that mountains are once again mountains, trees are once again trees, and people are once again people.

Midst all this, my son and his wife, both University of Alberta fine arts graduates, invited me to visit the famous art gallery at the foot of the mountain down University Street. They guided me through the chambers of paintings to a special exhibit—an installation of two paintings by

---

[14] Günter Wohlfart. (1997). "Haiku: Metaphor Without Metaphor." A talk presented at Simon Fraser University, Burnaby, British Columbia, Canada.

Gerhard Richter, a postmodern German painter. And there, I faced two paintings on adjacent walls (see Figures 1 and 2).

After a moment of silence, my son asked me, "Why are you positioned in this way when you are looking at the paintings?" I responded intelligently, so I thought. I gazed in concentration at this painting on the left (see Figure 1), then shifted to gazing at the other (see Figure 2), trying to make sense of the paintings. Then, he suggested, "Place yourself in the space between."

So located, I tried doubling: listening to the Zen parable and viewing the paintings simultaneously.

Figure 1: Gerhard Richter, *Wiesental* (1985)

Located in between with my eyes leaning to the left I heard, "For those who know nothing about Zen, mountains are but mountains, trees are but trees, and people are but people." Then, following my eyes leaning to the right, I heard, "For one who has studied Zen for a short while, mountains are no longer mountains, trees are no longer trees, and people are no longer people." So enlightened, one eye to the left and the other eye to the right, I listened: for those who understand Zen, "mountains are once again mountains, trees are once again trees, people are once again people."

Son engaging father in teaching/learning? Locating living gazing? Locating living pedagogy?

Figure 2: Gerhard Richter, *Mediation* (1986)

❱ (In)Different Spaces: Re-imagining Pedagogy in the Academy

Karen Meyer

Journeys have a way of finding our pathways.
Whether sought or circumstantial, each journey shapes how we walk in
the world.

We cannot help but learn by
being
> *some place*
> *at some time.*

Imagination becomes our ally,
connects us with the unknown and the breath of possibility.

Spirit edges us forward,
> *shaping*
> > *shifting*
> > > *shadowing*
> > > > *what is yet to come.*

This writing walks a journey through pedagogy in the academy.
It re-imagines pedagogy in disparate spaces between
belonging/estrangement;
what is said/what remains unsaid;
the orthodox/the untried.
[Co]creating a learning environment *with/in* a community is an inward path.
There are inspiring landscapes to walk. Possibilities run wild.
[Re]creating a learning environment in the academy is an outward path.

There are uneven territories to walk. Obstacles turn out.
It is here at the crossroad, in the space/place between we can transfigure
being in an academic setting.
Re-imagining is imagining again and again.
Here resides possibility.

In writing this journey I visit five places where I describe the
imagined, fictionalize the real, and repose (in) tensions. "**[Foot]notes
From the Edge**" are voices from subtexts that announce the
unsaid—that which remains unspoken in the day to day texts and
practices in the academy. Unspeakable disparities cannot help but shape
our pedagogy.

"Where are the Pink Flamingos? The Power of Tough Grace"
shows traces of a struggle in re-imagining pedagogy and tracks my own
footprints facing inwards and outwards in the soil. In the end, a tough
grace liberates us. We transgress the hardened beaten track.

In "**In the Somewhere Café**" and "The Coming of Kali Energy" I
explore a café metaphor as a place that breathes relevance; a gathering
place for travelers who find synchronous comfort in difference. It is
about the importance of place, community, and home within a learning
environment.

And in "Talk in the Centre That Is Not the Centre" I enter play
with words from a conversation I had with members of our learning
community which we call the Centre. We ask ourselves, how do I live a
life, a modern life, going through an academic institution?[1]

[Foot]notes From the Edge
(of the unsaid; of that which is not text)

Where are the Pink Flamingos? The Power of Tough Grace

My grandmother told me once that when she was troubled,
digging in the dirt resulted in some kind of grounded peace.

---

[1] I imagine many of us within the academy will admit to its indifference. We stare ahead
to the enduring weight of tenure approval or reflect back at a long series of hurdles
which in perspective look like a mirror image that endlessly repeats itself.

"Mother Earth," she promised, "will take care of you." My early memories of my grandmother's garden include rows of plastic flowers stuck in the ground around her house. While this gardening ploy sounds quite unnatural, even for the late 1950s and especially for the long growing season of southern California, it represents the nature of my grandmother. Barbara was a working woman, first employed during World War Two as many women were. After the war ended, she continued to work outside the home for many reasons until her retirement. I think she didn't have time to nurture a living garden but took pleasure in digging in the dirt and planting a medley of colorful plastic, the new material on the scene. And these manufactured inorganic flowers required replacement since the bright California sun bleached them within weeks. The faded remnants filled empty vases inside her house.

If Barbara were alive today and able to care for a garden of her own, I think she would lovingly plant a flock of plastic flamingos about the yard to keep her company while she weeded and mingled with the soil. She would talk to them as I heard her many times talk to a stuffed bear that sat on my grandfather's chair after he died. And midst the flowers, these flamingos—these Pink Angels—would remind her to dig in the dirt, and that Mother Earth would take care of her during her day-to-day struggles of living alone and being out of step with a modern urban world (Barbara was born on a farm in Alberta in 1904).

Barbara had an alchemist's skill for turning a jaded experience into a gem. As a young adult, I often entered her house carrying what I thought to be a devastating dilemma and later closed the door behind me on my way out holding a new perspective and vantage. She was graced with the sensibilities of experience. She was a wise teacher. While my youth has come and gone, my grandmother's pedagogy remains relevant in my life.

As a rookie administrator and director of a student-centered graduate unit I live between tradition and the untried as I seek to recreate a particular kind of learning environment. I believe it should promote the autonomy of students; elicit the preoccupations, passions, and lived experience students bring to the academy; and create a space for the articulation of and scholarly inquiry about these elements in their research and in their writing. The life of the Centre involves graduate students (faculty who teach and supervise Centre students are members of various departments). My priority is co-creating a learning environment with the community such that structures engage our participation and our participation shapes the learning environment. That is, I am not invested in "reproducing ourselves in the academy" by pulling students through overly prescribed programs and agendas. Of course from this position I encounter obstacles. The structure of our unit is unique. A student-centered unit has a different rhythm, a different focus from a traditional one. And more often than not, it appears to be out of step with mainstream organization. But as my grandmother told me many times, obstacles summon a critical stop. And rather than a moment of truth there is a moment of choice that *invites* rethinking and re-imagining if there is to be forward movement.

Specifically, this point about rethinking and re-imagining reminds me of the serious budget cut I received as a new director. It stopped me in my freshly laid tracks. Afterward I labored over how the Centre would continue beyond the curve thrown our way. Fortunately after I had whined to a friend about the situation, she reminded me that I had a severely limited notion of a resource. My friend addressed this point further by saying passionately that she thought universities are supposed to be resources for communities. That is to say, a resource is what a resource does.

As a community, the Centre continued to move forward in different ways both within everyday activities and in newly directed initiatives. For instance, because there was less money available to order food from campus catering (which is expensive and tasteless anyway) for our Tuesday cafés and seminar events, members of the community rolled up their sleeves, so to speak, and spent time cooking together or bringing in amazing specialty dishes from home. For a Thanksgiving potluck meal an international student from Nigeria cooked a turkey dressed in hybridities of garnishes. The point here is that our energy spent on day-to-day activities served to create a climate of collaboration.

From a broader perspective, members of the community wrote letters and arranged meetings with Faculty of Education and university administrators appealing the budget cuts and articulating the distinctive character of our student-centered academic unit. It is here at this stop that individual students began to (re)consider how they want *to be* in an academic environment. As a community, we began to own an appreciation of and advocacy for our greatest resource—ourselves. So in effect, a pathway around and between obstacles was laid in re-imagining pedagogical spaces in the Centre. Specifically, we have organized an informal writing group ("Rough Writers") and a study group ("Decolonizing Conversations") to fill the spaces around/between courses and program requirements as means to further scholarly discourse and our own inquiries. We continue recreating our brown bags, our cafés, our seminar series, and our on-line journal. Such is the inward path where possibilities live and run wild.

At the same time, for me personally and as an administrator, the climate and the politics surrounding the Centre have been difficult. What are the effects of an indifferent climate? There are numerous occasions when I feel like a Sisyphean laborer knowing the unknown—the possibility that one more budget cut or political gust around the corner could bring down the Centre. There isn't much room for difference on the hardened beaten track. With that in mind and having had to dust myself off numerous times, my confidence in my footing sometimes wavers. Like bell hooks, I am haunted by a dream that acts out in a weird tension between belonging (and what that means) and estrangement. For me it relates to the reality of being tenured, promoted, and an administrator while feeling like an impostor in the academy. I realized a few years ago that I wasn't the only one thinking about such a nightmare. A graduate student mentioned the same imposture scenario in a class discussion. And I have since talked in a serious way to colleagues about this counterfeit identification.

My fantasy is to act out this dream as a short skit with a group of colleagues. I believe the improvisation may prove to be healing to those of us who feel estranged, interrupted, ignored, or excluded. I think there could be fruitful discussion after such a performance.

Very briefly, the skit will go something like this. Several people wearing white overalls that have "University Movers" written on the back suddenly enter my office pushing empty clanging dollies with the intent to move me out. One mover tells me the academy has found out that I really don't belong here. I am an impostor. And, he shows me an official form that says so in triplicate. Of course I know nothing beforehand about this intrusion. The movers begin to take my desk, filing cabinets, pictures, and diplomas out of the office.

While this fraudulent fray feels to me like an inside job—my fault—it is really academicism gone wrong. And until now I never knew how to end the skit.

Here it is. In the final moment of the performance I say to the movers in a confident dramatic voice, "Take what you will, but LEAVE THE FLAMINGOS, THEY BELONG TO ME." I imagine the perennial path of my grandmother's footprints in her garden, place my feet in the outlines, and follow. I feel the power of grace. I dance with the Pink Angels across an empty room. [Curtain][2]

In the Somewhere Café

It would not have occurred to me to put my name forward for the position of director of the Centre. A colleague of mine suggested that I would be a good candidate. I wondered why I hadn't thought of that myself. Soon afterward, I gave myself a block of time, lunch away from the university, to dream about a place that I would like to call home in my university. As I sat and watched people in my immediate surroundings I wrote "The Somewhere Café." I read this short piece at the beginning of my presentation to the faculty administration as candidate for the position.

---

[2] Linda Tuhiwai Smith (1999) further points out that postcolonial discussions (part of academic discourse these days) meet with some indigenous resistance for at least two reasons. One is that the term "postcolonial" implies that colonization has "left." Secondly, the "fashion" of postcolonial re-authorizes the privileges of non-indigenous academics, leaving out indigenous peoples, their ways of knowing, and their concerns.

I found a place to think but in the moment drifted into being an observer—a self-marginalized corner-participant. The background emitted soft rock nostalgia which landed me back into fleeting sappy stretches of "been there, done that." The foreground twanged with clanging silverware finding a home. At my peripheries were earshot conversations resonating from cool copper tables set around an open kitchen. Staff in uniform behaved as such. Without speaking, the specialized crew tended to the unoccupied chore at hand, until a slippery hand broke the reticence and a glass dish. From then on these people at work appeared more animated with pairs and trios engaged in whispers of storytelling. The Somewhere Café. Its center stage pantry moved me to imagine a homespun living version. At the center is a kitchen with a 1970s chrome and veneer dinette that holds stirring heart-to-heart chat: chemotherapy, American troops in the Middle East, the British Boxing Board's decision that women are unfit to box because of pre-menstrual tension. These hybrid conversations situate in a place. Such places breathe relevance.

The Coming of Kali Energy

Kali's faded black backpack felt heavier now than ever before, like the way your heart feels after parting from a loved one. Half of the belongings embodied home where from time to time she longed to be. The other half exhibited her most meaningful keepsakes of a living journey. In so many ways this kindred tote that she preferred to keep close to her body portrayed Kali herself. She was a sojourner of sorts who, back in the 1980s and much of the '90s, lived in various immigrant communities and participated in community and popular theater, landing her on three continents. During those experiences, Kali dwelled between theater and disrupted narratives where memories and identities performed in dramas of being Elsewhere and Other. Here today Kali found herself, bag in hand, peering curiously into a room set up as a café, a sort of hybrid place packed with people and looking like a stopover for travelers who like Kali find synchronous comfort in difference. She remained at the open door, straightened the crumpled flyer—lifted off a chock-full bulletin board the day before—and read it again.

Centre for the Study of Curriculum and Instruction Tuesday Café
March 21, 12:30-2:00 Scarfe Building, room 310
The topic is CULTURE. Lunch is provided

As Kali repeated the words she realized that it was the word "culture" that attracted her to an invitation that was barely visible in a sea of notices. Because of that word, her presence in the Centre was not a happenstance, not a fluke. At least that's what it felt like to her at this moment as she longed for some kind of connection to an institution that transmits cutting indifference.

Kali walked in. She guessed that an unusual transformation had taken place in the room. Antique standing lamps and candles lit the seminar room overshadowing the standard fluorescent lights overhead. The room was furnished with office chairs and round tables draped with fabric from somewhere in the Middle East. Wall hangings shrouded two pedestrian white boards, and several Persian rugs covered the classroom carpet. Kali recognized each object in her gaze as somebody's story rather than a prop, more like a ring worn on a widow's left hand than a piece of jewelry in a display case. Her eyes turned toward a long table on one side of the room where a line of people conversed and at the same time loaded their plates from various containers of food that looked to be brought from homes. Background music and earshot conversations blended into an improvisational buzz, noticeable to Kali, still a silent observer.

Obviously, a typical seminar room had been converted into a salon-like veneer of patois and passionate dialogue. In that moment, the image moved Kali to recall a homespun version; friends in her kitchen around an old wooden table holding stirring heart-to-heart debates about local politics in Estonia. Conversations like the ones back home or in community gatherings always situate themselves in a place. Such places, she thought, breathe relevance.[3]

---

[3] Within Deborah Britzman's (1995) poststructural ethnographies, she narrates the stories of experience in learning to teach. In considering the position of graduate students, we can say they learn to research, to interpret literature, to write. Graduate students learn to be academics. As their mentors are we willing to enter the untenured spaces of what unfit to box because of pre-menstrual is not said, what is not written, what is not authorized, what is untried?

To push this point further, within the term "graduate student" there is no hyphen to probe the everyday politics that hide in the spaces between graduate (of the *academy*) and student. In *Working the Hyphens* Michelle Fine takes up the discourse that produces Self-Other within academic research, pointing out that the hyphen "both separates and merges personal identities with our inventions" (1994, p. 70). If we were to work the hyphen between graduate and student, we would begin to articulate the

Talk in the Centre That Is Not the Centre

I am still trying to express what this place is about and the pedagogy

I am still trying to express what this place is about

I am still trying to express

I am still trying

I am

I'm still
trying to express what this
place is about and the pedagogy. It began
by my trying to get a feel for this place and the
people and having many conversations. When I came
I was drawn to certain people, certain experiences, certain
spaces and I started, little by little, to feel like part of this
place. It has been quite amazing that this place has been relevant in terms of my whole life. I cannot see my life anymore
as a separation between the personal, the spiritual, and my
studies. Sometimes you don't realize so deeply what you
are searching for. Usually you have to go some other
place than university for your personal journey.
There's something wrong if it's not in the
place where you spend most
of your time.

How do I live a life, a modern life, going through institutions?

How can I bring my countless needs together and configure them in a story I love?

---

struggles of this in-between position and reveal the non-neutral boundaries and structures of the academy as a learning environment with politics and histories of power. What are the contradictions that proliferate at the frayed edges of the hyphen? What is implicated in our pedagogy? To answer these questions, we need to probe how we are as supervisors in relation to our students. And revisit how and why we teach what we do.

It's a place where characters and plots are somehow reconfiguring to allow us to pass through this complex institution we call a university. In effect we should be solving many of our life problems.

> There has to be a community of people. I have tried so desperately to see myself through all these theories of homelessness and go beyond thinking about the necessity of home.... All kinds of theories try to justify the floating and justify the common global facelessness. I began to think I wasn't telling myself the truth anymore. I was crying for a community, a home, a people I could relate to, especially in a new country.

> It's funny how some people decide what they are going to do for a dissertation. They look through all the literature to find something that hasn't been done and then do that. As if we're building up an accumulation of understanding somewhere out in the ether and somewhere someone's going to get the whole full picture. That's always been to me an absolutely ludicrous thing to do. If it doesn't arise out of your own sense of a need or a particular perspective that you value, I don't see why you should bother wasting your time doing it.

I was drawn here because I can see people working on such challenging projects that are risk taking. It's very bizarre that being true to yourself has become a risk in this society. When you were talking about your project I started crying without being emotional, just some sort of purification moment. I realized here are the people who are taking risks and their projects are relevant to real life goals and so meaningful to everybody's life. How rigorous, how challenging, how difficult these projects are.

> We have to have a place,
> We have to have a community,
> We have to have a home,
> That is what matters.

The Nearness of Place

We have to have a place.
It is the secret wish of a journey.

Nowhere else can you dig in the dirt
and be reminded that Mother Earth will take care of you...
or dream of Pink Angels whose graces can make Elsewhere home...

There is an incompleteness written into these subtexts. In the end, I bring only nearness to a pedagogy of place, of community, of heart that lives deep in the Centre that is not the center. In hindsight, the café metaphor I daydreamed in the Somewhere Café almost three years ago was merely a glimpse, like Kali's first impression as she peered into a room set up as a café. I wrote "The Coming of Kali Energy" as fiction to capture how the community realized so brilliantly a place that breathes relevance. When I walked into our first café, any doubt about the metaphor for our community fell to the floor like a discarded wrap.

The inward path of the journey with inspiring landscapes and the outward path with political territories have both led to a place where we imagine pedagogy again and again. At times I still ache with vulnerability and struggle with my footing. But it is in those moments that I learn the choreography of tough grace. All I know as an administrator is what I have lived as a teacher. I have never once been disenchanted with teaching and learning when the environment is engaging and inspiring. Recently a group of administrators asked me what secret ingredient was responsible for such a strong student community. What an odd question.

... Journeys have a way of finding our place.

Our (re)vision:
The Centre is committed to the inquiry into pedagogy as it is lived with the purpose of deepening understandings and re-imagining curriculum and pedagogical practices. Within spaces and tensions of interdisciplinarity, the Centre is a place where learners can gather to write and interpret new lines of curriculum, lines that communicate, collaborate, and connect.

References

Britzman, D. (1995). The question of belief: Writing poststructural ethnography. *International Journal of Qualitative Studies, 8*(3), 229–238.

Fine, M. (1994). Working the hyphens: Reinventing self and other in qualitative research. In N. K. Denzin and Y. S. Lincoln (Eds.), *Handbook of qualitative research* (pp. 70–82). Thousand Oaks, CA: Sage Publications.

Smith, L. T. (1999). *Decolonizing methodologies: Research and indigenous peoples.* New York: Zed Books.

Generative Interplay of/in Language(s) and Culture(s) Midst Curriculum Spaces

Sannie Yuet-San Tang

Prologue

My experience with translation has mainly been in and through research. As a person who has some fluency in both the Chinese and the English language, I often have the opportunity to do the work of "translation," whether it be translating interview transcripts, or doing ad hoc translation or interpretation in the health care setting for Chinese-speaking patients.

I remember when I was translating transcripts for my master's thesis, I took great pains to convert the Chinese text into English, word by word and sentence by sentence. I also remember that translation was no easy task, especially as the health care and research concepts that I am familiar with are mostly expressed in English. English words that had been natural to me often became "foreign" and unfamiliar when I struggled to clarify their meaning in order to convey them in Chinese. In order to keep the questions as close to their "original meaning" as possible, the questions that I asked of the research participants were "rigid" translations from English into Chinese, rendering the questions too artificial and difficult for the Chinese participants to understand.

Later on, as I gained more experience with translating research transcripts, I found myself less worried about translating the text word by word, but more concerned to grapple with the meaning of what was said, and "regurgitate" the meaning in the Chinese language. Even with this somewhat more flexible approach, the English language was still guiding what questions were asked, how they were asked, and how I made sense of what the participants told me.

What is often rendered non-transparent in the process of translation, however, is the "conversion" that was going on in my head as I translated a text from English into Chinese and vice versa. I now find myself asking questions such as these: What words or vocabularies were available to me? How did I go forward and backward between two meaning systems? How did I match one meaning with another? Could there be equivalent meanings in two cultures, two languages? What might get lost in this process? And what was renewed and generated? More importantly, where was my historical and discursive location as translator? And, what constituting effects might my translation have on the social landscape? As soon as these questions reappear on the surface of translation, the work of translation can no longer be assumed to be neutral or apolitical. Rather, the question of translation challenges us to look at the complexity of language, and to dig into the fascinating and challenging domain of language, thoughts, and culture.

My interest in the notion of translation was re-invoked recently by two persons. First, Dr. Ted Aoki has encouraged me to examine the movement of texts between languages and cultures in the hybrid space of intertextuality. Second, having gone to one of Dr. Mieke Bal's lectures in which she drew heavily on the work of Walter Benjamin, I became intrigued by how Benjamin has interpreted translation, and wanted to read more about it. In the following passage, I try to engage with the texts of a few scholars in order to examine the difficulty of philosophizing the culturalizing act of translation.

Some Philosophical Ponderings on the Question of Translation

> *What is translation?*
> *Where are translation and the*
> *translator located?*

Although the performativity of language is increasingly problematized and interrogated in terms of its effects in shaping the social landscape, translation as its literary "sibling" tends to receive less attention, which often renders the process of translation and its cultural function invisible.

In an important sense, however, translation seems to be at an even higher level of philosophical complexity than language. Translation, which requires traveling back and forth between two languages, is necessarily intertextual and intercultural. Intertextuality, according to Erika Hasebe-Ludt (1999), and following Julia Kristeva,

> implies a multiplicity of meaning present in any text, recognizing that the author's powerful creative act is supplemented by the reader's creative understanding of the text from a socially constructed and already existing worldview...any text is the absorption and transformation of another. (pp. 42–43)

Thus, the translator as reader is in a privileged position to rewrite an original text by rereading it and translating it from a particular linguistic and cultural location. *Translation as transformation* therefore challenges the criterion of "accuracy," one of the master signifiers in the scientific discourse of research, underlying which is the assumption that we are in a better position to make "truth claims" if knowledge construction is based on "accurate" translated materials (e.g., interviews conducted in a minority language).

But Bakhtin would have us see that the intertextual movement within a text and in between texts constantly resists any attempt to "crystallize" a text and reify it from the context in which it is uttered and understood. Distinguishing between language as a system of signs and language as text or utterance, Bakhtin insists that there can be no complete translation. As he tells us,

> Any sign system...can always in principle be deciphered, that is translated into other sign systems (other languages). Consequently, sign systems have a common logic, a potential single language of languages....But the text (as distinct from the language as a system of means) can never be completely translated, for there is no potential single text of texts. (1986, p. 106)

Questions to ask ourselves: In the research situation, are we trying to deal with the translation of signs, or the

translation of "text"?
If we treat translation as some unproblematic exchange of signs between languages, what might be lost or masked in the process?

Specifically, it is not as if the text is written and said once and for all. Rather, the text is constantly lived and re-lived in-between writers and readers in their encounter within the inter-textual space. The text is not a dead system of signs amenable to only "one true" translation. Every reading and rereading of the text by each translator is what Bakhtin might call "a new and unrepeatable event," that which "always develops *on the boundary between two consciousnesses, two subjects*" (Bakhtin, 1986, p. 106). Thus the inter-textuality of translation.

Walter Benjamin (1968) has also offered an interesting interpretation of the notion of translation in his "The Task of the Translator." Specifically, he has cracked open what I see as the metonymic space of translation in-between the original text and the translated text.

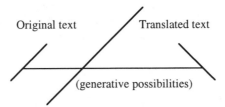

Original text   Translated text

(generative possibilities)

According to Benjamin, the translated text is *not the same thing* as the original text written in another language. By invoking the paradoxical relation between the original and the translation in terms of their likeness/unlikeness, closeness/remoteness, Benjamin emphasizes that the translation is something new, something beyond (both in the sense of its "literalness" and in the sense of its temporal location) what is inscribed in the original text.

The translation as a new-living of the original text in its "afterlife."

A text can only be read and translated *after* the original author has actually spoken through the text.

Metonymy in-between the present (absent) living of text-making and the afterlife re-living in text-translating.

The translated text is not the end but only the beginning of changes. *Translation as transformation.* As Benjamin argues,

> ...[n]o translation would be possible if in its ultimate essence it strove for likeness to the original. For in its afterlife—which could not be called that if it were not a transformation and a renewal of something living—the original undergoes a change. (p. 73)

What is changed in the original is not confined to what is translated. Not only is the original trans*form*ed, the translated is more than the original in the changed *form*.

Change/no change, foreign/home, present/absent, life/afterlife.

Thus, for Benjamin, translation goes far beyond the imparting of information. Information lives in the space of dead languages. But translation is alive. Translation takes place on the boundary of original and "alien" language, midst the echo of "original difficulties" (Jardine, 1992) as expressed in the human voice. In Benjamin's vivid words,

> Unlike the work of literature, translation does not find itself in the center of the language forest but on the outside facing the wooded ridge; it calls into it without entering, aiming at that single spot where the echo is able to give, in its own language, the reverberation of the work in the alien one. (p. 76)

The said and the unsaid. That which can be communicated, and that which is meaning*less* or non-amenable to semantic expression. The translated original, and the non-translated but no longer original.

Let Go

Benjamin (1968) challenges the translator to *let go* of the language of a translation so as to give voice to the intention of the original text. In particular, he emphasizes the significance of "the freedom" of the translator to break through the barrier (read *arrogance*) of his own language in "pure language" (which I understood as an ideology-free language representing *equally* the interest of every human being) a utopia? Could there ever be a pure language "without the mediation of meaning" (p. 82) and power? Benjamin himself seems to be pessimistic about this. He has quoted Pannwitz as saying, "Our translations, even the best ones, proceed from a wrong premise. They want to turn Hindi, Greek, English into German instead of turning German into Hindi, Greek, English" (p. 80).

Thus the inevitable politics of nations, cultures, languages.

Could a translation and the translator ever be free?

The Space of Translation: In-Between Home(s), Diaspora, Culture(s), and Language(s)

If translation cannot be assumed as some apolitical act of purely literary concern, then we must ask the question, where is the translator and his/her translation located midst the changing geo-ideological and cultural boundaries in-between peoples and nations?

Translation as aesthetic production has important "cultural functions" (Schwab, 1994).

Translation takes place in what I would call the "diasporic space" between cultures, or more specifically, between home and new-home or non-home. There is intermediacy between the "home language" and the "foreign language." There is negotiation between the dominant culture and the *Other* culture. There is traveling back and forth between the original text and the translated text, lost in the space of transformation.

But Where Is Ho(ME)?

Toni Morrison (1998), in her essay "Home," challenges us to make the radical distinction between the metaphor of house and the metaphor of home. It is all too easy to obfuscate human(e) presence as material existence. We can live in a house yet feel homeless. We feel the tension of being under shelter but at the same time being confined within the "prison" walls. We yearn to break free, to return to the nostalgic home in our writing and speaking.

But Again, Where Is Ho/me?

It is no longer straightforward for the diasporic person to define or find home. As I read in Fanon's and Schwab's writing, there is "diasporic tension" between cultures and languages midst the dislocation and relocation of self: the "homelessness" of one's identity, when one belongs neither to one group nor to the other, when one is a "mixed-up hybrid kid" (Aoki, 1999, p. 28).

Fanon has provocatively spoken of the diasporic tension felt by the colonized in the country of the colonizer:

> Jean Veneuse is a Negro. Born in the Antilles, he has lived in Bordeaux for years; so he is European. But he is black; so he is a Negro. There is the conflict. He does not understand his own race, and the whites do not understand him. (1967, p. 64)

In a similar vein, but speaking from a very different historical location, Schwab has also spoken of her experience of feeling alienated and homeless. As she tells us,

> No longer completely at home in the German academic world, but still a foreigner (or, as it says so nicely on my Green Card, an "alien resident") in my new academic home at the University of California, I often found myself an ethnographer in two foreign cultures. (1994, p. vii)

But cultures are like a train on a journey of change. Maybe we can never claim to be in a culture; we are always on the border of it, trying to hold it in our hands, like a slippery pig refusing to be caught. Or maybe we are that slippery pig who refuses to be restrained by the hegemonic Culture. Thus we see the importance and possibility of challenging dominant meanings about *Other* cultures through situated translation.

For Schwab, translation entails traveling back and forth "through the cultural space between two continents" (p. vii) and across different historical moments. I see this cultural space of translation as the "diasporic space" in which the translator constantly negotiates his/her identity in the new (ho)me. Could this diasporic space be the home for generative understanding in-between cultures? Or be that "Third Space of enunciation" in which the text can be "translated, rehistoricized and read anew" (Bhabha, 1994, p. 37)?

> Dia/spora, two/spora, two/origins?
> The imaginary of diaspora and the diasporic imagination.

Diaspora implies movement and change. "With a change of location, there is both change and no-change" (Radhakrishnan, 1996, p. xiv). The ambiguity of who one is and is becoming in the midst of displacement and re-location.

Radhakrishnan (1996) has eloquently spoken of the "doubling" inherent in the diasporic experience. As he argues,

> Diasporic subjectivity is thus necessarily double: acknowledging the imperatives of an earlier "elsewhere" in an active and critical relationship with the cultural politics of one's present home.... "Home" then becomes a mode of interpretive in-betweenness, as a form of accountability to more than one location. (pp. xiii–xiv)

So What Might Be the Effects of the Translator as a Diasporic Subject on the Translated Text?

Even when a translator is native to a particular culture and language, acquiring a second language will likely transform the translator who is now engaged in the ambiguous space in-between two languages, two cultures. Fanon reminds us of the power of language, in that "[t]o speak...means above all to assume a culture, to support the weight of a civilization" (pp. 17–18). After all, as Radhakrishnan maintains, "the use of language is no innocent activity" (p. xvii). But it is important to recognize the doubleness in the power of language. Just as language could be used to sustain the hegemonic position of a culture, acquiring a language also means "[possessing] the world expressed and implied by that language" (Fanon, 1967, p. 18), thus allowing the generative possibility of changing that world by manipulating the language in which it is constituted. In this sense, translation, like language, can be used as "intervention" (Chow, 1993) to disrupt colonial appropriation and inequalities in the existing world order.

Re-locating the Translator and the Translated Text
Within the "Third Space" of Intervention
So, can(not) the subaltern speak through the translator in the colonizer's language?

No-Ending: Translating Self by Letting Go

The Way of Life: Lao Tzu

The student learns by daily increment.
The way is gained by daily loss,
Loss upon loss until
At last comes rest.
By letting go, it all gets done;
The world is won by those who let it go!
But when you try and try,
The world is then beyond the winning.

My translation

English/Chinese

Chinese/English

Chinese-Canadian?

Cultured language

Languaging culture

(Who am I?)

Let go

Freedom

Humanity

References

Aoki, T. T. (1999). In the midst of doubled imaginaries: The Pacific community as diversity and as difference. *Interchange, 30*(1), 27–38.

Bakhtin, M. M. (1986). *Speech genres and other late essays* (C. Emerson and M. Holquist, Eds., V. W. McGee, Trans.). Austin: University of Texas Press.

Benjamin, W. (1968). The task of the translator. In *Illuminations* (pp. 69–82). New York: Harcourt, Brace & World.

Bhabha, H. K. (1994). *The location of culture.* London: Routledge.

Chow, R. (1993). *Writing diaspora: Tactics of intervention in contemporary cultural studies.* Bloomington: Indiana University Press

Fanon, F. (1967). *Black skin, white masks.* New York: Grove Press.

Hasebe-Ludt, E. (1999). The whole world in one classroom: Teaching across traditions in a cosmopolitan environment. *Interchange, 30*(1), 39–55.

Jardine, D. W. (1992). Reflections in education, hermeneutics, and ambiguity: Hermeneutics as a restoring of life to its original difficulty. In W. F. Pinar (Ed.), *Understanding curriculum as phenomenological and deconstructed text* (pp. 116–127). New York: Teachers College Press.

Morrison, T. (1998). Home. In W. Lubiano (Ed.), *The house that race built* (pp. 3–12). New York: Vintage Books.

Radhakrishnan, R. (1996). *Diasporic mediations: Between home and location.* Minneapolis: University of Minnesota Press.

Schwab, G. (1994). *Subjects without selves: Transitional texts in modern fiction.* Cambridge, MA: Harvard University Press.

❱ Terra Incognita

Constance Blomgren

Encountering identities…completely different identities…identities that share skin color and little more. My students were 15 and 16 years old; I was 41. I was female; 21 of the 23 students were male; I was female. They did not enjoy reading and many of them struggled with texts written above a Grade Five or Six level; I love reading and have ever since I learned. Writing was an equally undesirable task for them, whereas my love of reading has led to a love of writing. Most of the class members had fair skin, as do I, but some were First Nations students so this point of similarity was not more significant than the presence of the two female students. It seemed that our identities converged only slightly and lightly; sometimes I thought of this class as *Terra Incognita*.

Initially, I began the semester naïvely hopeful, my Celtic genetics flooding over the past difficult learning experiences that had made me a seasoned teacher. Being new to the school, I decided to address my students as the near adults that they were. Greeting them on the first day of class, I introduced myself to each one, extended my hand and used a formal, polite level of English. I asked each student for his or her name, and as awkwardly as the handshake, out tumbled the name. I repeated it, adding that it was a pleasure to meet him or her. Giggling or flushing red or looking with downcast eyes, my Wal-Mart greeter pushed the boundaries—of student self-identity and of his or her conceptions of teacher.

The monolithic adolescent peer culture that dominates media representations of youth did not reflect this class. They were neither urban affluent Californian or struggling Harlem high school students but such constructed images biased my students' perceptions of what high school life should or could encompass.

Instead, we were in the margins, the margins of Canada (rural), the margins of the school (non-academic), the margins of student valued curriculum (English). Once again, I was teaching students from the margins in the margins, a repeated theme in my professional life, like concentric water circles from a cast stone, contrasting with the linear growth model that foolishly misrepresents worldly success.

The clash of identities forced me to reconsider the content of my course, the stories and poems that would be the skeleton of any English class. Outcome based educational models bandied for attention yet I intuitively considered a theme regarding conflict, open conflict and in the aftermath of September 11, 2001, the relevance appealed to my students. A pacifist, I struggled with a focus solely on war, on the overt and intimidating display of power clashes and searched for a balance, for a title and a study that would give the counterpart to war, pain, and suffering. I decided on "Combat and Compassion," a unit that would openly explore the drive for power through physical force with its consequences of destruction, violence, and death. Like many people, in times of emotional stress, variations of violence—yelling, striking out, injuring through words—have formed my authentic and basal responses. Facing our fears, a Jungian response to the dark side of identity, influenced my turning to this exploration of combat and power, of a physical response to real and perceived injustices. The students, like many adolescents, were unsure of combat's power and potency, its ability to lead to heroic acts and simultaneously perpetuate massive destruction. Student curiosity and fascination issued a segue into an exploration of combat and compassion, of characters real and imagined and the expression of their overt and covert identities.

We studied *The War* by Timothy Findley, a short story written from the point of view of a nine year old boy during the Second World War whose father has decided to join the Canadian army. The narrator responds with fear, hides, and eventually throws a stone that knocks out his father. In selecting this story, I did not foresee that nearly every student would closely identify with the narrator, with his fear and irrational reactions. Perhaps Findley's skill as an author had brought them closer to insights offered to careful and sensitive readers, but such descriptors did not fit this group of learners. Rather, Findley's crafting of a fictional boy conjoined with the identity of most of these learners. Not many years away from nine, and with many of the same fears still intact, these students saw themselves in that frightened, confused young narrator.

Conjoining of identity also occurred with the reading of *Billy Bishop Goes to War*. In this play, the Canadian First World War ace recounts his life, beginning with failing at high school and eventually becoming the most decorated pilot in the elite British Air Force. Bishop narrates his life with minor characters moving the plot forward and the students saw themselves in this unlikely hero—a failure at school, someone who enjoyed carousing and eventually the successful underdog. Bishop's description of his suicide run into German territory, early one morning while he still wore his pajamas, emphasized how war makes soldiers temporarily insane, that post-traumatic stress syndrome has its seeds in the obscene violence, in the hell that makes any war. Somehow these students could identify with the possibility of coming face to face with such realities, within the context of a war. Unlike the short story, the play brought students in contact with a possible future identity, grounded in similar experiences to Bishop's poor school performance and in the realities of war currently being initiated and fought on foreign soil.

Discussions of compassion peppered class and written assignments, and brief references to the consequence of combat had students vaguely justifying war. *Universal Soldier* by Buffy Saint Marie broadened our definition of soldier and a newspaper article highlighting a fifteen year old Afghani warlord enlightened student understanding of current sites of combat. A tone of disbelief colored students' answers, most likely because at fifteen their world was safely small. The realities of combat and compassion were subjects to objectify, unlike this young warlord, who through circumstances of birth, had a life much different from that of his Canadian peers.

The unit ended and we turned to *Romeo and Juliet*, examining Bas Luhrmann's film and contrasting it to Zeffirelli's more conventional adaptation. With the exception of the two females, who saw a bit of Juliet in themselves, Mercutio, not Romeo, mirrored the self perceived identities of most of the male students. Hot blooded, hot headed, visceral Mercutio, who acts before thinking, who responds physically to his world, who dies young and tragically in a senseless fight provoked by the arrogant and baiting Tybalt—this mercurial character commanded the students' attention. In Luhrmann's *Venice Beach*, Mercutio played out experience and an identity familiar to many of my students. Despite his skin color and drag queen performance at the Capulet's masquerade party, Mercutio captivated their attention and covertly exposed surfaces of shared identity.

This class, this terra incognita, forced me to consider masculine interests and identities, within my students, the literature studied, and myself. We were, in the words of Adrienne Rich, "split at the root" (1995, p. 640), not into dichotomies as I and they had initially and superficially perceived, with the extremes of identities separating us—young or old, male or female. Instead, we were and are split into multiple identities, paradoxically aware and ignorant; fractured and disjointed we nurture yet starve our various exposed branches.

Fear begins and grows when we forget, ignore, or cut ourselves off from the root of our shared human identity and in this denial we feed the pseudo darkness and remain intimidated by its power. Fear grows, for me and my students, when we are split not just at the root, but from our root. Fear grows in terra incognita.

Figure 3: *Jesse Piotrowski* (October 2001)
Photographed by Constance Blomgren

References

Rich, A. (1995). Split at the root. In P. Lopate (Ed.), *The art of the personal essay* (pp. 639–655). New York: Anchor.

❱ "Behind Every Jewel Are Three Thousand Sweating Horses": Meditations on the Ontology of Mathematics and Mathematics Education

David W. Jardine
Sharon Friesen
Patricia Clifford

Preamble

[What if mathematics, or poetry, or the taxonomies of biology, or any other of the pieces of the world entrusted to us as teachers] no longer has the character of an object that stands over and against us? We are no longer able to approach this like an object of knowledge, grasping, measuring and controlling. Rather than meeting us in our world, it is much more a world into which we ourselves are drawn. [It] possesses its own worldliness and, thus, the centre of its own Being so long as it is not placed into the object-world of producing and marketing. The Being of this thing cannot be accessed by objectively measuring and estimating; rather, the totality of a lived context has entered into and is present in the thing. And we belong to it as well. Our orientation to it is always something like our orientation to an inheritance that this thing belongs to, be it from a stranger's life or from our own.
—Hans-Georg Gadamer, *Heidegger's Ways*

What possible good could come from a meditation on the *ontology* of mathematics and mathematics education?

Our answer to this question is simple to state, even though its practical educational consequences are enormous. Currently, the only discourses available in mathematics education are those of consumption or production. Becoming involved in mathematics, therefore, means becoming either a producer or a consumer. Mathematics, therefore, is something produced or consumed. Either one "makes meaning" of it oneself, or the meaning made by another is imposed "from outside" and simply "swallowed" because of the "authority" (which always means "power") of the maker.

Or, we "socially construct." That is, we are *all* producers and consumers of knowledge, and the whole known world is at the formative disposal of our knowing. Thus a thread of European history and the collapse of epistemology into the market begins:

> [Immanuel] Kant's dictum "the mind makes the object" were the words of blessing spoken at the wedding of knowing and production, and should be remembered when we contemplate what is common throughout the world. (Grant, 1998, p. 1)

> Accordingly, the spontaneity of understanding becomes the formative principle of receptive matter, and in one stroke we have the old mythology of an intellect which glues and rigs together the world's matter with its own forms. (Heidegger, 1985, p. 73)

And, accordingly, the Earth becomes a passive, malleable (and eventually disposable) "resource" for our consumptive and productive manipulation, and the term "math manipulatives" carries no irony or hesitation.

And children become "our greatest natural resource" with little thought given to what we've done to the rest of those things we've considered merely sources for our consumption and satisfaction, with no Being of their own, no reserve or character beyond our desire, our "wanting and doing" (Gadamer, 1989, p. xxviii).

But what if this is not the way that mathematics *exists*, as an object either produced or consumed, either individually or collectively? What if it somehow *is* different from what the economies of production and consumption, either individual or collective, can handle? What if the options of production and consumption (along with their consort images of ownership and the commodified exchange of objects between "individuals" whose only "world" is now "the market" [Jardine, Clifford, & Friesen, 2000] turn upon the same ontological ground and are therefore not especially options at all? What if, therefore, the epistemological quarrels over "production versus consumption" (and those over "individual versus collective"), which have been exhausting us, instead conceal a deeper, more dangerous debate that has been thus far successfully avoided?

What if mathematics is much more a world into which we ourselves are drawn, a world which we do not and cannot "own," but must rather somehow "inhabit" in order to understand it? What if we cannot own mathematics (either individually or collectively), not because it is some object independent of us and our (individual or collective) ownerships, but because *it is not an object at all*? What if, instead of production and consumption, the *world* of mathematics (as a *living, breathing, contested human discipline* that has been handed to us) needs our memory, our care, our intelligence, our work, the "continuity of [our] attention and devotion" (Berry, 1977, p. 32) and understanding if it is to remain hale and healthy and whole?

I

[Images] announce themselves, bear witness to their presence: "Look, here we are." They regard us beyond how we may regard them, our perspectives, what we intend with them, and how we dispose of them. (Hillman, 1982, p. 77)

Catch only what you've thrown yourself, all is mere skill and little gain. (From a poem by Rainer Maria Rilke, quoted as the epigraph in Gadamer, 1989)

Images have a most peculiar sense of arrival. They seem to *arrive*, out of nowhere, often unexpectedly, with a clear feeling of agency, of portent, of demand and deliberateness. This is phenomenologically undeniable. During the act of writing, of composing, of setting forth an idea in the already-imaginal (not simply signifying and signing [Gadamer, 1989, pp. 405, 412–418]) realm of words, images can, sometimes, become catalytic moments of experience, finally, it feels, saying what was silent, gathering what was dispersed, drawing us into the ways of a world of relations that has the center of its own Being beyond our "wanting and doing" (Gadamer 1989, p. xxviii).

Every word [-as-image, not -as-sign (Gadamer, 1989, pp. 405, 412–418)] breaks forth *as if* from a center. Every word causes the whole of the language to which it belongs to resonate and the whole world-view that underlies it to appear. (Gadamer, 1989, p. 458, our emphasis)

As signs, words re-present. They are mere stand-ins for the real thing, pointers to somewhere else.

As images, the real thing presents itself "in" words.

The title of this chapter is taken from Jane Hirshfield's wonderful work *Nine Gates: Entering the Mind of Poetry* (1997, p. 43). When we happened upon it, the first question was how to take care of it. This is because its arrival is first and foremost experienced as a claim made upon each of us (Gadamer, 1989, pp. 126–127, 297), an address spoken to us and for us (Gadamer, 1989, pp. 290, 295, 299).

This image we simply stumbled upon seemed to *require something of us*, seemed to require our attention and devotion and love and care and cultivation.

"Look. Here I am" (Hillman, 1982, p. 77).

The trouble always is, of course, that *the image itself* contains many, most, maybe all of the answers to the questions its demand provokes.

It pulls us into *its* question, *its* repose, *its* regard.

Therefore, first the question is posed not *by us* but *to us*. Good questions must be first *posed* (Gadamer, 1989, p. 363) and the writing that follows necessarily belies the writer's own emerging composure (an "exaggerated" [Gadamer, 1989, p. 115] reading of Gadamer's reading of *Bildung* [p. 9ff]) in the face of such questions.

And, too, if things go well, the writers and the readers might get a wee glimpse of the composure of the thing written about, its "repose" (Gadamer, 1977, p. 227) its *"Da,"* (Gadamer, 1994, pp. 22–25) its "standing-in-itself" (Gadamer, 1977, p. 226), again, over and above our "wanting and doing" (Gadamer, 1989, p. xxviii).

II

"Behind each jewel are three thousand sweating horses." This is an image from Zen Buddhism that invokes the tale of Indra's Jeweled Net from the *Avataska Sutra*:

> Far away in the heavenly abode of the great god Indra, there is a wonderful net that has been hung by some cunning artificer in such a manner that it stretches out infinitely in all directions. In accordance with the extravagant tastes of deities, the artificer has hung a single glittering jewel in each "eye" of the net, and since the net itself is infinite in all dimensions, the jewels are infinite in

number. There hang the jewels, glittering like stars of the first magnitude, a wonderful sight to behold. If we now arbitrarily select one of these jewels for inspection and look closely at it, we will discover that in its polished surface there are reflected all the other jewels in the net, infinite in number, not only that, but each of the jewels reflected in this one jewel is also reflecting all the other jewels, so that there is an infinite reflecting process occurring. (Quoted in Loy, 1993, p. 481)

This image of Indra's Net invokes an ontological claim: that things *are* their interdependencies with all things, and, therefore, to deeply understand any thing, we must understand it as *being itself* only in the midst of all its relations. Each thing, therefore, must be understood and experienced, not as some self-contained, self-existing substance ("a substance is that which requires nothing except itself in order to exist" [Descartes, 1640/1955, p. 255]), but as empty (*sunya*) of any self-existence (*svabhava*) apart from such living relatedness.

Each thing thus *is*, so to speak, what it *is not* while still remaining itself (Nishitani, 1982). This is a thing's reposing "in itself." It *is* the long and twisted entrails of all the interdependencies that gave rise to its being manifest just here, just now.

It *is* all the rains, all the breaths, that passed it along.

Each thing thus *is* all the codependent arisings that brought it here, and to understand this particular thing is to understand its standing in an "inheritance that it belongs to" (Gadamer, 1994, p. 192). Each thing, therefore, is not simply its own, isolated, subsequently-in-relation self, but is itself as center of a "totality of a lived context" (Gadamer, 1994, p. 191). This totality has "entered into and is present in the thing" (Gadamer, 1994, p. 192).

"And we belong to it as well" (Gadamer, 1994, p. 192).

"Thus in each dust mote is vast abundance" (Hongzhi, 1991, p. 14).

This inexhaustible emptying-out-into-all-their-relations is the deeply Earthly "repose" of things. They "stand-in-themselves," not by standing cut off from all things, but by standing *as* an opening, a portal, a way, an "e-vent," into a world of relations. This seemingly isolated object or word or glance, or even the seemingly most ordinary of classroom events (Jardine, 2000), *is* all of its relations.

As Martin Heidegger (1962) might have put it, even ordinary things sometimes "world," if we care to sit with them and wait a bit. Again, as Hans-Georg Gadamer (1994, p. 192) says in his lovely essays on his great teacher's thought, "there is a totality of a lived-context [a 'world'] present in the thing."

But this image of "sweating horses" does something more than simply invoke Indra's Net. It plays with the sense of ornateness and visionariness that Indra's Net entails—bright jewels, tapestries, heavenly arcs of space, time, vast, heady infinities, and great, swarming *ideas* of interconnectedness, interdependency, interpenetration, recursiveness, and dependent co-origination (*pratitya-samutpada*).

"Behind every jewel are three thousand sweating horses" disrupts the charming, entrancing composure of such delicious visions of "relatedness." Roaring behind each jewel, now, are not infinite refracted jewel-like visions, but *something coming at us*, something full of piss and blood and sweat, something crashing, stampeding, rough, vigorous, dangerous, full of life and death and the agonies in between, something animate that's spotted us beyond our spotting it, *demanding* attention.

III

> The point to the doctrine of interdependence is that things exist *only* in interdependence, for things do not exist in their own right. In Buddhism, this manner of existence is called "emptiness." Buddhism says that things are empty in the sense that they are absolutely lacking in a self-essence by virtue of which things would have independent existence. (Cook, 1989, p. 225)

> Lacking in self-essence resembles social and historical constitution, understands individual things as constituted by their relations to other things and especially to groups, families, species, and kinds. Emptiness resists the autonomy of the individual [which now appears] uniquely European American. (Ross, 1999, pp. 213–214)

We came across the title of this paper in the midst of a series of Grade 7 mathematics conversations, 60 students, two teachers, and a university researcher, over the course of several weeks. This was an ordinary classroom in an ordinary school undergoing what turned out to be, for all of us, an extraordinary experience.

All of us (students, teachers, and researchers) were deeply embroiled in heated talk and the heated display of differing mathematical explorations and differing mathematics solutions gathered around angles and their bisection, compasses and their workings, circles and their arcs and cords, and all the frustrating beauty of the dropping of perpendiculars. Living in the midst of these conversations day after day, this seemed like real, vigorous, embodied work, and mathematics seemed like a living, breathing discipline that drew us all in to an old, rich, Earthy place, a "topography" (Gadamer, 1989, p. 21): the deeply interrelated, interdependent, fertile (Gadamer, 1989, p. 32) terrains of geometry. Here were the sweating horses: arguments and frustrations and returns, pulling together and pulling apart the long and convoluted work of long-standing relations. And here, too, the sudden condensations of insight, moments of clarity, as they twisted pages sideways with breathtaking yells and smiles, took the pens over from each other, insisting on one more thing, one more thing.

Standing at one table. Four boys pushing a large piece of newsprint between them, given the task, with a straight-edge and compass alone, to drop a perpendicular line from a point to a line below it. We all know this one, and one student pressed ahead of us with moves we all recognized.

With the compass draw an arc through the line with the point as its centre. From each of the two points where the arc intersects the line, make two marks below the line. Use the straight-edge to connect the original point with the intersection of the two marks. This new line is perpendicular to the original line.

All of us at the table knew, *beyond a shadow of doubt*, that this solution was correct. But, equally, none of us knew *at all* why it was correct.

One boy insisted, with an insistence that we all recognized in ourselves, "That's just how you *do* it, ok?"

"But how do you know it's not hitting the line at, like, 89 degrees and not 90?" This simple question brought the whole sweaty roil to a halt all over again. We ended up in an odd place, stuck, almost dazzled by our own clarity and assurance, unable, at least initially, to "break open the being of the object" (Gadamer, 1989, p. 382). Many of us in this classroom had, over the year, talked about that odd feeling of having learned, having *memorized* a procedure and knowing how to *do* it beyond question or hesitation, and yet suffering the terrible silence and feeling of being stuck with it, a feeling of cold and deathly immobility (Jardine, Clifford, & Friesen, 2000) if anyone should have the audacity to ask a question about 89 degrees instead of 90.

All of us at this table did agree, however, that knowing this sort of flat, clear, mindless, unmoving way of understanding a procedure, unsurrounded and unsustained by the heated, tangled movements of relatedness that give it life, was not adequate. Here, in this classroom, we had come to understand that these arcs and lines and points, this compass movement, and the circles it hints at first through and then below the line all belong properly here together, together along with the ghosts of Pythagoras and Euclid and the whole cascade of memory and work that brought all this down to us. This "belonging together" is where this procedure actually *lives* as something sensible, something sane, something understandable in its living movement as a historically, humanly constituted inheritance to which our lives already and inevitably owe unvoiced obligations.

"That's just how you do it" mistakes what that procedure actually *is*. It is an uprising from this terrain of circles and lines and arcs, an uprising and a naming and an ordering and a setting-forth. As such, it is not a *substitute* for that terrain, but an imaginal coming-to-presence of it, a jewel-like condensation of the messy vigor of that terrain. Without this terrain and the risks that are involved in traversing it, the procedure remains merely memorizable. Within this terrain and our travels, it becomes memorable, like an old tale told by those who've been here before and have gathered us around a fire in the darkness to whisper to us. It is not a command, as mathematical procedures might often be experienced. It is a telling of where we have been, places we have witnessed *for ourselves*. We already know the roiling life of which this tale tells.

So one of the boys completed the circle that intersected the line in two places, and completed into circles the criss-crossing arcs below the line, ending, now, with a beautiful figure, reposing, full of the *Vesica Piscis* that we've since discovered (Lawlor, 1982; Friesen, 2000), a wee long-lost geopoetic ancestor caught kicking around in Greek sands.

"OK. I'm 49 years old and it never occurred to me that that crosshatch below the line was part of two circles." What did I think it was? Did I think about it *at all*? I expect the latter is important: I rarely *thought* about mathematics in the way I was witnessing here, in this classroom. I'd only rarely felt this living movement of understanding, this sense, in this case with geometry, of understanding its being what it is.

So over this diagram, one student said, "Oh boy. *Now* what?!" with a wonderful, weary sense of pleasure and exhaustion, but also this lovely, palpable sense of mathematical reality.

IV

> What man has to learn through suffering is not this or that particular thing, but insights into the limitations of humanity, into the absoluteness of the barrier that separates man from the divine. (Gadamer, 1989, p. 357)

> [We] belong to the text [we] are reading. The line of meaning that the text manifests. . .always and necessarily breaks off in an open indeterminacy. [We] can, indeed [we] must accept the fact that future generations will understand differently. (Gadamer, 1989, p. 340)

Mathematics *is*, in some sensible sense, all the actual, human, bodily work which is required if it is to remain hale and healthy, if it is to continue as a living practice which we desire to pass on, in some form, to our children.

"Every experience worthy of the name involves suffering" (Gadamer, 1989, p. 356). Thus, experience is not something we *possess* (like some commodifiable object) but something we *endure*, something we *undergo*. For mathematics to be deeply experienced, it must be drawn back into its suffering, its undergoing, its movement of becoming what it is, its living coming-to-presence, rather than its foreclosing *being* present. It *is* its "passing on." It *is* a fragile and finite and deeply human enterprise. This is the horrible mortality-insight of interdependency, that the seeming self-sufficiency of any seemingly isolated, self-referential object breaks outward into cascading interdependencies with all the ways it has arrived here, seeming so. "Future generations will understand differently." Mathematics *is* its being different in the future.

To understand mathematics free from the stultifying ontology of produced and consumed objects is to enter into the living movement of its "furtherance" (Gadamer, 1989, p. xxiv). Or, differently put, to understand geometry is to help keep it "open for the future" (Gadamer, 1989, p. 340). That is, to understand geometry is to keep it susceptible to being taken up and transformed anew and, it must be emphasized, to keep ourselves open to being transformed in our traversing its terrain and meeting our own ancestors in that terrain. In such a sojourn, we risk becoming people who bear the marks of having undergone such an adventure. We run the risk of bearing the marks of becoming *experienced* in mathematics in that wonderfully ecological sense that both Martin Heidegger (1962) and Hans-Georg Gadamer (1989) have identified as coming to "know your way around."

Given the dazzling allure of its rules and axioms and procedures, who would have imagined that, right at the heart of what once seemed to be the most cold and unforgiving and punishing of disciplines, is a generative, pedagogic heart? Who would have imagined that geometry *is* all the risk and pleasure and stubborn, sweaty work that brought it safely here to us?

"Behind every jewel are three thousand sweating horses."

References

Berry, W. (1977). *The unsettling of America*. San Francicso: Sierra Club Books.

Cook, F. (1989). The jewelled net of Indra. In J. Callicott and R. Ames (Eds.), *Nature in Asian traditions of thought: Essays in environmental philosophy* (pp. 213–229). Albany: State University of New York Press.

Descartes, R. (1640/1955). *Descartes selections*. New York: Charles Scribner's Sons.

Friesen, S. (2000). *Reforming mathematics in mathematics education*. Unpublished doctoral dissertation, Faculty of Education, University of Calgary.

Gadamer, H-G. (1977). *Philosophical hermeneutics*. Berkeley: University of California Press.

Gadamer, H-G. (1989). *Truth and method*. New York: Continuum Press.

Gadamer, H-G. (1994). *Heidegger's ways*. Boston: MIT Press.

Grant, G. (1998). *English-speaking justice*. Toronto: House of Anansi Press.

Heidegger, M. (1962). *Being and time*. New York: Harper and Row.

Heidegger, M. (1985). *History of the concept of time*. Bloomington: Indiana University Press.

Hillman, J. (1982). Anima mundi: Returning soul to the world. *Spring: An Annual of Archetypical Psychology and Jungian Studies, 40*, 164–181.

Hirshfield, J. (1997). *Nine gates: Entering the mind of poetry*. New York: Harper Collins.

Hongzhi, Z. (1991). *Cultivating the empty field: The silent illumination of Zen master Hongzhi*. San Francisco: North Point Press.

Jardine, D. (2000). *"Under the tough old stars": Ecopedagogical essays*. Burlington, VT: The Foundation for Educational Renewal.

Jardine, D., Clifford, P., & Friesen, S. (2000). Scenes from Calypso's Cave: On globalization and the pedagogical prospects of the gift. *Alberta Journal of Educational Research, 46*(1), 27–35.

Lawlor, R. (1982). *Sacred geometry*. London: Thames and Hudson.

Loy, D. (1993). Indra's postmodern net. *Philosophy East and West, 48*(3), 481–510.

Nishitani, K. (1982). *Religion and nothingness*. Berkeley: University of California Press.

Ross, S. (1999). *The gift of kinds: The good in abundance*. Albany: State University of New York Press.

In the Space Between the Threads: Reweaving the Yarns of Ethical Research

Jeannette Scott MacArthur

"Please, sir, instruct me further."
"So be it, my son. Bring me a fruit from the Nyagroda tree."
Svetateku picked a fruit and brought it to his father.
"Here it is, sir."
"Break it open."
"I have broken it, sir."
"What do you see there?"
"Little seeds."
"Break open one of them."
"I have broken it, sir."
"What do you see there?"
"Nothing at all."
"My son, that subtle essence which you cannot see, it is by
that very essence that this great Nyagroda tree stands."
—The Upanishads

As I recall, one of the more difficult questions with which I was confronted when I applied for graduate school was the inevitable—"What contribution do you expect your work to make to the present knowledge of teaching and of teacher education?" Apparently, as a newcomer to the academy, I was expected to have a plan for carving out the space myself, a design for filling it with what I would be expected to claim as new knowledge, most of which I would have unconsciously reconstructed from others, but all of which would have to be debated and defended as if it were my own. In retrospect, I wish that I had been able to share the Vedic story of the Nyagroda seed—although there is the possibility that the one who posed the question may have been no more open to Wisdom whispering an interpretation in his ear than I was to her prompting. Instead, caught in the stickiness of the student's desire for success, trapped in a desire to give the right answer, I sweated, confessed that I wasn't sure but, believing that the silence had to be filled, said that I hoped to provide some evidence for the need to change the criteria for selection of candidates entering teacher education programs.

The system tempts us to uncomplicate the world, to give the right answers, to speak of people as sifted through a grid of numbers or filtered through a mesh of words. I think of the students whom I have taught in public school and university classrooms. I see their faces. I know their stories—written on paper and in the bones of their bodies. But these are not the students who are described on the report cards that are sent home to parents or whose futures are determined by grade point averages on transcripts. Those students have no stories—just numbers and impersonal computer comments. And I think of colleagues who worked with me on previous research projects and those who shared in my recent work. They are not reducible to numbers nor to names. And their stories now also are written in me.[1]

Earlier in my career, I found myself involved in the sort of research which utilized t-values of scores on standardized tests in support of its claim to be telling the truth about students' abilities to read. Later, in reporting on an action research project, I contrived to meet institutional expectations for validity by designing scales which measured my perception of the shifts in teachers' stages of concern and levels of use of what I proclaimed to be the innovative instructional strategies with which I had evangelized their classrooms. That the subjectivity of the subjects of both of these research projects had been devalued by the subjectivity of the researcher was never seen by me or by others as an ethical issue. As a result, it is not surprising that in my application for study at the doctoral level, the proposals spoke of what I would do to and for some nameless others.

Fortunately, my work led me to a different understanding of ethics and of research. The research proposal I eventually submitted offered the playful suggestion that I might request a certificate of disapproval rather than a certificate of approval from the Screening Committee of the Office of Research Services, if working within the rules meant that I

---

[1] The research project which is recalled in this essay was an interpretive inquiry focusing on the following questions: What do teachers' stories tell us about the call of teaching? How does drama help teachers to remember and tell their stories?

could be seduced into again letting my colleagues become subjects of the prepositional phrase instead of subjects of the verb.[2] I felt sure that I wanted my research to be the result of my working against the rules, outside the ivy-covered over-arching principles of research which would have me digging into the hearts of teachers looking for some particular essence that might be torn out, isolated from the messy work of teaching, and then described quantitatively or qualitatively.

What had happened to foster this transformation was that "the eyes of the other" had come over me, overtaken me, pulled me up short.[3] I found myself caught in "a whole network of obligations," a multiplicity of me's pulling at the threads of the re's in my research plan so that I was forced to (re)cognize that I should not, I could not, dance this work on my own. I had been changed and, as a result, my work had to change. The choreography of my teaching and of my re/searching had to allow space and time for improvisation. My research had to make way for our researching.

For a number of years, I passionately pursued Ethics in this place and in that. At one time, I even planned to conduct a research project that would help me to chastise my colleagues for their breaches of the teachers' professional code of ethics. However, the more that I shared responsibility for the research with others, the more certain I became that I had no choice but to sever the relationship. So, I left Ethics to spend his time with cynics and pragmatists. I had been warned of his inconstancy but had chosen not to pay attention until it was very nearly too late. I had been about to take his hand and allow him to lead me into a phenomenological forest. But I changed direction; I chose Obligation instead of Ethics, radical hermeneutics[4] instead of idealistic essentialism, foolishness instead of sensibility. Following John Caputo's lead, but keeping my distance so that I could bypass the fissures and cracks of relativism, I chose to pay attention to that which continues to bind me to

---

[2] Ted Tetsuo Aoki. (1988). "Toward a Dialectic Between the Conceptual World and the Lived World." In William Pinar (Ed.), *Contemporary Curriculum Discourses* (pp. 402–416). Scottsdale, AZ: Gorsuch Scarisbrick.

[3] John Caputo. (1993). *Against Ethics*. Bloomington: Indiana University Press.

[4] I confess that there is an irony here in that, on the one hand, I am expressing an obligation to those whose stories I have taken and shared; on the other hand, I have placed my work within the deconstructive mode of radical hermeneutics. Nevertheless, I believe that to pretend that the message-bearer is capable of delivering the message exactly as it has been seen to have been sent would be more deceptive.

the dust rather than to that which caught me in custom, handcuffed me to a set of rules, arbitrarily created and arbitrarily enforced.

In journeying away from familiar and comfortable places, I found that a slippage had occurred between what I previously had assumed to be right and wrong. Having promised to conduct my work ethically and to report my work in such a way that it could be taken seriously, I found myself standing, not on moral *terra firma* as expected, but, like Caputo (1993), on ground which tended to shift (p. 3). Estrangement allowed me to discern what previously I had been incapable of seeing. I realized that ethical eyes/I's have great difficulty in distinguishing between what is wrong and what is different. I do not know when I developed the habit of judging others, how I came to imagine myself placed on high, but I am grateful to have been drawn into a *metanoia*, in a turning from those old habits (p. 112).

What happened was that I found myself, like Jonah, tumbling head over heels in the foul-smelling belly of the whale, forced to give up my journey to Tarshish. Then, having pulled myself up from the vomit of the beast and crawled away from the beach, I finally admitted that I had been trying to escape my obligation to go to Nineveh. Later, in the silence, "the whisper of the will of God" (p. 19) reminded me that though I might be able to wash my dirty self, my dusty self will forever remain. I am dust. From dust I have come. To dust I shall return. I remain caught by the vulnerability of an earthbinding between my self and my other selves, by an irresistible connection between the humus in me, by the obligations that I owe to others, that others owe to me. The only way that it was possible to complete my work was to take off my shoes, to touch the earth, to join in her moving and shifting, to dig beneath the surface, to get my fingernails dirty and to let the stars take care of themselves (pp. 5–6).

Unlike Ethics which come from on high, Obligation, Caputo cautions, happens "down low, well below the range of philosophical conceptuality" (p. 72). Ethics are subject to reductionism, relativism, deconstruction; Obligation is not deconstructable. Pulling on Obligation is like pulling on bindweed or rhizomes. Wherever it is, its roots are there; wherever it is, its roots are not there.[5] The application of ethical

---

[5] rhizome—underground rootlike stems which produce roots and shoots (from the Latin *rhizome*, a mass of roots, from the Greek *rhizoma*, roots of a tree, *rhizousthai*, to take root, from *rhiza*, root). I have often wondered when and where and who has given a

standards, like the attempt to be rid of the bindweed, gives the appearance of neat closure but it always leaves something behind. Obligation is what is left over. Like "a remnant, an undigested morsel, a loose fragment, a shard."

---

new meaning to this word. See Gilles Deleuze and Félix Guattari (1983). *On the Line.* New York: Semiotext(e). What circumstances have denied the roots and valorized the stem? As a gardener, I think the qualities of *convolvulus* (bindweed) express Deleuze's and Guattari's intention more clearly.

❯ Radical Contingencies in the Words of a Student: (Dis)placing, (Re)marking, Languaging

Marylin Low

Dear teacher,
You marked me low level student. Why? I think you mark just my grammar. I not low level. I think my writing maybe confused you reading me. I write more than English words say only. I like my Japanese hide in between English words. You can't se it but I think you know. Maybe you don't like not know exactly meaning. Can we meet? I want us to read me together. (ji, international student)

Contingent 1. liable to happen xiv. 2. dependent upon or subject to conditions xvi.—L contingens, -ent-, prp of contingere be CONTIGUOUS, in connection or in contact, befall. So contingency xvi.
        —Oxford Concise Dictionary of English Etymology

An invitation to respond to a mark is returned and, in its return, I am marked. The performative words of this student, dwelling in a global(ized)[1] site, disrupt a comfortable certainty of how I had come to

---

[1] Dwelling in the middle of things, and attuned to the words of a student, I have come to understand classrooms of international students as sites that are both global and economically globalized, in this paper signified by the inscription *global(ized)*. I gratefully acknowledge the permission granted me by the five students whose voices are inscribed herein. I am further indebted to their willingness to risk those articulations that were, for me, deeply felt pedagogical moments.

mark her English. In life complicated by intertexts of *différance*,[2] cries from the margins of a pedagogical place called English as a second language (ESL) could be heard—a location the student continued to agitate and contest. And she is not the only one.

These words of a student reminded me of other recent "disturbing" readings. I had taken an interdisciplinary journey to a place where issues of language and signification are vividly apparent, yet they had previously escaped my work. That is, until I offered to type a handwritten invited address for curriculum scholar and sensei, Ted Aoki. As I entered his words on the screen, new meanings were invoked in such significations as *imaginary, hybridity, doubling*, and *difference*. It was this text that invited me to take a pedagogical turn and read elsewhere. The work of postcolonial scholars such as Homi Bhabha, Trinh Minh-ha, and Rey Chow troubled my desire to read the other as a temporary translation from one language to another. The intertexts of these scholars led me to Foucault and Derrida, readings that made me suspicious of my own work as a teacher and led me to question my longing to be certain of the other—a way of being with the other so familiar to me, a way of keeping intact a binary of teacher/learner that unwittingly privileged me, the teacher. Reading elsewhere disturbed a marking of the other outside of myself and unsettled the need to fixate students in a rhetoric of place (beginner) and name (Japanese). Instead, scenes of dynamic relations complicated and blurred distinctions between student and teacher, opening me to the complexities of self in other and other in self.

Reading out of education as a way of reading in, I sought the work of other educators who engaged in the same way. Ted Aoki's (2000) living pedagogy began as a psychoanalytic curiosity that invited an inter-disciplinary rereading of education and its "difficulties" as vibrant sites of tensioned anxieties—sites that are not clean and controlled as I had been taught they should be, but as sites always already incomplete, complex, and ambiguous. Tracking ambiguity, I read the work of

---

[2] A Derridean *différance* combines complicated relations of difference and deferral—meanings that never quite arrive—that are always in-between or in-the process-of arriving and constituted in resisting forces of difference. It is a way of reading "ESLness" elsewhere and otherwise that troubles traditional notions of "pure" difference. See Bennington's (1993, pp. 70–84) tracking of Derrida's written traces of *différance*.

educational scholars David Jardine (1992) and David Smith (1994/1999a), and their questioning of the pedagogical cover-up of ambiguity—a cover-up I had learned to skillfully maintain through a "standard" marking of the other, while blaming the difficulty of my work on my own inadequacies as a teacher. Opening to the possibility of reading difference and difficulty elsewhere and otherwise disrupted the necessary illusions of an Enlightenment model of curriculum—of fixity, of mastery, of identity—that I had come to rely on in the classroom. The hegemony of my "standards" was displaced as I listened to the words of a student.

What do global(ized) sites, as places of international students learning in English, mean for me as a teacher of language? How have I come to (re)mark and (dis)place students and myself in these sites? How do such experiences rewrite life in the classroom? For those in global(ized) sites—for students labeled ESL and for teachers given the responsibility for assessing students' ESLness, these are significant questions. In many school systems, students becoming literate in their new language, English, have been relegated to a classroom called "ESL" because of their assumed special or different needs. Marking *différance* through technical acts of labeling, segregating, and quantifying (numbering, grading, leveling) has been important work in second language pedagogy. Such processes mark people as having an*other* language and (dis)place them to a site of *différance* that is often pathologized as a place where language can be fixed. It is a place that often assumes the work of correction and purification as a removal of interlanguage's ambiguous and "faulty" sites of dis-ease. Now I see this place as a kind of predatory consumption of language in its (re)production and its totalitarian assumptions of homogenizing and assimilating a *différance* that refuses the call. It is a place I resist while learning to live well within its structures.

Storied cartographies in global(ized) sites—especially those of assessment—are saturated with difficulties (Low, 1999). Opening to these difficulties creates the conditions for a happenstance of radical contingencies in the classroom—what Ted Aoki inscribes as metonymic moments of living pedagogy—a living pedagogy that brings under suspicion the traditional distinctive binary of teacher/learner and rewrites teaching as a messy text (Low & Palulis, 2000)—a messiness constituted in moments of relational misfires, resistances, and failures.

Foregrounding those moments as sparks of contingency (Bhabha, 1999), as readings of "ESLness" elsewhere and otherwise—readings that disturb the normalized discourse of ESL and its educational structurings of assessment—becomes the "sweet" labor of my work, opening to a vibrant tensionality in the classroom. Writing out of the difficulties of pedagogy, this project textually incites the messiness of curricular practices not yet tolerated in education.

In the words of a student—a flicker, a spark ignites. There is no easy way to enter this conversation.

I

I want to know how you know my mark. It's not me. I am more than this number. You said just say simple. I can't do that. So I use computer and word check. It changed what I say to right way but I still got low mark and wrong place. (yk, international student)

I had not heeded these words until now. For many years I had been teaching (in) my first language, English, the only language I thought I knew. My work as a teacher led me to quest(ion)s midst pedagogical/assessment practices with international students. Part of my work was in wired classrooms and, for a while, I indulged in the fantasy of a global village and what I presumed to be a culturally neutral medium of local and international computer-based communication. What I had neglected to notice was the interested nature of *universality* within the global-village narrative and its web interconnectivity as something constructed specifically within the framework of Western politics, economics, English language, and culture (Hawisher & Selfe, 2000). Aside from belying the myths of cultural neutrality, the computer increasingly became a tool of efficiency, assisting me in an "ideology of progress" that dominated my work with students. As they wrote essays in this abstract and "neutral" medium, word processed and supported by electronic checks of the "universal" laws of English, I evaluated and recorded such judgments digitized by numeracy and accurate to two decimal points. Now, I realize the enframing at work in the dis-embodiment of an always already performative language in translation—languaging in subjectivities of performed relations—a writing that nervously "takes its pulse from the *difference* rather than the *identity* between the linguistic symbol and the thing it is meant to represent" (italics in original; Pollock, 1998, pp. 82–83). It has been difficult, *heavy* work in my resistance to come technologically clean.

Students from all around the globe come to us in search of a place—an imagined classroom of belonging, a place where over time relationships of respect and trust can develop. Yet, our well-intentioned acts of assessment reduce students' humanness to the technical power of a number—the "essence of technology" (Heidegger, 1954/1977) at work—the self comes to presence under the spell of technology and resists (or insists on) its "accuracy." In the words of a student, *it is not me*. Technology persists with a dissection and dis-embodiment of "correctable" parts of language, inviting an evaluation that can be established and accessed through the efficiency of dead numbers, a lifeless summation that is misaligned with the living text of the student, a mark that privileges mastery and censures textual misfires and resistances that are always already integral to the performativity of the text—a text in which the whole is always already more than the sum of its parts: *I am more than this number.* Technology becomes an efficiency aspect of consumptive assessment that attempts to reduce living pedagogy to plain language, where students, labeled and marked, are held in place by the power of a "simple" number, segregated to a place(ment) legitimated and controlled by an identity indebted to a number and to the linearity of the place it holds (beginning, intermediate, advanced)—a heavy debt accumulated through the active consumerism at work in teaching.

Resisting the desire for plain language, I turned to a Lacanian reading of teaching and was at once both startled and affirmed by Doug Aoki's (2000) claim that this "translation of complex materials into plain language is actually a refusal to teach" (p. 347). The plain language of a number as a refusal to teach—the negation and alienation of communities of relations in which we are living together—a life complicated by the daily intertexts of anxieties and ambiguities in the classroom cannot be written in plain language. I cannot "be" without others—a troubling of imaginary binary distinctions of self and other complicated by the doubling of other in self. (Inter)texts and their evaluation cannot "be" without acknowledging the incomplete and recursive movements of relational investments in their social meaning. From the words of a student, a radical contingency speaks in/of complexities in response to a mark. I am learning to resist the (dis)placement of others; to resist relegating them to the marginal spaces of ESL; and to resist (dis)placing and segregating them through numerical reduction to the layered and leveled life in schools. It is the mark(et)ed life of an (ESL) student. And, I can no longer carry the burden of plain language.

II

Sometimes, I don't like question. It just repeat what study in class. I know more so I try to say but sometimes it worse. I make many mistakes and I get low mark. Teacher say it my Japanese way. I sometimes think I can't say anymore what I want. (os, international student)

The scoring of a student inscribes his place. A dis-embodied mark works to exhaust and collapse difference; the subject is reduced to a numerical "thing" easily categorized, labeled, and consumed by those who know. Consumption becomes, as Arjun Appadurai (1997) terms it: the process of "disciplining the imagination" (p. 102). What is at issue is the cultural production of a pedagogical imagination that reifies ESL learning as a mechanical, linear production under construction. This is an imaginary some diasporic learners collectively resist. But such resistance is hard to sustain.

Increasing numbers of students cross the borders of their homelands to reach other landscapes, a journey further complicated and problematicized by entering the intertexts of more than one language and culture. While most administrators and teachers seek ways to master, ascertain, and correct only one language—an ordering and reducing by number of the textured complexities of *différance*—resistance is heard in the words of a student. A radical contingency, now inscribed at the point of the non-visible gap in the frame, is enacted; an erasure at the moment of exposure—Bhabha's (1999) "tiny spark of contingency" emerges as "a flickering moment, a restless movement of the darkness that befalls the exposed frame and sutures without letting them turn into a binary relation, or a unitary synthesis" (p. xi). The student's work had been stripped of its mysteries, complexities, ambiguities, and situational character by teachers who care. Formal educational paradigms based on conditions and assumptions about language teaching continue to insist on debilitated letters and precise—often fixed—pronouncements from a pen that reveals the "clear" presence of cultural and political authority in the classroom. Conditions that betray the very notion of pedagogy incite radical contingencies.

I sat with the student and we talked together. All the while I was reminded of David Smith's (1999b) notion of teaching as "an act of coming together between teacher and student under the transcendental sign of "thinking'" (p. 112). We talked of writing, its destination, the risk of detour, and the multiple readings along the way. Through complicated conversations, we struggled to remain open to a difficult space of ambiguity and unreadability: a space *in-between* us teeming with intertextual flaws and peculiarities, a text re-markable in its complexity and uncertainty. Resistances enacted this *becoming*—an always already doubled movement of the "disembodied evil eye...that wreaks its revenge by circulating, *without being seen*" (Bhabha, 1994, p. 55), a site of the split-space of enunciation open to misfires, failures, and rereadings within and across at least two languages. And so we struggled to dwell at that aporetic site, Bhabha's Third Space, "the cutting edge of translation and negotiation—the in-between space—that carries the burden of culture" (Bhabha, 1994, p. 38). We penetrated the silence surrounding the intertexts of the other, re-marking and dis-placing selves with/in doubling movements across translation. There was no reduction to plain language. No numerical intervention to cover up the mess.

III

I try to write like my teacher. I want her correct everything. But my Japanese is big problem. I can't get rid of it. (international student comment)

Languaging from a hybrid place, as Trinh Minh-ha (1992) confides, "resists any easy category" (p. 137). The difficulties encountered by this international student had much to do with resistance against conformist borders, those mark(et)able categories and academic regulations imposed on writing that insist teachers be concerned with the hybridity of writing itself. What is this normative territory called "good writing"? Is it writing that must be constructed in a way recognizable to and validated by us as teachers—the ones who "know"? Is this pedagogical work?

Acts of languaging—especially from a hybrid place wherein a mixing of different texts becomes the mutual interchange of discursive and "non-discursive" languages—break from the fixed norms of prevailing discourses and are easily misread, dismissed, or obscured as "second language" writing. As a question of translation and the valorizing of the "original" language, Rey Chow (1995) offers a lesson "about the 'original'…[for us to] take absolutely seriously the deconstructionist insistence that the 'first' and 'original' as such is always already *différance*—always already translated" (p. 193). What does it mean to read and then mark a text of *différance*? By focusing on accuracy and correctness, have they "brush[ed] aside…creativity and genius, eternal value and mystery" (Benjamin, 1968, p. 218) in a translation whose uncontrolled application would render the conventional categories and regulations of the academy useless? It seems ESL work never quite corresponds to what teachers are seeking.

What are called "international" practices are often the mere juxtaposition of a number of different languages/cultures. In such a politics of pluralist exchange and dialogue, the concept of "inter" (trans)formation and growth is usually reduced to a question of proper accumulation and acquisition. It is a form of human capital wherein the possibility of universality presumes too much. Languaging in this context tends to become narrow, specialized, professionalized, unified discourse(s) that remain(s) closed to writing from a hybrid place. Languages/cultures are simply added, kept in place—in my example, participants continue to speak as experts of Japanese and novices of English. Yet, stretched to the limits, "inter" pulls down barriers of languages/cultures, and borderlines remain strategic and contingent as they cancel themselves out in translation, in an invitation to Aoki's (1999) enunciatory, hybrid space of Ko-jin, "both divided and undivided, an admission perhaps that in translation there is some slippage, something left untranslated, and thus incomplete" (p. 35). It is the site where the very idea of a language, a culture, is challenged—a space no single group can own—a space in-between conventional opposing pairs. Could this be dwelling in a metonymic moment of tensioned borderlines, an Aokian living pedagogy with all its generative possibilities? Is this international student part of a diasporic generation who lives in dis-ease as boundaries are safeguarded on either side of the borderlines of Japanese and English? These borderlines resist fixedness and remain fluid from language crossings, intertextual markings caught in Derrida's performative contradiction: "I ever only speak one language. Yes, but, I never only speak one language" (Derrida, 1998, p. 7).

What *does* assessment want from a hybrid text? Object-oriented evaluation where the marker focuses on catching the object —objectifying the text—ignores the subjectifying "non" text always already there, a hybridization between and within languages/cultures. The division separating "normal" or "native" English and "abnormal" or "second-language" English is not discovered but socially produced and is legislated and enforced by the ideological law by which normality is invented and maintained. It is an enframing so powerful that many teachers, including myself, have only begun to become aware of what such structures force us to do.

Epilogue

Residues and traces of the Enlightenment era continue to emerge in the most unsuspecting places. Ashis Nandy's (1989) comment, that "colonialism may have vanished from the world scene but its smile lingers in the air" (p. 276), now speaks to me more poignantly than ever as I, a teacher and teacher educator, continue to struggle with the question, what does it mean to be an English teacher in these global(ized) times? Who are the students I teach and for what purposes and under what conditions are they learning English?

Having fallen prey to a cultural narrative drawing on the Enlightenment dream, I question with Hawisher and Selfe (2000) the potent desire for a global village. Attending to the multiple and culturally specific literacy practices that influence not only web communications but all forms of "technical" literacy alerts me to the political, corporate mindset of computers in the classroom. However, more significantly, I now see how my teaching of English—especially in a wired classroom—was a continuation of the "colonial smile," as I imposed and sustained the phantasms of a global(ized) village, using technology and its unsuspecting digital confinement to (dis)place students of the globe from their hybrid place, doubled in languages/cultures, to a place insistent on the impossibility of rigid borders and pure languages.

For some, establishing discursive borders through tense language acts of labeling, segregating, and quantifying have become necessary illusions for second language students' survival in schools—necessary illusions in which arbitrary and artificial frames of reference often contain and restrict rather than benefit those they are meant to serve. They become instances of reified, objectified practices of commodification, providing a rationale for perpetuating socially produced and discursively sustained dehumanizing acts of teaching. Instead, I listen to the disturbing words of students. A repositioning of a pedagogy *with* international students opens to a scene of teaching that leans on Bill Readings' (1997, p. 19) notion of a complex "network of obligations" and debts mediated by teachers and students. It is a reclaiming of the public realm, a socially constructed "public," a doubled movement of self/other, an imaginary that presumes the interconnectedness of people and their responsibility for and to each other. It is a (re)marking and (dis)placing of current discourse, shifting to languaging practices that invite Pasha and Samatar's (1997) intercivilization dialogues midst notions of hybridity and *différance*: imagined selves that can never be completely unified, a global village that becomes undone (undisciplined) by the very system that works to protect its production. For assessment, it is a rethinking of what it means to be just and fair with/in the complexities and uncertainties of *différance*.

Radical contingencies are invoked by the words of students, each "tiny spark of contingency" locating a moment of living pedagogy in assessment, a place in which wary and tenuous face(t)s of pedagogy can resist the call to be clear, where teachers and students can learn to live well with/in a troubling vibrancy of *différance,* a place where language cannot be fully "known" but is always already incomplete in its doubled movements of a Derridean performative contradiction. Dwelling midst the fissures and rumblings just might incite a challenge to the seductiveness of an "efficient" technology of language and its global capital powerfully at work in education today.

I refuse to be involved in language and processes that keep us "simple," by which othered bodies are (re)marked and (dis)placed within a technological and consumptive language of mastery, clarity, and certainty while commitments to social responsibility and a living pedagogy remain contained and marginalized. As a performative contradiction, in the words of a teacher, *I simply refuse to refuse to teach.*

References

Aoki, D. S. (2000). The thing never speaks for itself: Lacan and the pedagogical politics of clarity. *Harvard Educational Review, 70*(3), 347–369.

Aoki, T. (1999). In the midst of doubled imaginaries: The Pacific community as diversity and difference. *Interchange, 30*(1), 27–38.

Aoki, T. (2000, April). *Locating living pedagogy in teacher "research": Five Metonymic moments.* Paper presented at the International Conference on Teacher Research, Baton Rouge, LA.

Appadurai, A. (1997). *Modernity at large: Cultural dimensions of globalization.* Minneapolis: University of Minnesota Press.

Benjamin, W. (1968). The task of the translator. In H. Arendt (Ed.), *Illuminations,* (pp. 69–82). New York: Schocken Books.

Bennington, G., & Derrida, J. (1993). *Jacques Derrida* (G. Bennington, Trans.). Chicago: University of Chicago Press.

Bhabha, H. (1994). *The location of culture.* New York: Routledge.

Bhabha, H. (1999). Arrivals and departures. In H. Naficy (Ed.), *Home, exile, homeland* (pp. vii–xiii). New York: Routledge.

Chow, R. (1995). *Primitive passions: Visuality, sexuality, ethnography, and contemporary Chinese cinema.* New York: Columbia University Press.

Derrida, J. (1998). *Monolingualism of the other or the prosthesis of origin* (P. Mensah, Trans.). Stanford, CA: Stanford University Press.

Hawisher, G., & Selfe, C. (2000). *Global literacies and the world-wide web.* New York: Routledge.

Heidegger, M. (1954/1977). The question concerning technology. In D. F. Krell (Ed.), *Basic Writing* (W. Lovitt, Trans.) (pp. 287–317). New York: Harper & Row.

Jardine, D. (1992). Reflections on education, hermeneutics, and ambiguity: Hermeneutics as a restoring of life to its original difficulty. In W. Pinar and W. Reynolds (Eds.), *Understanding curriculum as phenomenological and deconstructed text* (pp. 116–127). New York: Teachers College Press.

Low, M. (1999). *"Difficulties" of integrative evaluation practices: Instances of language and content as/in contested space(s).* Unpublished Ph.D. dissertation, Vancouver, BC, The University of British Columbia.

Low, M., & Palulis, P. (2000). Teaching as a messy text: Metonymic moments in pedagogical practice. *Journal of Curriculum Theorizing, 16*(2), 67–79.

Nandy, A. (1989). Shamans, savages and the wilderness: On the audibility of dissent and the future of civilizations. *Alternatives, 14*, 263–277.

Pasha, K., & Samatar, A. (1997). The resurgence of Islam. In J. Mittelman (Ed.), *Globalization: Critical reflections* (pp. 79–85). New York: Sage.

Pollock, D. (1998). Performing writing. In P. Phelan (Ed.), *The ends of performance* (pp. 73–103). New York: New York University Press.

Readings, B. (1997). *The university in ruins.* Cambridge, MA: Harvard University Press.

Smith, D. (1994/1999a). *Pedagon.* New York: Peter Lang.

Smith, D. (1999b). Economic fundamentalism, globalization, and the public remains of education. *Interchange, 30*(1), 93–17.

Trinh Minh-ha, T. (1992). From a hybrid place. In T. Trinh Minh-ha (Ed.), *Framer framed* (pp. 137–148). New York: Routledge.

❯ conSCIENCEness Land(e)scapes

Kathy Nolan

translation: escaping to lands of
being
with science

the division between
my body, my mind is never so sharp
moving away from the computer
    to hear the SNAP
    SyNAPses ceasing
    joints reminding
my mind, my body
I've not stood for hours
and where am I after all?
    the minutes tick by
    the pages
        unfinished links

[insert here]
by the asterisks ***
outside the box
weaving a web of colour
and on the porch
the tangled fly reminding
my body, my mind

I've not eaten for hours

and where am I after all?
on the landing escaping
laptop hum
unending references
unfinished busyness
the power surges
and my back is to the wall reminding
my mind, my body
mind and body
[caught in dichot...]
o my
bodymind
[SNAP]
and where am I after all?

❯ Stories of an Itinerant Wayfarer: Narrative in the Space of Healing

Patrick Verriour

Each morning I take the same walk, starting out from one seacoast and not returning home until I have glimpsed the sea again at the other end of the road. When I first started walking this road nearly two years ago I was still in the early stages of inoperative and incurable cancer. I could barely reach the top of the first hill before turning back. In spite of my frequent protests, my wife, physicians, and nurses told me to keep on walking.

As I continued walking, my mind connected with other roads I had walked in my life; my daily journal started evoking images of roads from my childhood and my early days teaching in England. "Imagine a misty May day in Worcestershire walking past the Knyght's Meadow on the way to school," I instructed myself. As I wrote, I discovered that each road I recalled and each walk I had taken had a deep and personal significance for me. Scattered across three countries on three different continents there are roads for which I still believe I need no charts to guide my way and which I walk frequently in my imagination.

"There is a lovely road that runs from Ixopo into the hills," writes Alan Paton in *Cry the Beloved Country*. "These hills are grass covered and rolling, and they are lovely beyond the singing of it" (1948, p. 1). Paton's words thrilled and moved me as a child, creating a yearning to walk across the grassy hills of Africa and an undiminished passion for stories. Throughout my life the roads I have walked have become entwined with the dusty trails, narrow country lanes, and moorland tracks I have encountered in literature. Even though all these paths are familiar to me, I am always thrilled to start my journey, knowing that with each step I am making fresh discoveries and writing new stories. When I was diagnosed with cancer I felt like Judith Zaruches that "the destination and map I had used to navigate my life before were no longer useful" (quoted in Frank, 1995, p. 1). It was a time without hope, full of bitterness and depression. I sat for hours at the kitchen table staring through the window at the road which I now walk each day. I could see it snaking up the hill away from me. I never thought then that this road so familiar to me for 20 years would give me the hope and the strength to story my life once more, and would reveal to me that each footstep in the journeys I take is the shifting compass point I now use to navigate my life.

Once I was a traveler with my eyes narrowly fixed on my destination, but now I have become a wayfarer lingering to hear the plop of a maple leaf landing on the road beside me and reveling in the glory of the sun casting silver shafts of light through tall Douglas firs and morning mist. Landscaping this country of which I am now a citizen with images, impressions, and stories has been my joy and my passion. The stories other cancer patients shared with me on their journeys have strengthened me and enriched my understanding of the power of narrative to heal.

In my life and career as a drama educator, I have aimed to teach my students to story their lives, to be playful, to be prepared for the unpredictable and unexpected, to value their intuition and to be always shifting their perspectives of themselves and others. Like Peter Brook, I believe any physical space can provide opportunities for people to create theatre for themselves. Brook writes, "I can take any empty space and call it a bare stage. A man walks across this empty space whilst someone else is watching him, and this is all I need for an act of theater to be engaged" (1967, p. 1).

But no spaces are really empty: Each one is filled with a myriad of story possibilities waiting to be told, depicted, and reflected on. Embedded within each of these stories there are always possibilities of other stories as yet untold leading us in fresh directions. When I first contracted cancer, life for me became "an empty space" void of any personal meaning or future direction. I believed I had no more stories to tell and that my life story was over. In this essay I shall explore the power of story to heal the body and the spirit, and to transform the view of one's self in relation to others. I shall dialogue with myself at other times in my journey, and reflect on how ill-equipped I was to face the sudden change of direction in my life. Above all I shall explore the open spaces that still lay waiting to be discovered as I became a wayfarer listening to other voices and other stories that now inform my life.

On November 26, 1996, I walk into the Vancouver Cancer Agency on the corner of Heather Street expecting to arrange three weeks of daily radiation treatment for my recently diagnosed prostate cancer. I am assuming that the treatment will be fitted in between teaching my final university classes that same day and Christmas week. This, I have calculated in my weekly planner, will allow me a few days with my family before resuming classes in the New Year.

Three hours later I walk out of the agency clutching two plastic containers of white pills. Seated in a tiny cubicle, I have been informed by the examining oncologist that there is only a remote possibility of my ever being cured of cancer, and there is an even chance I will be dead in five years. I am 58 years old. The oncologist suggests I take early retirement. At this advanced stage of the cancer, surgery or immediate radiation treatment are both out of the question. The pills I have been given are hormone tablets designed to shrink the tumor through "chemical castration."

"We'll start you on hormone therapy. Can't cure you but it might help control the cancer spreading. Best of luck."

I can only imagine I have been given bottles of aspirin to treat terminal cancer and that my case is so hopeless there is little the medical profession can do for me. I have been dismissed. In three short hours I have made one of the longest journeys of my life from the place Susan Sontag calls "the kingdom of the well" to that other citadel "the kingdom of the sick" (1978, p. 3).

Two separate kingdoms divided from one another.

Sontag suggests that we all hold citizenship in both kingdoms but "although we all prefer to use only the good passport, sooner or later each of us is obliged, at least for a spell, to identify ourselves as citizens of that other place" (1978, p. 3). That afternoon, after visiting the cancer agency and finding my "good" passport revoked, I teach my last university class, pack my 35-year teaching career and my stories away in my knapsack, and exile myself to become an unwilling citizen and traveler in "that other place."

"That other place." Even Sontag, once a cancer patient herself, seems to have difficulty in avoiding the euphemisms that are used to conceal illness and speak the unspeakable.

Reading through my journal entries of those days that immediately preceded my first visit to the Cancer Agency, I discover my reluctance to admit I had cancer, how I avoided any use of the word, and how I told no one except my wife that I was ill. I am reminded how angry I was when she passed on the news to other people. I am astonished how blissfully ignorant I was of my medical condition and of what it means to be sick. In so doing I tried to hide the truth from myself with either a show of bravado or a pretence that a diagnosis of prostate cancer would not disrupt my busy schedule.

Here I am on October 31, 1996, laughing at "the dancing, prancing Hallowe'en skeletons festooning the ceiling of the hospital room" when I am summoned to the radiology unit for a bone scan. I hum "Il mi tesori" from Mozart's Don Giovanni as my body slowly passes through a long cylindrical metal tube, and I am rebuked by the attending nurse for fidgeting. On November 4 my 80-year-old father-in-law, who has "a ready wit and a twinkle in his eye," tells me a dream he once had about dying and I squirrel it away for some unnamed and unforeseen future writing project. Now here on November 13 I am complaining about having to report to the Cancer Agency on November 26 for three weeks of treatment which will occupy sorely needed time for writing and course preparation. And on November 25 I reflect on the narrative journey my students and I have been sharing in a doctoral seminar which is just ending.

So many voices, so many stories in those early journal entries, but none directly and honestly told the whole story of what I had been experiencing.

And then there is silence for six weeks.

January 9, 1997

Out of the gray morning mist the orchard trees peer at me dimly through the kitchen window. I feel the damp cold in my bones. Hard to get moving. Already 10 a.m. and I have barely finished my breakfast and taken my pills. Energy is sapped, wanting to start but not knowing how. Every step I take to the top of the stairs is labored. When I reach the top the phone rings in the kitchen and I ignore it. My immediate priority is the bathroom and it will be hard to reach the phone before it stops ringing I tell myself. I stand waiting for silence, which comes swiftly, and I wonder who it could have been. I want someone to call. I need to be in contact with but I have difficulty finding the words. I returned to the Cancer Agency with Angela on December 3 so she could ask the questions I was unable to frame, and listen to the answers I seem to have difficulty in hearing. I do remember that when the oncologist leaves he turns to Angela, not me, and says, "I would like to wish you a happy Christmas but there seems no point under the circumstances." Since that moment I have endured the worst and darkest days and weeks of my life. If there had been a gun to hand on Christmas Day I think I would have blown my brains out.

As I write now, over three years later, I find myself revisiting another person trapped in a body that is in pain, exhausted, incontinent, and impotent. I hear a single voice, at times angry and bitter, and I sense the daily erratic mood swings. The handwriting is cramped, the content rambling and digressive. And yet I feel a stronger personal connection with this writer than I do with the one who was still living blind in the "kingdom of the well." I experience a sudden rush of love and compassion for that person struggling to find words and a voice. It is as if I am opening a time capsule buried by my other self in the deep recesses of "the kingdom of the sick."

At this stage in my illness my writing was purely cathartic and the task of journal keeping had only tenuous connections with the daily discipline of my working life. I would rise each morning sometimes quite late, eat breakfast, and then write. The writing probably never took more than 20 minutes but I wrote fast and intensely. Scant thought was given to the stories I told or matters I discussed. My entries are a pot-pourri of events in my life recalled, emotional outbursts, snatches of conversations with my wife, thoughts about music and books, and most of all much personal recrimination. Through my writing I discovered that in addition to being overly self-critical, I had given little thought to myself as a whole person beyond meeting the day-to-day demands of work. Like those of other cancer patients my words convey my sense of guilt for having been diagnosed with the disease, and most of all, in my case, not for insisting that my local doctor examine me earlier for prostate cancer.

This is the voice of a man not unlike other men of my age or older I have met as fellow travelers in the kingdom of the sick. Few have ever given much thought to what it means to have a debilitating disease, and most never consider discussing the possibility of its presence in their bodies with other men. Thinking back to the few support group meetings I have attended, I can recall much talk about diet, recent research findings, and the importance of receiving an early diagnosis. The lengthy and arduous process of self-healing, the ever-present existence of cancer, and the means of dealing with one's sense of loss as a man are rarely explored, and are, for the most part, camouflaged with the kind of bravado that probably suggests deep unvoiced underlying fears, anxieties, and a sense of failure.

Susan Sontag writes that "the cancer personality is regarded...with condescension as one of life's losers. Napoleon, Ulysses S. Grant, Robert A. Taft, and Hubert Humphrey have all had their cancers diagnosed as the reaction to political defeat and the curtailing of their ambitions" (1978, p. 49). Even now as I write in the year 2000, a leading American politician has withdrawn ignominiously from a Republican senatorial race amidst revelations about scandal in his personal life and the news that he has prostate cancer. When I was first diagnosed with cancer, the head of my department wrote to me, "Who can tell the damage that the _____ affair has done to your health, and whether you will ever be able to repair the damage to your reputation?" She was referring to an academic dispute concerning a biography written by one of the graduate students I had supervised.

"I do not forget cancer for very long, ever," writes Audre Lorde, a breast cancer victim, in her journal. "I live with the constant fear of recurrence of another cancer" (1980, p. 14). I have shared that fear for the past three years, at first very intensely, less so now. But it is still there, a persistent nagging fear, which surfaces every time I report for blood tests and medical examinations. I think I have learned to live with and work through that fear as others have in their own way, but anxiety is insidious and crippling. Lorde describes anxiety as "an immobilizing yield to things that go bump in the night, a surrender to namelessness, formlessness, voicelessness, and silence" (1980, p. 14). Like Lorde I was to discover that the real problem of being seriously ill becomes the problem of finding a voice.

February 7, 1997
I lay awake last night wondering if I was becoming obsessed by my illness, dwelling on it in my journal. I already fear the silence. After my biopsy in mid October, the news that I had cancer, and the ensuing

scans, I kept on teaching. I felt very tired, and I lost myself in my teaching. Worked in the morning in the office and then slept there until my afternoon class. When I awoke I ran into class and completely immersed myself in the drama at hand. Sometimes I would go in with my arms plastered with band-aids concealing injections. The students looked surprised but I told them nothing. Apart from one drama we created about the aftermath of a young girl being badly injured in a car crash, which momentarily touched me emotionally, I quickly learned to cope with my double life of appearing well and energetic (I thought) and living with the dark knowledge I had cancer. Looking back now I realize how silent I was becoming as I continued to separate my career and work from my illness.

By remaining silent about my illness, I had contradicted much of what I had been teaching in drama education about trust and openness with others in the interest of what I believed to be the kind of academic detachment I should be projecting to my students. I have always treasured the intimacy that I thought has existed between myself and my students in many of the drama classes I have taught. Because I could not find the words to confide in them, I think I was afraid of risking that relationship.

Discussing the bond that is forged between writer and reader, Gillian Rose writes, "Suppose that I were now to reveal that I have AIDS, full blown AIDS, and have been ill during most of the course of what I have related. I would lose you. I would lose you to knowledge, to fear and to metaphor" (1995, p. 152). Writing about a terminal illness, suggests Rose, is like breaking your contract with your reader. Rose, who died of ovarian cancer in 1995, believes she must take this risk, "otherwise I die deadly, but this way, by this work, I may die forward into the intensified *agon* of living" (1995, p. 153). When my colleagues eventually discovered I was sick, I found myself reverting to words and phrases that trivialized my problem. Often I spoke disparagingly of my medical condition as if confessing to some personal misdemeanor I had committed. The journey that I have taken to finding the voice to write publicly about my personal encounter with cancer has been as long and painful as the physical healing itself.

Arthur Frank says there are three ethics of self story: the *ethic of recollection*, the *ethic of solidarity and commitment,* and the *ethic of inspiration.* The three ethics refer to responsibility in storytelling. *The ethic of recollection* involves taking responsibility for what was done, the story providing "a moral opportunity to set right what was done wrong or incompletely" (1995, p. 132). The other two ethics require the storyteller to offer his voice to speak *with*, not for, his fellow sufferers and to ground the story in the truth of his experience, whatever the pain or agony, to "show what is possible in impossible situations" (1995, p. 133).

When I think of the drama classes I taught at university for 20 years, I see myself sitting in a circle of students talking with them about storying their lives, living playfully, and being prepared for the unpredictable. We discuss the importance of the imagination, of intuition, of always shifting perspectives to examine an issue or problem and learning how to present the work metaphorically in dramatic form. Above all, we talk about risk taking and how people may discover their public voice through drama.

In one class, Amel, a beginning teacher of East Indian origins, whose family had fled Uganda during the dictatorship of Idi Amin in the 1970s, found his voice to tell a story concerning his childhood which we dramatized. When his family arrived in Canada as refugees, Amel attended an elementary school in the British Columbia lower mainland and found the cultural and social adjustment difficult. The boy's parents became actively involved in the school. When the school organized a potluck social evening for parents and their children, Amel's parents brought a plate containing a variety of East Indian delicacies. To Amel's deep and long-lasting distress, not one person took any food from his parents' plate. Watching the other plates empty he confessed feeling humiliated and rejected by his peers and their parents. It had taken 20 years for him to find the voice within him to organize and tell that story. But in doing so, even though the other drama students were most supportive, he found difficulty in coming to terms with the emotions that this story had evoked.

In the middle of the year Amel left our drama class and resigned his teaching position to return to Uganda for the first time since his childhood, and journey in his former homeland. Two years later, back in Canada, he told his story again, this time in the public forum of a narrative conference for educators from across North America. I often wonder if in his retellings, Amel has ever described the meta-narrative surrounding that story involving the painful process and circumstances of finding his public voice.

February 12, 1997

How do I describe the morning here? How can I paint the different shades of greens and browns highlighting trunks, branches, and leaves, and the hazy purple of the distant hills? How do I capture the sudden shafts of sunlight that glance through clouds at the dark sea? How can I depict the noise—two crows scolding a thief a hundred feet above me and the slow rhythmic beat of the departing raven's wings? I can track the sound as it moves across the orchard. How can I evoke the silence and the ripple of a breeze in the long grass? I, who am breathless, surprised by the perfection of morning.

In taking sick leave after my initial visit to the Cancer Agency, I felt as if I was in flight, retreating to the only place I knew where I could escape from the poor prognosis I had received. I craved silence. Not the continued silencing of my voice nor my failure to share with others the knowledge that I had cancer. Instead, I was searching for the silence of a space that would allow me time to heal if that was to be my destiny.

I was blessed with being in a job and living in a society that permitted me that time. I was also blessed with being in a marriage of over 30 years where I received the kind of support that I would need. However much I instinctively rejected Sontag's separation of two mutually exclusive kingdoms, by my actions I had tacitly accepted it. Like Judith Zaruches, I "needed...to think differently and construct new perceptions of my relationship with the world" (Frank, 1995, p. 1).

In my silent space of healing I learned to cry, sometimes out of self-pity perhaps but mostly I suspect for the comfort and physical/emotional release that weeping provided. I cried when I listened to the prisoners' chorus in Beethoven's *Fidelio*, I went downstairs and sobbed in the middle of the night after I awoke from a dream in which I met my wife for the first time, and I cried for no reason at all. "Was weeping such a weakness?" writes Salmon Rushdie. "Was defending to the death such a strength?" (1995, p. 80). My weeping physically engulfed and convulsed me. My whole body shook when I cried and on one occasion I let out a primeval anguished howl which I barely recognized as being mine. Often I wept when I wrote in my journal as the power of my own words moved me in a way I had never before experienced. "The continuing hormone treatment seems to be propelling me along on an emotional roller coaster," I wrote dismissively in my journal, presumably trying to excuse myself for this unmanly behavior.

In my silent space of healing I tried to learn to be invisible like Kirpal Singh, the Sikh sapper in *The English Patient.* "Quite early on I had discovered the overlooked space open to those of us with a silent life" (Ondaatje, 1992, p. 200). My teaching and university career required me to be in the public spotlight where there was little or no opportunity for invisibility. Now I stand in the orchard, sometimes in the rain, motionless like our old gray horse, head bowed. Will I still be here when this place no longer contains me, watching the branches of the apple trees reaching out and touching one another? Is this the overlooked space in my life? The space that I occupied at university is already shrinking the longer I stay away. My voice, the public pedagogical voice, is as silent as the one I had failed to discover when I was first ill.

February 27, 1997
Your eyes tell me you are not here.
Do your thoughts include me?
I am young, awkward, and gauche again,
Wanting to attract your attention
Not knowing how.
How can I reclaim your love?

> *"There are two kingdoms," I say.*
> *"I belong to the one populated by invalids.*
> *You are in the kingdom of the well."*

Deflecting the poison, you say
"Don't try to separate us,"
"We are and always will be one."

I am not alone in my silent space of healing. While my public space is shrinking, my private personal space is expanding in a way that has not occurred since I was first married. At that time we were teachers in an isolated school in the African bush, sharing our day-to-day experiences, storying our lives together. During those three years there was rarely a time when we were apart from each other. Our circle of friends was limited to a handful of people but the pleasure we discovered in one another's company sustained us in our everyday lives and during some very difficult and challenging crises when the country descended into civil war.

I learned the excitement of seeing the world afresh through a different pair of eyes and from a different perspective. I experienced the discomfort of having my strongly held views challenged and the joy and pain of sharing my life with someone else. A loner by inclination, I learned to enjoy not being alone. When I spoke I started to recognize her voice speaking through me. Today, being together again after pursuing two separate careers and almost two separate journeys for so many years, we seem to have slid comfortably and easily back into the relationship we enjoyed in our early married life but I know this to be illusory.

John Bayley, husband to the novelist Iris Murdoch, cared for his wife at home in her final years as she suffered from Alzheimer's disease. Bayley writes,

> Looking back now, I separate us with difficulty. We seem always to have been together. But memory draws a sharp divide, nonetheless. The person I was at that age now seems odd to myself—could I *really* have been in love? Could I have felt at least some of the time, all that jealousy, ecstasy, misery, longing, unhopefulness, mingled with a fever of possibility and joy? I can hardly believe it. (1998, p. 80)

Like Bayley I saw myself as a far different person from when I was first married, but I believed my wife to be the same as I always remembered her. In the intervening years, I had failed to notice how strong she had become, how self-assured and articulate in public spaces. How people sought her opinions and looked to her for leadership. Underlying all this she has retained the same gentleness and uncompromising sense of fair play I can always remember. While I had been in the city teaching, she had been in the country running our home and nurturing our family. I was only a part-time participant in her life, and our love for one another had changed from that which we had enjoyed when we were first married.

My journal entries in my first months of having cancer reveal how much I had retreated into myself, and how much I relied on her to be my voice, coping with asking questions related to my condition and then summarizing the responses later. When she left the house in the morning to go to school, I felt the emptiness. Through her I learned to discover the immediate natural world that now surrounded me. On the Christmas Day following my diagnosis, my wife gave me a present, a hand-made wooden bird feeder. "Now that you have to stay at home and convalesce you can watch the birds," she said. This was the strangest present she had ever given me, rather like a father who gives his son a train set so he himself can play with it, I thought.

March 5, 1997

What have I learned, what new knowledge have I gained? I know the difference between a male and female downy woodpecker. I know that the chickadees and nuthatches prefer sunflower seeds to millet but they love suet most of all. Sitting alone at the kitchen table, eating my lunch, I know the closeness and love of Angela. A hawk, with slate gray wings and a mottled white and brown breast, is sitting on the fence by the bird feeder. The small birds have darted away save for a downy that has climbed quickly into a branch of the plum tree where it hangs motionless, frozen, creating the illusion of being invisible. I lean out of the window and clap my hands at the hawk, which flies lazily, arrogantly away. The woodpecker remains still for another five minutes and then when other smaller birds return it clambers down backwards onto the suet. A dark desolate sort of day. One of thin, cold rain.

There is a space that lies between the two kingdoms. I imagine this space as being broad, treeless, and with sweeping vistas. The kind of physical space traveled by Christian in *Pilgrim's Progress* or across which Don Quixote might have scattered and vanquished sheep or tilted at windmills. My diagnosis of cancer was my first real encounter with solitude. There have been times in my life when I have deliberately chosen to be alone, tramping in places like the Western Highlands of Scotland, conducting research in a library, or losing myself in some large city. But I had never faced the stark sense of aloneness that I felt now.

Up to that stage in my life I don't think I had ever really known people with cancer. There was no one with whom I felt I could talk about a shared experience and I dismissed the thought of meeting with a support group of complete strangers to talk about my problems. When friends and colleagues phoned me they were loving and supportive but our points of contact in university life were slipping away. Some were uneasy in talking about cancer. Perhaps I was most surprised by the lengths that they seemed to take to protect me.

July 17, 1997
  The heat has been unbearable. On my arrival at the cancer lodge last night to start my seven weeks of radiation treatment the sight of all the elderly patients sitting, watching television game shows, or huddling over jigsaw puzzles devastated me. So many people crowded together, bald women—some with turbans and some with wigs, elderly gray-faced men creeping around, and then there were the smokers on the outside porch talking at me endlessly. There was no space for quiet—nowhere to escape. I phoned Angela asking her to promise to talk to me on the phone every night at 9:30 p.m. I have spoken to no one. Fortunately there was no one sharing my room but I did not sleep. Kept staring at the hours ticking away on the illuminated dial of the clock radio. This morning I was prepared for radiation treatment. A thickset male nurse in a green smock with short stubby fingers shoved a catheter tube up my penis through to the prostate and left me lying on a stretcher in a closet sized room for 30 minutes. The pain was excruciating. Alone, I screamed and swore at my tormentor. No one heard me. He came back eventually, nonchalantly wheeled me down the corridor to another room, and left me by myself under the radiation machine. We had not spoken a word to each other. I was in terrible pain and suddenly the catheter popped out and I was sobbing with rage and embarrassment. More figures in green smocks rushed from behind the window where I was being observed. As I urinated all over myself a voice called out, "not to worry, we don't need it anyway."

"As a relation to events," writes Shoshana Felman, "testimony seems to be composed of bits and pieces of a memory that has been overwhelmed by occurrences that have not settled into understanding or remembrance, acts that cannot be constructed as knowledge nor assimilated into full cognition, events in excess of our frame of reference" (1992, p. 5). My journal is a kaleidoscopic jumble of bits and pieces of a memory, a memory that is overwhelmed by the disruption that has occurred in my perceptions of myself in relation to others and to my perceptions of my body.

White, male, married, overweight, middle-aged, and in a secure academic position, I found myself at that moment in my life stripped of all the wisdom and understanding I mistakenly believed I had acquired. Reading over the entry on my arrival at the lodge I ask myself, "Where is the tolerance and the empathy for others I had prided myself on?" "Where are my abilities not to stereotype people and to engage in conversation with others whatever their circumstances?" "Where is my ability to observe an event and analyze it critically and objectively?" The process of rethinking and reshaping my life had only just begun. In many ways I felt myself to be a child again.

On the second night I was at the cancer lodge, an elderly man immaculately dressed in white shirt, shorts, and sandals entered my room and announced he was moving in with me because his roommate snored loudly. He sat on the edge of the other bed stiffly and addressed me as if he was presenting his credentials for sharing my room, "My name is Karl. I am 75 years old. I was in England in 1947 after being released as a POW. I joined an amateur dramatic society. I didn't act, just helped with the stage management side. Then one day the director said, 'There is a part for a German officer in this play, Karl. Would you play him please?' Of course I did and do you know that after that performance I had all sorts of girls. No one wanted to come out with me before that."

Everything in that speech was designed to overcome the prejudices against him that were written all over my face. I resented anyone invading my space. He was the first self-declared World War Two German soldier I had ever met. My father had been one of the first British soldiers to discover and liberate the Belsen concentration camp at the end of the war. That and other wartime experiences had brutalized him and eventually scarred my lifelong relations with him. Poor Karl. My dislike for him was evident, and all he wanted was a bed to sleep in and a sympathetic fellow sufferer to talk to who would understand that his greatest fear was losing his sexual potency because of radiation.

Karl was refreshingly open and had a genuine concern for others. The next morning at breakfast, I watched him taking the time to talk to other patients and I started to follow his example. The radiation treatment occupied only about an hour of any day. The rest of the time I spent reading, writing letters, walking, and talking with other patients. My journal is packed with their stories. They suffered from every type, condition, and severity of cancer. We talked about our families and our lives. We laughed a lot, complained about the food, and talked about how many days there were to go before the end of our treatment. Amid all the noise and turmoil of the lodge we learned how to respect one another's privacy, and how to respond when someone needed our help. Sometimes two or three of us would talk long into the night about cancer and how the disease had changed our lives. I learned that the most casual word, glance, or gesture can be of great comfort.

Returning daily to the lodge from my radiation treatment, I was always struck by the sudden change of social dynamics with the departure of some patients and the arrival of new ones. One morning as I was setting out for my treatment, an elderly woman who had been there for at least two weeks saw me in the entrance lobby. "Are you leaving?" she asked. "No," I replied. She walked away, came back, and kissed me on the cheek. That was all. When I returned to the lodge later I found she had gone, her treatment over. She had promised to teach me to knit. Another time a man with a brain tumor and only three months to live, with whom I had been talking for several days, seemed to have vanished in the middle of his treatment. On inquiry, I discovered that because he had lost much of his memory, his friends had only just discovered that he was at the lodge. They had whisked him away so he could be with them.

For that moment in time all of us at the lodge were held captive in each other's company saying the words we hoped would make us better. We never disputed what the doctors told us or denied the correctness of anyone else's diagnosis. The second hot sultry evening I was at the lodge, an 80-year-old woman sat on the front porch repeating to me over and over again, "I am going home tomorrow. My doctor told me, 'Edie, I am sending you home, cancer free.'" I knew it would be months before the X rays would reveal whether or not she had been cured but I told her how pleased I was for her. Every new prognosis was shared and discussed at length. We tolerated the present but wanted to stake our claim in a future beyond radiation and life at the cancer lodge.

Mark, a young, gentle Chinese Canadian suffering from throat cancer, had bought a stereo system while he was in Vancouver. Looking forward to playing it when he arrived home in the north gave him something to hold onto. He had lost everything else. When he was first diagnosed with cancer his wife of one month had left him and he had lost his job as an engineer in the local pulp mill. Like so many others, one day he left suddenly and I had no chance to say "Goodbye." Carol, a middle-aged woman with breast cancer, told me that she had recently sold her business, which had taken her 20 years to develop, to her daughter for a minimal amount and when her husband discovered she had cancer, he left her destitute. I was constantly reminded of ways in which the sick are discarded, and the dreadful punishing life blows being delivered to my fellow travelers and storytellers.

In Janet Hobhouse's autobiographical novel, *The Furies*, her last chapter is entitled "Alone." Suffering from terminal ovarian cancer herself, Hobhouse recounts the final moments of her main character's life in New York. Her former husband now living far away in London is quite unable to handle her news, and later thinks he is consoling her by saying that friends have expressed their sympathy for him as if they are still married. Hobhouse writes,

> But we weren't together because he was in the death-free zone, where there was all the time in the world, nothing but pink, hazy future, and you could simply cast off the past. This new place I was in was quite different. There was high emotion and fear and a lot of drudgery: the sudden world of doctors and waiting rooms, insurance forms and constant appointments, of boredom muffling terror. It was a world full of portents, too, secret codes and deciphering, where you read professional faces for 'true' information, learned doctors' euphemisms and what their sudden silences could mean. All words were scanned for some double entendre, some secret message from out there. (1993, p. 107)

I can think of no other description that so aptly describes the deadly fear and day-to-day tedium and stress of cancer treatment as that written by Janet Hobhouse in the final days of her life. I would be less than honest if I said that I enjoyed staying at the cancer lodge. When the time came for me to go, I left at the first possible moment after my last radiation session. There were no times for "good-byes." I was so eager to leave I forgot to hand in my room key, rushing for my bus without a backward glance. I do wonder if people missed me in the same way as I missed patients like Michael. I exchanged phone numbers with several people but apart from one or two short telephone conversations, I have not had any further communication with my fellow patients at the lodge.

October 10, 1997
We need in love, to practice only this:
Letting each other go. For holding on

Comes easily; we do not need to learn it. (Rilke 1989, p. 85)

Memory is the only afterlife I have ever believed in. But the forgetting inside us cannot be stopped. We are programmed to betray. (Ignatieff, 1993, p. 4)

I am writing and storying myself into re-birth and re-being.

I often think about my fellow patients at the cancer lodge and the journeys they have taken since we were thrown together for those few brief weeks. We became such close confidants, I wonder why we have not kept in touch, why we let each other go so quickly and easily. But then I realize that although we may have enriched each others' lives, this was not a time about which we would ever wish to reminisce. We may never meet each other again but the stories we told one another are now collectively shared by all of us. For me the healing I experienced at the lodge was just as powerful as the radiation treatment I underwent at the cancer agency, and an important stage in my ongoing quest for the restoration of my health and my search for the voice that would story my journey.

Across the open space that lies between and beyond the two kingdoms, I was to make many personal changes in my life with regard to diet, exercise, and health but none has been so demanding as the personal examination of myself in relation to those around me. In becoming "a witness to my illness" in my daily writing, I was forced to confront my own life in terms of my sickness and the actions I would take to secure my recovery. As an academic in the field of drama, I had worked through narrative for many years in theatrical spaces, in my research, and in my students' writing and research. I promised my students protection in finding their own voices and telling their stories but I rarely exposed myself and my life to the public scrutiny I demanded of them. Revisiting "the empty space" many years later, Peter Brook writes, "another aspect of the empty space is that the emptiness is shared: it's the same space for everyone who is present" (1993, p. 6). I believe I am still in the process of finding the voice and the language to story my life more openly and honestly; to break the silence that crippled me even before I was first diagnosed with cancer.

Audre Lorde writes, "I was going to die, if not sooner then later, whether or not I had ever spoken myself. My silences had not protected me. Your silence will not protect you....In the transformation of silence into language and action, it is vitally necessary for each one of us to establish or examine her function in that transformation, and to recognize her role as vital within that transformation" (1980, p. 20).

One of the first people to confide in me as a fellow cancer patient approached me quite unexpectedly. She was a secretary in my department and we had rarely spoken to one another. "I had ovarian cancer," she said. "I didn't know," I replied. "I don't tell anyone. It was long and painful but I feel I have changed as a person as a result of my experience." At the time I wrote in my journal I recognized the common bond between us, and the courage she had shown in breaking her silence in order to comfort, encourage, and strengthen me. Such a few words, such a brief personal contact, but her disclosure transformed our relationship with one another and gave me some early insights into the importance of sharing one's cancer story with others however discomforting that might be.

This incident like so many others I have described was jotted down months ago. Selecting and disclosing entries from my journal for this essay has been difficult. Many of them are still quite raw and painful. This is the first time I have written publicly about my cancer journey and I have been particularly aware of Primo Levi's (1988) warning that while frequent evocation of an event keeps memories fresh and alive, a memory evoked too often can become fixed into a stereotype.

In choosing the metaphor of the wayfarer and his journey to describe my illness I found myself continually checking myself to ensure I was not writing the stereotypical sickness story, in which the patient casts him/herself in the role of hero/victim with the medical profession as villains/oppressors, and travels back and forth between Sontag's two kingdoms, finally arriving back transformed and whole again in the "kingdom of the well."

Although the journey metaphor has been used by other writers afflicted with life-threatening diseases, I wished to avoid the "struggle or battle" metaphor I had encountered in so many books, largely because I believe there are no battles to be waged, only lives to be lived and stories to be told. I shall probably tell my story quite differently if I choose to revisit my journals. Although I would argue that this present description and examination of my life as a cancer patient is as honest as I can write it at this point, I do not claim to be telling you the whole/literal truth. The metaphor has in itself shaped the truth I have shared with you, and the stories I have told about others and myself. Even the stories themselves have already changed and will continue to change in the retelling(s) as I gain greater power and control over the voice I have discovered to story my life and share it with others.

References

Bayley, J. (1998). *Iris: A memoir of Iris Murdoch.* London: Abacus.

Brook, P. (1967). *The empty space.* Harmondsworth, England: Penguin.

Brook, P. (1993). *The open door.* New York: Pantheon Books.

Felman, S. (1992). Education and crisis. In S. Felman and D. Laub (Eds.), *Testimony: Crises of witnessing literature, psychoanalysis, and history* (pp. 1–57). New York: Routledge.

Frank, A. W. (1995). *The wounded storyteller: Body, illness, and ethics.* Chicago: University of Chicago Press.

Hobhouse, J. (1993). *The furies.* New York: Anchor Books.

Ignatieff, M. (1993). *Scar tissue.* London: Chatto & Windus.

Levi, P. (1988). *The drowned and the saved* (R. Rosenthal, Trans.). New York: Summit Books.

Lorde, A. (1980). *The cancer journals.* San Francisco: aunt lute books.

Ondaatje, M. (1992). *The English patient.* London: Picador.

Paton, A. (1948). *Cry the beloved country.* New York: Charles Scribner's Sons.

Rilke, R. M. (1989). Requiem for a friend. In S. Mitchell (Ed. and Trans.), *The selected poetry of Rainer Maria Rilke* (pp. 73–87). New York: Vintage International.

Rose, G. (1995). *Love's work.* London: Chatto & Windus.

Rushdie, S. (1995). *The moor's last sigh.* Toronto: Alfred A. Knopf Canada.

Sontag, S. (1978). *Illness as metaphors and AIDS and its metaphors.* New York: Anchor Books.

❱ Reaching Haiku's Pedagogical Nature

Bruce David Russell

The state of Nature has a law of Nature to govern it, which obliges everyone, and reason, which is that law, teaches all mankind who will consult it, that being all equal and independent, no one ought to harm another...
—John Locke, *Of the State of Nature*

This reworking of a traditional short form of poetry begins with the voice of a giant of legal philosophy whose ideas came forth during a period of expanding nationalism and are still echoing through the workings of Western justice today. How the legacy of Locke influences our discussions on responsible citizenship today is not my main concern, for my hope is to widen the curricular space surrounding historically conceived "nature" (as capitalized above) and reconsider these diverse understandings positioned in the pedagogy of haiku. This will involve an intersecting of culture and aesthetics that highlights the individual's place in earthly and human nature, informed by the historical location of language. Ultimately, this is a view toward an intercultural consideration of the poetic, historical, and spiritual values that lie at the heart of a Japanese aesthetic sensibility, aspects of which we already find in our schools. The inherently spiritual teachings and practices of haiku will be revealed as a proposal for new linguistic and cultural themes in humanities education.

Awaiting snow
Poets in their cups
See lightning flash
—Basho, *Basho: Haiku*

The question is whether a short form of poetry provides the structures, practices, and rituals that open the curricular spaces of individual creativity and group sharing that transform a lesson or unit into an enriching cross-cultural experience. These well-traveled, frequently translated poems indigenous to Japan have been floating through North American language arts classrooms for decades. Their allure for teachers and students has perhaps been the surprising flexibility of a striking brevity that invokes an instantaneous, silent reflection on an event, while highlighting the importance and expressive potential of thoughtful word choice and placement. We are drawn to their portability partly because a structure limited in syllables has not held haiku poets back from producing deeply thoughtful language full of symbolism. Haiku adapt to experimentation with various devices—assonance, alliteration, and internal rhyme—while Zen-inspired simplicity continues to inform and instruct us that a poem that is too extravagant with words may risk putting an over-played description between the reader and the lived experience the poet hopes to capture and convey. Beyond the challenges of translation and the inevitable loss of meaning as Japanese ideograms give way to the symbols of other languages, the basic objective of composing haiku in English remains universal. That is, the essence of haiku—immediate life experience—provides a powerful basis for adaptation. In fact, haiku display an amazing resilience in changes in the traditions, customs, and conventions of the original form by experimentalists around the world who represent a wide range of cultural experience. Stopping to consider the persuasion of fewer words is a powerful process, given the way we are inundated with language text and print in our daily lives. The shared history of haiku, then, re-textualizes fundamental human emotions to the extent where it is time to ask ourselves what this form may teach educators about the limitations of our predominant approaches to imagery and temporality, thus providing students with an opportunity to explore their own contributions to a historical, linguistic learning experience attentive to time and place. The "lightning flash" for us might well come in finding ourselves located between states of nature.

My foray into haiku should not be construed as an attempt to deconstruct the supposed mystical, spiritual side of this poetry, but should lead us to consider a Japanese sensibility that on one level locates a poem in nature as it pulls the reader into an appreciation of the symbols that trigger a sense of the human place in the ritual and cyclical movement of the world (Hass, 1994). Familiar vocabulary allowed a Japanese reader to acknowledge the season of the poem's setting, and recognize what we might in the West call the "mood," exposing a second level of the haiku's character, as these natural references allow the poet to bypass elaborate attempts to set an atmosphere for the reader because of the transient nature of Buddhist thought underlying these traditional renderings. Popularly understood as a sense of the contingency of nature assimilated into Japanese thought, we might first recognize how such a perspective may be transferred across cultures—even generations—pointing to the undeniable importance of the poet as aesthete, seeker, humanist, and naturalist. And what of the reader? There is a sense of an exposure to the elements in the way the readers of the poems connect to common themes and references. Entering a haiku provides an example of the difference between a text of *pleasure* —reinforcing one's comfortable beliefs about the world—and the text of *bliss*—creating a disturbance of the reader's historical, cultural, and linguistic assumptions (Barthes, 1975). Developing such a literary appreciation is a profoundly instructive example of how readers delve into the moment of a writing and locate themselves within a poem. When we encourage students to cultivate word usage that appeals to the senses, whether the vehicle is one of natural phenomena or of material surroundings, a space of individual and collective intergenerativity for the writer and the audience begins to develop. What is more essential to teaching than providing images for the imagination? Teachers can call upon traditional or contemporary haiku to place a thoughtful movement of words in an intersecting context of nature, expression, and understanding. These little poems are instrumental in helping us ask the class: "How do we locate ourselves within a poem?"

Within the nature of haiku is an opening and closing of history and culture that is offered to us as a reinterpretation of personal experience. It comes packaged as an "act of a mind and spirit that has collected and gathered itself historically" (Gadamer, 1989/1999). Haiku's characteristic appeal to immediacy produces an intimacy that provokes us to reflect upon how our poetry or prose will integrate history with our present desire to describe our experiences naturally. Where is North America's current fascination with endless forms of communication and often fast-paced stimuli leading us? The haiku moment might restructure the context of our relationship with popular culture in a more complex view of temporality that involves the cyclical, spiritual, and chronological. The dominance of empty images today does not override our need to continue to ponder the importance and influence of the lived moment. Social commentators lament the lack of ways to slow down the pace of life, while many students wonder what all the fuss is about. There is a possible space of repose in this intergenerational dialogue, a step toward a mediating process that addresses the inclinations of different ages and cultures while pulling back from the influence of overwhelming technological change; it may remind us of our need to be aware that in the process of interpreting a tradition the cultural aspects are experienced not as something over and done with, but as something still important for the present (Gadamer, 1989/1999). In addition, we need not worry about attempting to capture the full measure of the poet's intentions; we should focus on how the words reveal possibilities that prepare us for future interpretations of experience.

If teachers approach haiku as an unfinished event, the classroom will become less focused on the terminated, finite poem as end product, and more on playing with word order and searching for thoughtful communication as important themes. Striving to achieve a clear structure via rereading then becomes less an excessive framing and binding of expression than an invitation to enter into creating a shared experience. In a semantically seductive way this transforms us into a conduit of our moment before we even realize we have been pulled into the process of imaginative meaning-making. By eliciting a profound, immediate response and by creating a thoughtful silence, both individual and collective, we participate in the strength of the pedagogy of the event, in construction as a reflective happening. I do not believe that last phrase is an oxymoron, only a habit we do not feel we have the luxury of time to engage in and develop. Haiku allow us to ask, "In what ways has the poet taken us to other places, and what might we generate in these new locations?" Interpreting haiku helps in establishing a platform that allows our students to pursue a constructive reliance upon lived, known experience in a move toward writing that helps us appreciate what it means to be understood in all of our unspoken contradictions. This locates us in the context of individuals as part of a larger whole, interwoven (like a haiku) with the fabric of history, culture, and personal experience that helps us to make a connection to the writing we produce and other interpretations we encounter. The quality of actuality in haiku teaches us to be aware of how we dwell in a state of grace when we do not forsake our origins in a state of nature. We then open up a historical moment when we are aware of our place, melding an interpretive opportunity with the fact that our lives often fall between past, present, and future into a reflective time of substantive insight into what it means to live out an experiential understanding of life. We return to the present, but not before we have been endowed with an outlook that changes our view of the past, allowing us to experience reflective occasions differently in the future.

At times we need to recognize that voices from the past—both our own and others—break through our thoughts and inform our current thinking. The ambiguity of haiku's pedagogy lies in the fact that how contemplating an event may or may not pull the individual into a space of intersecting temporalities. The struggle with words and syllables that represents an individual process of giving meaning to a captured moment has its own teaching, but becomes secondary to the search for those elusive times when we are able to understand and connect with ourselves as located in interpretation. Such is our part in the whole of a natural human experience. The haiku form is a hybrid of interconnected and independent lines of deeply cultural thought which offer a play upon a relationship of part to whole that is found in so many aspects of life. I refer to our inability to take the time to reflect upon moments of personal significance. It is important to guide students in expressing emotion—but I'm alluding to something separate from a description of the latest experience that has moved us. There is a different kind of rationality involved when one attempts to interpret the importance of the understatement. Haiku has been called in essence "a metaphor without metaphor" (Wohlfart, 1994). This speaks to the silence invoked by the seeming lack of description, a kind of truncated simile at best, creating a shift in perspective that pulls us away from an appeal to our senses by the use of figurative language that is so common to poetry. I've hinted that this feature attracts many to haiku, but we cannot underscore the importance of this move away from a dependence on comparative devices to a space where language is suspended in the nonverbal and the potentially non-poetical. This halting of language leads haiku to a point of counter-description that continues to emphasize the experience, but in a new language, one that is usually beyond us (Barthes, 1982). This loss of meaning paradoxically engenders a pedagogic opportunity that allows the classroom to explore the importance of not simply knowing a concept, but interpreting events in a way that allows an understanding that is pertinent to our lives.

It is in this non-figurative moment that our words move into a space between the concepts of nature made famous by John Locke. The first is the "state of Nature," which I will call a metaphor for all that we are born into (Latin: *natura* or *nascor*; to be born). This metaphor combines the *state of nature* we are born into with a *state of grace* which emphasizes that we begin life surrounded by the social, the cultural, and the linguistic, and must struggle to achieve the reason that makes us civilized humans. Rituals and responsibilities develop along with us as we mature, as do the forms of communication we use to understand our place in society. The law of nature becomes the codified rules we must learn to be responsible citizens and dwell peacefully in society, and yet we sense there is more than this to our existence. What is it to be constantly reminded that we are poised between a state of nature and a state of grace? How can education help us to accept that we will always exist between the two, not alienated by either, but learning from both? Our practices often take us further from an appreciation of the physical, planetary nature we are closely connected to, and many contemporary movements are reminding humankind of its responsibility to earth. In the haiku's insistence upon an adherence to time and place there is a "breech of meaning" that subverts our usual understanding of appreciating poetry to a degree where we are dealing with traces of meaning that result in "a vision without commentary" (Barthes, 1982). We need to continue to experience moments that help us to reflect upon our ability to hang on to historically informed images long after they have passed. The mystery lies in how significant many of these experiences remain for us throughout life. This is not a call to romanticize a mystical, silent Zen approach to language, but a suggestion that it is best to sink down through the levels of the haiku and practice an attentiveness to the particular human consciousness a poem reflects (Hass, 1994). In bringing our experience to bear on appreciating a haiku, reworking our understanding of our captured moment, we learn to focus upon the situated, textual importance of words. The metaphor has long been a teaching tool used to carry students from the sensual-visual level to the abstract-conceptual level. Savoring a haiku leads us to consider where comparison stops and compassion begins. We undertake a journey through words using our own combination of experience, emotion, and culture. In a haiku we learn that at times what is literal and what is metaphorical become less important than the student's take-off into a world of brief literary expression, incorporating past experience, present knowledge of vocabulary, and future possibilities for the unpredictability of memory. We have then entered a space of Metonymy and the role of language in interpreting what is remembered and forgotten, changed and unchanged, when we engage different forms of nature (human, earthly) through an accessible, immediate text. This entails an opening of many middle spaces in the curriculum (Aoki, 1991) that teach through uncertainty and difference. By seizing upon the moment, exploring the variety and intensity of experience we encourage haiku to develop in us a metonymic skill of spiritual poetics.

The haiku moment can be appreciated for what it represents, rather than as a comparison with other experiences. Interpreting or composing a haiku involves a degree of historical reconstruction that loses its anachronistic qualities as we bring the event forward to a rediscovery of what makes it intelligible and insightful in the present. Composing haiku loosens a hold on historical distance that can make literature less appealing to new readers, shaking a fixation on chronology, and allowing learners to play with the expanded boundaries of a nonlinear temporality. The advantage of following the traditional syntactic structure of haiku is that it becomes a tool in exposing other demarcations of time, like seasonal or spiritual moments. A non-modern Japanese literary genre that has foundations supposedly far removed from our postmodern lives somehow brings us back to what it means to experience something plain, manageable and profound. Consider the ever-present clash of opinion—again, often intergenerational—surrounding the importance of history in our lives. Reading and understanding the subtle qualities of haiku can give an individual a sense of the intertwining temporalities which we must resensitize through seductive images. A linear understanding of history has failed us by persuading us to trivialize and subjugate all other ways of experiencing time, and as a result we have difficulty reflecting on the beliefs of others who seem to have little stake in our present world. Haiku position our thoughts to consider the importance of the moment in our lives, and provide a space of reflection for us to consider that we do not access our most memorable experiences in a linear way, but play them out through our continuing emotions and thoughts. The implications for a point of view that includes more than one temporality for our students lies in helping them to see that our thinking constantly diverges from chronology. We are then able to expose historical moments that transmit importance to the present. The recognition of an event makes it possible for a careful consideration to begin. Granted, the compact structure of haiku establishes a comfort zone at the same time as it potentially limits expression by minimizing words and syllables, but here lies the strength of getting beyond metaphor to a language that cuts figurative description down to the bare essentials of poetic understanding. We learn to present a playful event within a five-seven-five structure that celebrates a brevity with certain advantages over longer modes of expression.

Working outside of the customary seasonal signposts of the Japanese, relied upon for centuries as a kind of locating referent, we can ask students where word choices locate and position them in relation to nature and to people in their lives. In fact, it is empowering to note that we recognize many historical references while creating more, in the context of those issuing from contemporary culture. It is fascinating that for students in Japan who now have little attachment to the agricultural society that produced haiku themes, seasonal images continue to hold significant nostalgic power. Something in the nature of both the reader and the poem has the potential to place us in the moment and appreciate its living quality, even though few of us may have a personal experience to draw upon. We need to ask when a hermeneutics of silence helps us to arrive at an event's meaning differently from a hermenutics of speech (Sundara Rajan, 1991). A haiku poet searches out those moments in nature—in our nature—that return to become significant for us, and may be so for others. This tells me that the themes for haiku are limitless, so long as we seek to work with language that is potentially multivocal and communal because of its experiential quality. The generative characteristics of this poetry lend a life-affirming intertextual flavor to our writing that gives us the confidence to explore the placement of events in many genres of literature. By asking students to play with an original poem, we might demystify the process of capturing a moment, to allow other interpretations. Here is a student's reworking of the earlier Basho poem, replacing the last word of each line:

> Awaiting *words*
> Poets in their *ink*
> See lightning *dance*

A return to Locke's passage causes me to ask what human nature is in its natural state. If we explore with our students why reason must be legislated, we must also discuss the human qualities found in moments of reflection that allow us to treat each other with the respect that informs our need to feel connected to the communities we share. What locates us reflectively is the knowledge that we can articulate our experiences as we learn from the significance of our contact with others. One area in which to begin a drawing together of the natural and the social is an increased awareness of the cyclical forces of nature and the ritualistic movements of community in our lives. This means exploring the influence of events in our lives, as well as the rites of passage that mark birth and death in our midst. In a profound way this entails us facing and reflecting upon a pedagogical universality in the difference we experience and describe as individually profound. In mentioning a trans-historical discourse within haiku my intent is to reveal an intertextuality that eludes the generalization we try to place upon it. These images or ideas of nature are not traditional because they are not locked in time but move through temporalities to become meaningful in our present-lived lives. We become positioned between the historical moment of individual significance and the universally recognizable event. Not only do we learn to appreciate a new sense of how temporality works in our personal histories; we also begin to see that the truly lasting qualities of human character are like nature, beyond our attempts to generalize them.

References

Aoki, T. (1991). *Inspiriting the curriculum: Talks to teachers*. Edmonton: University of Alberta.

Barthes, R. (1975). *The pleasure of the text*. New York: Hill and Wang.

Barthes, R. (1982). *Empire of signs*. New York: Hill and Wang.

Basho. (1985). *Basho: Haiku* (L. Stryk, Trans.). New York: Penguin.

Gadamer, H-G. (1989/1999). *Truth and method* (2nd ed.). New York: Continuum.

Hass, R. (1994). *The essential haiku*. Hopewell, NJ: Ecco Press.

Locke, J. (1959). *An essay concerning human understanding*. New York: Dove Publications.

Sundara Rajan, R. (1991). *Studies in phenomenology, hermeneutics and deconstruction*. New Delhi: Indian Council of Philosophical Research.

Wohlfart, G. (1994). *Haiku: Metaphor without metaphor*. Paper presented to the Asia-Pacific Foundation of Canada, Vancouver, BC.

❯ On Being a Disciple of Memoir[1]

Cynthia Chambers

Just as I walk the coulees where I live, searching for animal tracks, beaten paths, deer trails, old cairns, and holy rocks, trying to know and understand this place and my place in it, so too am I drawn to the landscape of memory. Just like my memory, at first glance, the coulees do not seem particularly remarkable. They appear as a series of undulating hills that simply relieve the boring flatness of a silent prairie. Yet with a second look, points of color become visible: a pear cactus in yellow spring-bloom, rose hips fully ripened midst brittle autumn leaves.

Sometimes out walking, I feel I am alone in the center of some windy and barren universe. Yet I know I am not. I learn to recognize a small herd of deer nestled into their earthen beds, chewing and watching. I hear the meadowlark hidden in the spear grass but rarely see her. When I first came to the coulees I didn't know what a meadowlark was, and didn't notice its distinctive call. Moving down toward the river, I am startled by the huge hare that hops out of the brush and then disappears over the hill, his white tail flashing in the chinook-dry grass.

Another day, I suddenly notice a coyote tracking me from the safe distance of a parallel ridge. Maybe she has tracked me before. She trots along glancing at me over her shoulder: no need to watch her steps, she knows this place. This is her home. When I stop, she stops. She turns in my direction, sits down on her haunches, watches and waits. I too watch and wait. Then as if to end the standoff, she points her snout skyward and howls. I imagine her song means something like this:

I hunt in this coulee with my pack.

---

[1] Originally presented as part of a performance session titled "What Does Writing Autobiographically Do to Us?" at the American Educational Research Association annual conference held in New Orleans, USA, on April 26, 2000.

I live in that den with my cubs.
I was born right down there.
I will die here somewhere,
And so will my cubs.
But you, you are a stranger.
I warn you.

Coyote's howl-song reminds me once again that I am an immigrant in this place, and I always will be.

The drama and texture of the coulees just across the road from my house are revealed only as I walk there day after day. Then weeks go by and I don't go into the coulees. Perhaps I resent the cold and the snow, or I want to hide from the July sun and the mosquitoes. But when I stop visiting, I stop seeing (or hearing and feeling) in the way the coulees invite. And when I finally return, the landscape appears once again empty and silent. I have to learn all over again how to walk and watch, learn and listen in this space, which at first seems to have little to show, little to say.

Like the coulees, I share my memory with others. I am neither alone nor the true center of what is remembered, even when I think I am. Memory is a densely populated landscape and without much difficulty I easily notice those I love and care to remember. When I am in the habit of returning to memory, just as when I walk in the coulees, I quickly conjure up the images of those I used to love but no longer do, as well as those I hardly remember. And if I am disciplined enough to return regularly and consistently, I begin to imagine those I don't know at all.

My memory is also inhabited by beings—like Athena, the Greek goddess, or Yamozha, the Dogrib creator of the world, Socrates and Plato, Wasagiachuk, the Cree trickster, or Lao Tsu, or Winston Churchill whom my grandmother told me over and over how much she hated because he ordered the police to stop the women demonstrating in the streets for the right to vote and the police did stop them, with their billy clubs.

In my memory, I carry around characters from family stories like Uncle Sandy Scott who moved to Italy from Edinburgh to start his own religion, 50 years before I was even born. Or my great-grandmother, whose prophecies of war have apparently all come true, even though she died in 1936. Or my great-grandfather who, my grandmother always told us, was a gifted surgeon but turned out to be a hospital orderly repeatedly hospitalized with delirium tremors.

I don't know about you but my memory is all of this.

Some of the memories I carry around are from photographs I have never seen and stories I have never heard. I imagine my mother's family, moving from England at the turn of the twentieth century to the small prairie town of Cartwright, Manitoba, astride horses that are strung out along the horizon in an uneven line, the women sitting sidesaddle holding parasols, the men, backs erect, grasping their reins, in that British manner of casual mastery over beast and landscape. I have never actually seen the photograph, only heard of it. I know few if any stories about these people.

Alongside images of my mother from a recent visit, her hands gnarled by arthritis, struggling with the buttons of her blouse, lives my memory of the 1934 black and white newsreel which featured her and her brother diving off the 10-meter board at the old Kitsilano Pool in Vancouver, cheered on by their one-armed swimming coach, Phil French, who had trained Johnny Weissmuller, of *Tarzan, the Ape Man* fame. Even though I have never seen the actual newsreel, I know she was only two years old at the time of the film which then showed in movie theaters everywhere.

My early memories of romance include Gilbert Blythe pulling Anne Shirley's red pigtails in Avonlea, P.E.I., as much as they do my first lover and his 1960 convertible Ford Montcalm with bucket seats, even though I never saw P.E.I. until long after I was divorced, my children had grown, and I had outgrown *Anne of Green Gables*, or thought I had.

In the remembered place of memory, I feel all of these ghosts as well as others, some from tribes with whom I have only a passing acquaintance or none at all: Chairman Mao, Marie Antoinette, and Akaitcho, the great peacemaker of the Dene. In this landscape of memory, those we do not know are as important as the ones we do. Memory is home to them all.

I don't know about you but my memory is all of this.

In the coulees, the west wind gusts up to 50 and 60 kilometers an hour for days on end. (Such a wind keeps you inside, hiding under the bedcovers, grinding your teeth.) Although the wind blows in all directions, it is the prevailing west wind that bends branches, twists tree trunks, and sweeps and grinds the coulees.

In my memory, it is the hard blow of English that drowns out other languages. But when the roar abates, tongues I once knew, like Dogrib, come to me in my dreams. And when the wind is still, I can sometimes hear fragments of languages I never knew, but might have learned, like Latin or Tutchone. And, I must remember, all of these languages, with their varied sounds and multiple meanings shape and reshape this place of remembering.

When I walk in the coulees, I stumble over bleached skulls and clumps of fur. I find hawk feathers and pieces of wood too far away from the river to have drifted here. Aspects of my memory are like this: They appear random and episodic. Words I have seen but never heard, such as "verisimilitude," ambush me from the most unlikely places. My mind is full of words I think I know but don't. I always thought a jukebox was a jute-box, with a /t/ instead of a /k/, probably because in our family we threw two bits into a Wurlitzer if we wanted to hear the latest 45-rpm record. Hiding and appearing at the most inconvenient times are other ancient words like "beauty-parlor" or Canadianisms such as "chesterfield." I say idiotic things like "The Lord stone the crows" or "Get up off your duff" and my children gawk at me like I am using a foreign tongue and I suppose I am. For them, Duff is the beer that Homer Simpson drinks.

Ugly conversations that I wish I could erase keep surfacing in my memory like stones on my trail down to the river. Like when one of my lovers was leaving me and I screamed at him: "I have wasted four years of my life on you."

Things left unsaid haunt memory as well. A few weeks ago, the lover I speak of—whom I hadn't seen in a dozen years or more—was changing a tire on the side of the road outside of Denver when another driver hit and killed him. Death alters the landscape of memory drastically like a volcano or an avalanche. I never told Tom that the time I spent with him was not a waste but a gift. And now I never will. The landscape of memory is filled with these bits and pieces torn from their original circumstance, now bleached and tattered but still turning up like bad pennies. There is another one of those sayings I have inherited from somewhere and I don't really know what it means.

I don't know about you but my memory is all of this.

And of course, I know the skull belonged to a deer, which belonged to a herd, which belongs to a species that descended from a prehistoric genus I never knew the name of. And I know the stones over which I trip come from a mountain via a river formed by a glacier from an age when ice was infinite. I know most things are connected, but sometimes memory feels random and episodic. Tom and my children, my mother and the newsreels are interrelated through stories, and those stories are connected to other stories, big ones like the Irish potato famine, immigration, and colonization, and these big stories are connected to the other big stories, such as myths and legends that go back thousands of years.

I remember hearing about Dogrib elders who knew stories that took several days and nights to tell. And people would come to listen. All of these stories—the ones I remember and the ones I never knew—make the landscape of memory worth exploring and knowing well. And if these stories were all connected they would form long intertwined tales that would take days or even months to tell, if only there were still people who could tell stories that long. If only there were people who knew the stories, and knew them well. And if only there were audiences who could still listen for that long, audiences who cared enough to remember.

Sometimes you have to hear one good story to remember another waiting to be told. And I confess that is why I turn to memoir. I read memoirs—good and bad—always looking and hoping for that one good story, the one that shows me the beauty and the way in what at first appears to be a barren landscape. I'm a critical reader because I know even memoir can't turn drivel into literature or angst into insight. I'm a crabby reader because I have to plough through so much badly written memoir and autobiography. But all it takes is one. So I continue to read, watching and listening for the story that I can follow, for the trails—ancient and new—that make this landscape navigable for me and for others. You need these stories, too; you need these trails, these maps. Why? Because like me, you are in a dream, you are lost always trying to find your way home.

I don't know about you but my memory is all of this. Memory is the homeland from which you are always in exile. It is the one place you can never go home to but must always remember, because while the past is forever gone it is also always present. So although I feel like an immigrant here, and I'm lazy and hate the wind, through the discipline of walking I become a disciple of the present. And although I am an exile there, and I hate writing my way back and forth, through the discipline of memoir, I become a disciple of the past. I tramp the trails that often lead nowhere, always hoping to find myself on the one going somewhere. I continue to scout memory for the significant bits and pieces and then I carry them home to tell the one good story that must be told.

❱ Auto'•geo'•carto'•graphia'
(A Curricular Collage)[1]

Wanda Hurren

> **auto'•geo'•carto'•graphia'** [æto jiokarto grðpfið] *n, v.* **1** the representation (through various expressive forms, including maps, text, poetry, dance) of the mingling of self and place. **2** the representation itself is both a noun (thing) and a verb (action/process) in the same moment, acknowledging the constitutive role of signification—*the map is the territory is the map is the territory...*, or,...*the word is the world is the word is the world...*

As a curricular scholar working in the areas of social studies/geography and curriculum theory and research, I am interested in exploring ways in which curriculum might enhance what we know of our places and our selves and I am interested in exploring how what we know of our places and selves might enhance curriculum theory and research. Notions of "identity" and "place" are central to both social studies/geography curriculum and curriculum in its most general sense. Curriculum has been described as the medium in and through which "generations struggle to define themselves and the world" (Pinar, Reynolds, Slattery, & Taubman, 1995, p. 848). Autobiography and geography would seem to be intimately connected to the notion of curriculum. Ivor Goodson (1998) suggests that understanding the emergent process of identity requires "an attention to...social geography and social theory...a social cartography of the self" (p. 47). So, then, I am intent on exploring the

---

[1] Originally presented as part of a performance session titled "Autobiography as an Ethos for Our Time: Living Well With Each Other" at the American Educational Research Association annual conference held in Seattle, USA, on April 14, 2001.

connections between autobiography, geography, and curriculum within teaching and learning and living and theory and research, and I want to explore these connections in ways that attend to embodied knowing: sounds, sights, smells, feelings, memories, gut reactions. I want to pay attention to the physicality of our various places and spaces: prairie or coast or river edge, classrooms and hallways and offices and parking lots and conference rooms.

Cynthia Chambers (1999), a Western Canadian curriculum storyteller, invites us to begin at home in our curricular theorizing. Accepting her invitation, I will share aspects of my own geographical and autobiographical curricular stories, and I will do so in cartographic form. My choice of cartography is designed to draw attention to the common metaphorical references to curriculum as landscape, curriculum as map, and curriculum as field or territory, and to disrupt the typical bird's eye view associated with these cartographic references. In this collage of auto′•geo′•carto′•graphia′, I am choosing to drop down closer to ground level in my curricular storytelling or map-making, to impose and compose stories of place and self within the lines of my everyday maps of teaching, learning, living, and researching. I believe there are many ways to map a territory, and while visual maps and charts are the expected products of cartography, my desire is that the curricular cartography that follows will be more of the "uncharted" type; invoking images/sounds/feelings/smells/memories rather than presenting the dream of exacting territories. In Michael Ondaatje's (1992) *The English Patient*, Caravaggio imagines being in a place that is "under the millimetre of haze just above the inked fibres of a map, that pure zone between land and chart between distances and legend between nature and storyteller" (p. 246). Perhaps this is the zone in which we are all walking, as we compose our various curricular stories/maps, and as we pay attention to embodied knowings of place, self, and curriculum.

WITH APOLOGIES

stepping off a bus
leaving a phone booth
or the laundromat
i am never quite sure
if I have gathered all of myself together
always

a backward glance is necessary
i do not wish to leave a trail of panties
and socks
bits and pieces of my living
scattered along transit lines
forgotten within folds
of weathered yellow pages
(Hurren, 2000, p. 105)

I have chosen to use collage as a textual strategy in order to indicate how these elements, self, place, and curriculum, happen in mingling ways. That is, notions of self are influenced by notions of place which are influenced by notions of curriculum theory and research, and not necessarily in linear fashion. These processes are always already mingling in the moment. In any given moment, it is impossible to freeze-frame this mingling dance and say "oh, this is just about self" or "this is just about place" or "this is just about curriculum." Collage work requires a deliberate overlapping arrangement of bits and pieces. Within collage there are no clean edges or borderlines between the bits and pieces. In my cartographic arrangement of bits and pieces of teaching and living and learning and self and place and theory and research, my desire is to create a collage that catches the constitutive role of the mingling dance of signification.

TEACHING AND LEARNING AND LIVING ON THE EDGE OF PINK

In September
I tried not to press too hard
on the tips
of my freshly sharpened Laurentien pencil crayons
colouring the world
I saved my favourite colours for the big spaces
USA was #5 Purple
#4 Cerise was for the British Commonwealth of Nations

If I was just colouring Canada
#1 Deep Yellow was for my province
a place where men in malls in winter
had #17 Smoke Grey coats, hair, whiskers, and skin
Manitoba was #10 Brown

Alberta was #2 Orange
  the colour of the Camrose grain elevator on our calendar
  beside the fridge
Quebec was #16 French Green
British Columbia was #22 Sky Magenta
I would have chosen #9 Deep Green because of all the trees
except that I always saved #7 Peacock Blue for the ocean
I thought there was a rule about green and blue
not going together: *Green does not go with blue*
my older sister told me one school morning
eyeing my carefully chosen pedal pushers and pop top

In July
living on #22 Sky Magenta
sailing in #7 Peacock Blue
my husband takes the tiller and moves us through the waves
as if we are on the #1 Deep Yellow space of a prairie wheat field
instead of leaving a #10 Brown line
of astonishingly moist overturned soil
behind us in #7 Peacock Blue
we leave a #23 Cotton White line of air mixed with water
(Hurren, 2000, p. 53).

Dear Professor Hurren:
Thank you for agreeing to review the book Under the Tough Old Stars:
Ecopedagogical Essays. *I have enclosed a copy of the Notes for Reviewers.*
Please use this as a reference but feel free to create your review in a way that
you believe best suits the book and your audience....

Breathing through yet another week of −30° C air, trudging through
crisp, dry snow, living through endless dead, fallow fields, I interrupt my
prairie winter to read David Jardine's (2000) collection of
ecopedagogical essays, "Under the Tough Old Stars." And I emerge from
the reading glistening with river spray. Such a moist, scholarly text. His
writing is a performance of how place and self mingle in curricular
theorizing. His notions of ecopedagogy are filled with autobiographical
accounts of places in his world where he is inspired, where he learns to
listen, where he watches himself being watched, at the river edge or in a
stand of aspen. He is demonstrating how place and self are intimately
connected to what we know and how we know it.

On the prairie (an ancient, dried up riverbed) I am always conscious
of the grid system. The landscape easily lends itself to neat and tidy

parallels and perpendiculars. Roads and streets and highways are highly organized here. Never mind that the earth isn't truly flat. It is close enough, and anyway, we have incorporated, at regular intervals, town lines and correction lines to keep the earth's curves in check.

Here, on August afternoons, dust rises up in grids as vehicles move along farm roads, and on cold November days, exhaust collects and hangs suspended in grid formation above town and city streets. If space makes a difference, if location matters when we are concerned with issues of teaching, living, and learning, then how might we acknowledge the autobiographical and the geographical in our curricular endeavors—whether theorizing, researching, or "practicing"?

LIVING A LANDSCAPE OF GEOMETRICAL PROGRESSION

warm
early summer evenings
the upstairs window open to the prairie breeze
my sisters already breathing their sleep breath
I listened to the traffic
living on an edge
inside an intersection
I heard travellers leaving town
sounding off into the depths
until the anticipated click
as they reached the point of intersection
where the railway tracks crossed the highway
upstairs in my bed
blowing over my face and body
a breeze so soft the same breeze
that skimmed over the hood of the car
as it crossed the tracks
years later
still living inside an intersection
but on an opposite corner
on warm sunny afternoons
with my strollered baby
I leave the town behind
the prairie landscape a perfect study of perspective
lines moving off
in ever widening angles
I am always at the vertex
reaching the railroad tracks

I turn back toward town
welcoming the same breeze
that has blown over my body
all these years
(Hurren, 2000, p. 90).

Wayson Choy (1997), a Vancouver-born writer, tells us in his autobiographical writing, "I had been writing fiction about life in Chinatown; Chinatown, all these years, had been writing me" (p. 22).

PROGRAM OF RESEARCH

discuss the objectives
research purpose in context
social and educational context
and the theoretical context for your study
(maximum 25 words)

this research
is framed within a poststructural perspective,
wherein structures of public schooling, both
physical (space allocations, architectural
design) and non-physical (curricular
practices, policies, and procedures), are
examined for their inherent role in identity
formation...

this research
will draw upon the work of Lefebvre (1991)
in defining space as socially produced; of
Mouffe (1992) in defining identity as non-
essential and always in process; and of
Foucault (1986, p. 122) in defining identity
as something that is "proposed, suggested
and imposed on one by one's culture, one's
society and one's social group"...

this research
will focus on the shifting and changeable
nature of both places and identities, and the
theory that "space is at once result and

cause, product and producer" (Lefebvre, 1991, p. 142)...

this research
proposal is 115 words beyond the maximum
and is taking up too much space.

> *Well, the prime real estate in our school, for the girls, definitely, is the bathroom. Not so much now that I am in Grade 12, but in Grade 9, we spent a lot of time in the bathrooms. I don't think it's the same for the guys.* (J., with permission; Hurren, 2001)

> *My daughters were the only children in the school who did not speak English. All the ESL is taught in one school, and it was downtown and we lived too far away for that. I did not want to put my daughters on a bus and send them across the city. They could walk to our neighbourhood school. But they could not speak English.* (B., with permission; Hurren, 2001)

> *Well, there is one hallway and I don't know how it got this name, but it's called Loser Lane, and well, it is the more "loser" types of students that walk there and hang out in that hallway.* (R., with permission; Hurren, 2001)

> *How do we imagine our geographical location, and does it influence our notions of teaching and living and learning?* (Wanda)

Curriculum & Instruction 804

Choose three words to describe your imaginative landscape, and complete this sentence:

If I could tell other curricular theorists one thing about my physical location I would tell them about...

> *Struggling, introspective, underappreciated. If I could tell other curricular theorists one thing about my physical location, I would tell them about my isolation. This is physical isolation that comes from living in a province that is not highly populated and the population is spread out. There is also isolation in a cultural sense. The community I live in is over 95% white, with English as a first language. There are basically no people who are first generation Canadian. We are cocooned....*(Prystay, 2000)

Wild, boring, developing. If I could tell other curriculum theorists one thing about my physical landscape, I would tell them about the opportunities to enjoy to vast and varied land. Our physical landscape is like the people who live here—different, interesting, and worth discovering. (Bast, 2000)

Land of plenty, natural resources, great exporter (of people due to location of other centres with more opportunities and resources). If I could tell other curriculum theorists one thing about my physical location, what would I tell them? I would probably indicate the diversity of it. Saskatchewan has a lot of resources. They include trees, prairie, topsoil, and lakes. There is a misconception that Saskatchewan is nowhere. (Tourigny, 2000)

STATEMENTS OF PLACE

just like any other map
with dots punctuating places
small dots for small places
large dots for large places
on this map a large dot shows this place
Vancouver
like a period at the end of a statement

rolling down the map on prairie afternoons
we looked for places
we read the words beside the dots
not our dots
someone else lived in the dots we found
unlike the dot dwellers we lived in an unedited space
a dotless territory on the map
full of wind and gravel roads and sun
and in our sky jet streams left wispy lines
playing their game of connect the dots
(Hurren, 2000, p. 108).

It is a funny thing about addresses where you live. When you live there you know it so well it is like identity a thing that is so much a thing that it could not ever be any other thing and then you live somewhere else and years later, the address that was so much an address that it was a name like your name and you said it as if it was not an address but something that was living and then years after you do not know what the address was and when you say it it is not a name any more but something you cannot remember. That is what makes your identity not a thing that exists but something you do or do not remember. (Stein, 1985, p. 55)

A List of Seven Small Pleasures: Self-Portrait at 42

I
gin and tonic on Friday evening
ice cubes clinking inside a thick glass tumbler
Van Morrison playing *Into the Mystic*

II
driving home around the lake
on Wednesday evening
planning for the Friday evening gin and tonic

III
raising the window blinds on Saturday morning
running a finger along the sill
painted white high gloss
no dust

IV
April snow storm
burning the last of the birch cord
doggie splayed out in front of the fire
wet traffic noises sometimes sifting through

V
finding a new shop
buying a small lamp
seeing how the mottled shade
yellows the light around the hall table

VI
a weekend
in a hotel
eating alone
sleeping alone
waking alone

VII
lunch in an Irish pub
Murphy's amber
stilton, roasted pear
and toasted pecan salad
strawberry vinaigrette

And identity is funny being yourself is funny as you are never yourself to yourself except as you remember yourself and then of course you do not believe yourself. That is really the trouble with an autobiography you do not of course you do not really believe yourself why should you, you know so well so very well that it is not yourself, it could not be yourself because you cannot remember right and if you do remember right it does not sound right and of course it does not sound right because it is not right. You are of course never yourself. Well anyway I did tell all about myself, telling about my brother was telling about myself...(Stein, 1985, p. 53)

I am intent on exploring connections between autobiography and geography and curriculum. I think that in telling about myself I am telling something about my place, and in telling about my place I am telling about myself, and curriculum is the medium that creates the spaces for the telling. Perhaps it is true that "certain spaces equal certain identities" (Natter and Jones, 1997, p.152). Perhaps it is true that spaces and identities are in a constant state of change. Attending to our place, and encouraging students to do the same, is one way of acknowledging the autobiographical and geographical cartographic imperative within curriculum. How we know and what we know is always within a context of who we are and where we are. I am reminded now of Vipassana insight meditation and the practice of mindfulness. Becoming aware of where our bodies touch the earth is part of this practice and it is this same awareness—being mindful of where our bodies touch the earth and noting the sensations that arise—that I want to bring to the practice of curriculum.

References

Bast, S. (2000). Written communication to author, July 2000.

Chambers, C. (1999). A topography for Canadian curriculum theory. *Canadian Journal of Education, 24*(2), 137–150.

Choy, W. (1997). The ten thousand things. In C. Rooke (Ed.), *Writing home: A pen Canada anthology* (pp. 13–22). Toronto: McClelland & Stewart.

Foucault, M. (1986). *The history of sexuality, Vol. 2: The use of pleasure.* (R. Hurley, Trans.). New York: Vintage Books.

Goodson, I. (1998). Storying the self: Life politics and the study of the teacher's life and work. In W. Pinar (Ed.), *Curriculum: Toward new identities* (pp. 3–20). New York: Garland Publishing.

Hurren, W. (2000). *Line dancing: An atlas of geography, curriculum, and poetic possibilities.* New York: Peter Lang.

Hurren, W. (2001). *Spatial practices in public schools.* (Unpublished pilot study).

Jardine, D. (2000). *Under the tough old stars.* Brandon, VT: Foundation for Educational Renewal, Inc.

Lefebvre, H. (1991). *The production of space.* (D. Nicholson-Smith, Trans.). Oxford: Blackwell.

Mouffe, C. (1992). Democratic citizenship and the political community. In C. Mouffe (Ed.), *Dimensions of radical democracy: Pluralism, citizenship, and community* (pp. 225–239). London: Verso.

Natter, W., and Jones, J. (1997). Identity, space, and other uncertainties. In G. Benko and U. Strohmayer (Eds.), *Space and social theory: Interpreting modernity and postmodernity* (pp. 141–161). Oxford, UK: Blackwell Publishers.

Ondaatje, M. (1992). *The English patient.* Toronto: Random House.

Pinar, W., Reynolds, W., Slattery, P., & Taubman, P. (1995). *Understanding curriculum: An introduction to the study of historical and contemporary curriculum discourses.* New York: Peter Lang.

Prystay, S. (2000). Written communication to author, July 2000.

Stein, G. (1985). *Everybody's autobiography.* London: Virago Press.

Tourigny, P. (2000). Written communication to author, July 2000.

❱ Paying Attention and Not Knowing[1]

Antoinette Oberg

Through the writing I present here I am paying attention to my practice of paying attention and not knowing. I begin by paying attention to my response to the proposal I wrote for this writing.

The proposal began with the title "Paying Attention and Not Knowing," followed by a quotation from the *Tao Te Ching* by Lao Tsu: "When wisdom and intelligence are born/The great pretence begins" (*Tao Te Ching,* 1972, p. 18). I then wrote that I eschewed generalized knowledge claims, which I called pretentious, claiming (!) that they distracted me from responding authentically (that is, with my own authority) in specific situations. I wrote that the situations in which I am most interested (from the Latin *inter esse,* literally, already in the midst of) are meetings with individual graduate students unfolding their inquiries. There I find that paying attention and not knowing (which I

[1] Originally presented as part of a performance session titled "Autobiography as an Ethos for Our Time: Living Well With Each Other" at the American Educational Research Association annual conference held in Seattle, USA, on April 14, 2001.

have characterized as suspending expectations and delaying the desire to conceptualize) invites another layer of a student's inquiry to unfold itself.

Over a period of six months following the writing of this proposal, I made notes of meetings with graduate students in which something notable happened. When I began to write this paper, however, instead of looking at the notes of those specific events, I focused on Lao Tsu's words in the proposal, "When wisdom and intelligence are born/The great pretence begins" (p. 18), feeling obliged to say more clearly what they meant. After all, I reasoned, I had selected this statement because it meant something to me. Surely explication of its meaning would compose the essay I had committed myself to write. In fulfilling this obligation, I wrote about what the "great pretence" was and what the alternative might be. Eventually I realized that I had taken a path I did not want to follow, explicating theoretical concepts disconnected from a specific situation.

Feeling frustrated but having learned my lesson (or so I thought), I went back to the quotation and focused on the specific event of engaging Lao Tsu's words: "When wisdom and intelligence are born/The great pretence begins" (p. 18). When the idea occurred to me that Lao Tsu's words themselves were possibly somewhat pretentious in the generality of their claim, I wrote about the kinds of writing I experience as pretentious and the kinds of writing I do not experience that way, and I analyzed the difference. Again I found myself in theoretical territory, explicating general concepts disconnected from the specific event with which I had begun.

Looking for inspiration, I went to my bookshelf where I was greeted by the *Tao of Pooh* (Hof, 1982). Reading Hof's little book, I recognized a way of being that was familiar to me—not in my approach to writing, but in my supervisory practice with graduate students: paying attention without prejudgment to ongoing inquiry and then articulating what I noticed. In this way of being, the task is to pay attention to what a student presents and then make a response that crystallizes the student's inquiry.

I noticed the difference between this familiar way of being with graduate students and the way I had proceeded to write this essay. In writing (the essay), I had imposed a pattern of beginning with general concepts instead of paying attention to a flow of specific events, allowing a pattern to form, and then responding. Ironically, I had done what I was using the quotation from the *Tao Te Ching* to resist: I had tried to make wise and intelligent statements about the concepts of wisdom and intelligence, only to find that in doing so I was hiding behind the pretence of knowing what I was talking about!

Having come out from behind that veil of pretence, I turned my attention, at last, to some specific situations with graduate students where my practice of paying attention and not knowing are in evidence. I will recount two of these situations (with the permission of the students concerned) and reflect on them.

A student in my research methods class who was also a counselor came to talk with me about her study. She had already collected the data for her research and through writing freely from her own interest she realized that the methodology she had planned to use to interpret her data didn't make sense to her any more. She said she felt confused and muddled. She had tried another approach, but this didn't fit either. Since finding herself in this predicament of having no method, she had sought out new literature related to her topic. Her topic was the practice of mindfulness in counseling. At first she found reading no help. She had no response to what she read. She simply took in the words. Then she found a book called *Women's Ways of Knowing* (Belenky, Clinchy, Goldberger, & Tarule, 1986) that prompted her to see that her relationship with knowledge was what the book authors called "received knowing." Just as the book authors described, she had been setting aside her own experience to make room to receive the words of others, believing her own experience and understanding to be inferior to the insights of published authors. When she returned to her interview transcripts, she noticed that she had prompted her interviewees to do the same, that is, to speak more frequently of theory and philosophy than of their own experiences of mindfulness. Still uncertain what to do about the persistent problem of method, she started reading a book I suggested on creativity (Nachmanovitch, 1990). She had what she called a breakthrough. She began to see the many ways she had been blocking her own creativity and stopping her process of inquiry.

She said that she had come to realize she was not in fact an empty vessel waiting to be filled with others' knowledge. Indeed, she had had lots of responses while reading the book on creativity which, even though they were not easy to put into words, she had finally gotten down on paper. After that she had gone back to the interview transcripts with new eyes and had begun to write her responses to what she saw there. All the while she was speaking, I made notes of what she said, especially all the ways she paid attention to what stopped her inquiry process and how she got it started again. "But," she said in desperation, "I don't have a method!" Then I made my offering. I said, "It sounds to me as though your method is mindfulness and here are the procedures you use," and I handed her the list I'd made of what she'd told me she'd been doing.

Another day a student came to ask about how to approach the review of the literature for her thesis, given that her topic was very broad. Her topic was inviting adolescent students into genuine inquiry instead of simply telling them what they should know. She believed that introducing students early on in their school careers to the indeterminacies and complexities of issues was more reflective of real life than were the predigested curricula delivered up by the ministry. I asked how she taught her students to inquire. She said she began with issues that were connected to students' lives. When an issue came up, she first told them everything she knew about the topic, taking care to point to things she didn't know. Then she and the students set out to find out more about the issue. They went to libraries, searched the Internet, did interviews. They felt their way as they went, tracing promising leads, reading, writing, sharing, and talking together. "Well," I said, "it seems imperative that you proceed in the same way in your thesis literature review, using all the ways you have just listed to find out all you can about your topic."

In these narratives I am interested in the moment when I became aware of a congruence between the topic and the method of inquiry. This congruence runs so deep that the topic becomes the method through which the topic is pursued. In the first situation described above, mindfulness became the method of studying mindfulness; in the second, emergent inquiry became the method of studying emergent inquiry.

At some point during my meeting with each of these students, I perceived a patterning in what had up until that moment appeared to be formless. The moment of awareness seemed like a revelation, as if something that was already there waiting to be found had disclosed itself. Yet I also sensed that in that moment something new had come into being, and my articulation crystallized it.

In fractal geometry (Capra, 1996), patterns repeat themselves on varying scales such that the pattern of the whole is present holographically in the smallest part. When I perceived congruence between topic and method in these two students' inquiries, I discerned a patterning in each that existed on a scale larger than the scale of the inquiries presented to me. The presence of this patterning was signaled by the fact that without a formal research method, each student *already knew* how to proceed. Each was reproducing a patterning that existed elsewhere in their lives, in their cases, in their professional work outside the university. However, within their university thesis research, the students themselves did not recognize this patterning. My articulation of this patterning in their research both brought it to their attention and legitimated it within the university.

In chaos theory (Briggs, 1992), the meeting of opposites (such as hot and cold air masses or a fluid medium and a solid object) generates a pattern of spirals. A spiral is dynamic, balanced, and transformative (Schneider, 1995). I noticed that the patterning I discerned in students' professional work and saw repeated in their thesis inquiries had been produced by the meeting of some natural impetus or flow with a limitation represented by a prescribed form. In their professional work the students had not been stopped by this limitation but had responded creatively to the prescription. The person in the first story had transformed conventional counseling skills and procedures into mindfulness practice. The person in the second had replaced prescribed school curricula with student-led emergent inquiry.

However, as university students, both had encountered prescriptions about inquiry to which they felt obliged to adhere: respectively, the requirement for a standardized method, and the requirement for a conventional review of the literature. Both students had experienced these prescriptions as an obstacle to the flow of inquiry. My response showing them that they already knew how to proceed, removed that obstacle, and allowed the patterning that already existed in their professional work to become the patterning of their inquiries. What they had done in their professional work, they now did in their inquiries. Both students responded creatively to the limitation of a prescribed form, the first by designating mindfulness as her method, and the second by designing an emergent approach to her literature review.

Two key features of these students' inquiries are the repetition in the inquiry of patterning present elsewhere in the inquirer's life, and the generative response to the limiting effects of prescription. These features have something, that I cannot yet articulate, to do with the congruence of topic and method. Allowing this connection to remain elusive for the time being, I now return to examining my own inquiry. Picking up the threads of the story begun at the start of this essay and using my interpretation of students' inquiries as a source of inspiration, I seek to discern the patterning of my own inquiry into my practice of paying attention and not knowing.

For a long time, I have been aware of the patterning of my professional practice. As I supervise graduate student inquiries, I advise students to pursue their interests, allowing both topic and method to evolve. I offer research methods as tools to be used creatively in the pursuit of interests. I listen as students describe the course of their inquiries, paying attention and then articulating what I notice. However, this patterning evident in my professional practice did not manifest itself as I began the inquiry for this paper. Instead, the patterning of my inquiry was a kind of approach-avoidance as I repeatedly followed then rejected prescriptions for writing abstractly about generalized knowledge. Thinking that my challenge was eschewing prescribed forms of writing maintained this approach-avoidance patterning. Eventually, turning my attention to specific events with graduate students' inquiries opened the way for a different pattern to form. Paying attention to differences between the initial patterning of my inquiry and the patterning I perceived in graduate students' inquiries, I came to appreciate the difference between resisting prescription and responding creatively to it. In its limiting effect, prescription is like the shore of a river or a boulder in midstream. As it meets these obstacles the flowing river forms a complex spiral patterning of backeddies and whirlpools. Meeting an obstacle is an opportunity for a response that is both dynamic and transformative, like the spirals in the river. Resisting prescription perpetuates a pattern of opposition in which movement is confined within the two poles of a dualism. Responding creatively to prescription transforms opposition into a flow that is dynamic, balanced, and transformative.

My inquiry has begun to flow as I have allowed the patterning of my professional practice to manifest itself in my writing. The patterning of both my professional practice and my writing is to pay attention without knowing what comes next and to notice the patterning. I have just noticed that my topic and method are congruent.

References

Belenky, M., Clinchy, B., Goldberger, N., & Tarule, J. (1986). *Women's ways of knowing: The development of self, voice, and mind.* New York: Basic Books.

Briggs, J. (1992). *Fractals: The patterns of chaos: Discovering a new aesthetic of art, science, and nature.* New York: Simon & Schuster.

Capra, F. (1996). *The web of life.* New York: Anchor Books.

Gadamer, H-G. (1986). *Truth and method.* New York: Crossroad.

Hof, B. (1982). *The Tao of Pooh.* Markham, ON, Canada: Penguin Books.

Nachmanovitch, S. (1990). *Free play: Improvisation in life and art.* New York: G. P. Putnam's Sons.

Schneider, M. (1995). *A beginner's guide to constructing the universe: The mathematical archetypes of nature, art, and science.* New York: HarperPerennial.

Tao Te Ching/Lao Tsu. (1972). (G-F. Feng & J. English, Trans.). New York: Alfred A. Knopf.

❱ Backyard Questions Written in Stone and Water: Alchemic Possibilities in the Space of the Heart[1]

Carl Leggo

Pre-Rumbles of Rumination

We spend the first decade of our lives in a state of suspended consciousness, endlessly receptive to the floods of sensation that overwhelm us, as though we were sieves through which being flows almost unimpeded. That decade shapes us for a lifetime. Looked back at, there are only a few memories that cohere to anchor us, but these will be repeated again and again in the depths of our unconscious throughout our lives.
> —Rosemary Sullivan, *Shadow Maker*

AS BOYS

Cec Frazer Macky my brother and I
constructed intricate networks
of roads and tunnels in the autumn
after Skipper dug up the potatoes
where we drove our trucks, cranes, and tractors

we built snow tunnels so long and deep
we could ride toboggans through them
and snow forts like King Arthur's Camelot

we held daily endless competitions
to prove
who could walk furthest the narrow fence

---

[1] Originally presented as part of a performance session titled "Autobiography as an Ethos for Our Time: Living Well With Each Other" at the American Educational Research Association annual conference held in Seattle, USA, on April 14, 2001.

around Billy Mercer's yard

who could spin up Lynch's Lane on a bicycle
all the way to Old Man Downey's house

who could climb highest in the alders
in Cec's backyard

who could dive from the highest place
in Margaret Bowater Park

we dreamed about Charles Atlas ads in comic books
stuffed jute bags for punching bags
and admired tough rough guys
who smoked and swore and got into fist fights

we pretended to be cowboys, soldiers, gladiators,
knights, conquistadors, pirates, flying aces

we hammered and fired swords, shields, bazookas,
battering rams, sling shots, bows and arrows,
snowballs, and catapults, an arsenal
of weapons for fighting Nazis, Communists,
aliens from Pluto, and one another

and when a few weeks ago I saw
Cec for the first time in years

now middle-aged like all of us
we chuckled together shyly
and hid in dark corners of the Majestic
with Mark Wahlberg in *Planet of the Apes.*

In *Holes and Other Superficialities*, philosophers Roberto Casati and Achille C. Varzi (1994) note that "a philosophical theory originates from astonishment" (p. 7). On first reading that observation I was excited, but the second part of the statement asserts that a philosophical theory "is judged from its ability to silence astonishment" (p. 7). My objection to this is that astonishment is a good place to begin and a good place to linger. In sharing the following poems and ruminations about backyards, autobiography, poetry, and the heart, I am not seeking to silence astonishment. I hope instead to astonish silence.

I am a poet, not a philosopher, but like the American poet E. V. Rieu, I am entranced with the questions of philosophy. Rieu, in the poem *Night thought of a tortoise suffering from insomnia on a lawn* (1975, p. 209), wrote:

The world is very flat—
There is no doubt of that.

Like me, the tortoise is entranced by questions of epistemology.

For more than a decade, I have been writing autobiographical poetry about growing up on Lynch's Lane in Corner Brook, Newfoundland. So far, I have published two books of poems and I am currently completing a third, and I now acknowledge that the stories of my backyard are inexhaustible. I began the first autobiographical poems about growing up when I was 34 years old. I write about people and experiences that I never wrote about in school where I tried to mimic the writing I read in class anthologies. For years and years I heard an insistent voice of warning that it is not sufficient to write about ordinary people with ordinary emotions in ordinary situations. What is needed is an extraordinary subject or an extraordinary perspective on the ordinary.

In *Pedagogy of the Heart*, published posthumously in 1997, Paulo Freire acknowledges from the perspective of a long life nearing its end that his childhood backyard was a space connected to many spaces. Freire writes:

My childhood backyard has been unveiling itself to many other spaces—spaces that are not necessarily other yards. Spaces where this man of today sees the child of yesterday in himself and learns to see better what he had seen before. To see again what had already been seen before always implies seeing angles that were not perceived before. Thus, a posterior view of the world can be done in a more critical, less naïve, and more rigorous way. (p. 38)

In the preface to *Pedagogy of the Heart*, Ladislau Dowbor observes that

in Paulo Freire's reasoning, rationality is rationally clamouring for the right to its emotional roots. This is the return to the shade of the mango tree, to the complete human being. And with the smells and tastes of childhood, it is much broader a concept than that of right or left, a deeply radical one: human solidarity. (p. 28)

As Freire understood, "a new reading of my world requires a new language—that of possibility, open to hope" (p. 77).

> In my poetry I ask questions
> as part of an ongoing quest
> to know the spaces of my childhood backyard,
> and to know the circular, circulatory, and curricular
> flowing of life, blood, and memory
> that constitutes the heart of the writer and learner and teacher.
> I seek to disclose and know again
> the location of my backyard,
> and how this specific geographical space
> represents a location for locution in the bigger world.
> In an ongoing act of memory and remembering
> I return again and again to my childhood backyard
> in order to write autobiographically and poetically and cogitatively
> in a quest(ion)ing filled with wonder
> for the possibility of alchemic transformations
> of water and stone that can compose
> the lined and layered art of (a) life.

Even in this beginning of the quest(ion)ing,
I am learning that the heart
of any pedagogic endeavour
is learning to breathe.

I am interested in knowing
the space between the systole and diastole
of the heart's quest, the space
where questions are too little asked.

Some of the questions I am asking/might ask include:

1. How are the senses connected to the body, to the places where bodies leave traces?
2. What constitutes memory? How does memory live?
3. What is the ecology and economy of emotion and reasoning?
4. What constitutes a life?
5. How is the present related to the past and the future?
6. What is novel about an autobiography and what is autobiographical about a novel?
7. How are memory and creativity and imagination and invention connected?
8. What is the difference between adorning the self and adoring the self?
9. How are autobiographical energies linked to the self and the world?

Freire encourages me that "the more rooted I am in my location, the more I extend myself to other places so as to become a citizen of the world. No one becomes local from a universal location" (p. 39).

In middle age, I went to a counsellor.
I said, I do not find it easy to be a human being.
She said, What was it like in your home in the first year of your life?
I said, All I know are the stories I've been told. Times were hard.
I recounted stories of death, grief, anger,
young parents now living with a widowed grandmother.
The counsellor said, Your first year is written in your body;
your life is a series of revisions.

Wherever I am,
all I need is the smell
of clover in fresh-cut hay
to return in imagination

and heart-memory
to the Lynch's Lane
of my growing up.

> From my patio on the west coast
> I can almost see you,
> five time zones away,
> on the east coast
> while I spin out my lines,
> seeking the sun moon and star,
> the light lunacy of love in your eyes.

I will not record the lines only
of shadow's sadness, leaning on light,
a rumination of rough cut stones,
all always recalled in the blood
with its own circular course.

> *In my autobiographical poems,*
> *I am learning how to live with wellness in the world.*
> *I am learning that life/living is a verb,*
> *a process, a flow,*
> *not necessarily evolving,*
> *perhaps revolving,*
> *but definitely not static.*

Rosemary Sullivan (1995) writes:

> The houses we are born into are always more than domestic architecture. They
> are mental spaces that define the power dynamic of the world we enter
> unwittingly; those houses will surface repeatedly in our dreams and we will
> reconstruct them throughout a lifetime. (p. 3)

MY MOTHER'S HOUSE

Last spring I returned to my mother's house.
Like living in a Volkswagen van
each move had to be exact and slow and smooth.

My mother's house is a museum

of artifacts from Woolworth's and K-Mart,
every room crammed, everything in place.

My mother has two or three of everything,
just in case, because it was on sale,
because she found space not filled:

stacks of satin-bound blankets in cellophane,
more than the Glynmill Inn,
enough dish towels from Duz detergent

to wash all the dishes in all the restaurants
of Corner Brook, salt and pepper shakers
and pots pans mugs jars jugs cups cans tins
filling every cupboard corner crack cranny,
nothing ever used, just collected and stored
and protected like the treasure in Ali Baba's cave.

My mother's house is not a house
for dancing in, and yet I recall I once danced
in rubber boots. I was a Cossack from Siberia.

Every Wednesday night I wrestled
my brother in a match to the death
or the end of Skipper's patience.
My brother and I played pool in the kitchen

on a table with collapsible legs,
sometimes opening the fridge door to make a shot.

I was going to be the first Newfoundlander
to make the Canadian gymnastics team,
somersaults and handstands on the sofa cushions.

My brother and I shot ceramic animals
with darts from spring-loaded guns
like Hemingway hunting elephants in Africa.

But last spring in my mother's house
I was like a reformed bull who knows
how to behave in a china shop.

If I moved quickly I would upset
the balance. I learned to move little,
always slowly, but that is not how

I once lived in my mother's house:
    perhaps I have grown bigger,
    perhaps I have grown smaller.
(Leggo, 1999, pp. 1–2)

> *In my autobiographical poems,*
> *I am learning how to live with wellness in the world.*
> *I am learning that I bear the traces*
> *of everybody I have known*
> *and many I have not known,*
> *sacred connections to be acknowledged.*

Janice Kulyk Keefer understands: "To write of family can be an act of homage and of trespass" (p. 6), and the autobiographical writing is "not a fairy tale, but a story, made as all true stories are, out of the fallible flesh and blood of perfectly ordinary, perfectly remarkable people" (p. 323).

WEST COAST PRAIRIE

last Saturday while biking the dike around Lulu Island, born out of sand swept and gathered by the Fraser, Norm asked why I had moved to Richmond economic necessity, the only place I could afford, no other reason, and Norm said he chose Richmond because it is flat and has farms like Saskatchewan

how when he first moved here, years ago, the Coast Mountains around English Bay held only threats, the world written in the geography of our growing up, and I told him

about Corner Brook curled in the Humber Arm with the world's biggest paper mill belching steam smoke sulphite all day, every day, except Christmas and Labour Day

and how I always thought the world had come to Corner Brook with Ann Landers Ed Sullivan Hollywood Eaton's catalogues and Millbrook Mall with an elevator

and visits by famous people like Pierre and Margaret Trudeau Gordon Lightfoot Ian and Sylvia Gordie Howe Hollywood actors (though I can't remember any) the queen even
until I left Corner Brook for the first time at 15 and went to Montreal and couldn't believe how big the world was, so much bigger than TV and Saturday matinees

and after growing up perpendicular on the side of a hill like a robust merlot, kissed by wild autumn, spring ice, summer blast, and winter light with long shadows on the retina

of the heart, I now live in Richmond with one long wet season, flat like Saskatchewan, and remember jigg's dinner, dark rum, cod's tongues, stewed moose, fish and brewis,

jigs and Celtic rhythms, Al Pittman's poetry, Skipper's rants, storms sturdy enough to knock you off your feet, and stripping the willow with Eddy Ezekiel on accordion
always going back in my poems, knowing I have left and never left, knowing I can always go back and never go back, the world written in the geography of our growing up

In my autobiographical poems,
I am learning how to live with wellness in the world.
I am learning that each of us
is responsible to countless others,
seeking ways to respond in our responsibility.

Jean Vanier (1998) asks:

> Is this not the life undertaking of us all…to become human? It can be a long and sometimes painful process. It involves a growth to freedom, an opening up of our hearts to others, no longer hiding behind masks or behind the walls of fear and prejudice. (p. 1)

DAISY GRIFFIN

crawling through the tall grass
in Sammy Baker's back yard
hunting for grasshoppers
I saw Jimmy Griffin's mother
framed in her picture window,
the only time I ever saw
her, a phantom, a character
in a story, not that I knew much
about Jimmy Griffin, the only
Catholic on Lynch's Lane

Cec, Frazer, Macky, my brother,
and I, all Protestants
whose only protest was going
to church, had little to do
with Jimmy Griffin who wore
a blue blazer and was an altar boy,
but I saw Daisy Griffin
in the window, her eyes fixed
on the harbour or the sky or beyond,
and the neighbours hinted Daisy was

> : a lush
> : married to God
> : always pregnant
> : too good for anybody
> : a looney

but I saw Daisy Griffin,
a pale face framed
in black hair, framed
in the window, like a child
on a stormy day, both fascinated
and fearful with the world outside,
and I wanted Daisy Griffin

to crawl through the tall grass
in Sammy Baker's back yard
hunting for grasshoppers, too
(Leggo, 1994, p. 23)

In my autobiographical poems,
I am learning how to live with wellness in the world.
I am learning that wisdom
is searching together,
seeking truth in hope and heart.

Jane Rule (1986) warns that "homesteading an emotional territory . . . takes a lot of simple hard work," (p. 60) and she suggests that "we have to begin not only by lying less but by telling the truth more" (p. 92).

CROQUET

Mel Mercer built the first patio in Humber East,
a rectangle of concrete slabs no bigger
than a family cemetery plot, and he built
the first barbecue, too, an oil drum cut in half,
filled with charcoal briquettes, and all summer
long he called the neighbours together
to sip Scotch and croon with Perry Como
and eat tenderloin steak wrapped in bacon.

Billy Mercer sat on his verandah in the dark,
rocked in a white wicker chair, and watched
the parties on Mel Mercer's patio, more
fun than anything on CBC, he said. Even
though Mel Mercer always waved, Join us,
Billy Mercer wanted only to watch, knowing
the see-saw balance between nephew and uncle
augured accurately the alignment of planets.

But everything changed the forest fire summer
Carrie counted her Gold Stamps from Coleman's
where every payday she picked up groceries
and burned a Gold Stamp shopping spree
like a winter-crazed prospector across the catalogue:
lawn chairs, plastic tumblers, a card table.

Everything we wanted Carrie got with Gold Stamps,
till there was nothing left to get except a croquet set.
A few times I had seen croquet played on TV,
aristocratic, civilized, genteel, British, but
on Lynch's Lane with no level yard for croquet,
we had to pound the wooden balls up the hill,
nudge them down the hill through stubbles of grass,
and never smack the balls into Skipper's rows
of potatoes. Everything connected, like one ball
conking another, Carrie's croquet convened chaos.

Day after day Billy Mercer watched us play croquet.
So his daughter bought him a set at Canadian Tire, but
Billy Mercer wanted what no one on Lynch's Lane had:
a level front yard like a TV suburban manicured lawn.
He worked out the mathematics (asked to help, I
nodded at his sketches with my grade nine geometry)
of moving the back yard to the front yard, and excavated
and dumped tons of clay and rock, a new Antaeus.

Mel Mercer looked out his kitchen window
and saw a wall of grass and gravel like a tsunami
poised to crash on his patio. Angry hot, he told
anyone who would listen, some who wouldn't, all
the stories best kept between uncles and nephews,
stories bumped stories, the hard crack of croquet balls
caught in the slate gray sky over Humber East, echoes
off a patio, verandah, yard, now always winter empty.
(Leggo, 1999, pp. 27–28)

In my autobiographical poems,
I am learning how to live with wellness in the world.
I am learning to trust in the paradox of agnostic knowing,
less and less arrested with the claims of agonistic knowing.

Paulo Freire (1997) contends:

Critical acceptance of my inconclusion necessarily immerses me in permanent
search. What makes me hopeful is not so much the certainty of the *find*, but my
movement in *search*. It is not possible to search without hope, not even in
solitude. (p. 106)

WHAT'S IN A NAME?

I was named
after Carl Hunter,
my mother says,
a family acquaintance,
a bush pilot
who went away
to the mainland
and flew Cessna's
into northern Ontario
and sent a Christmas card
each year, a card
signed Carl, and I
sometimes thought
I had sent the card
myself and forgotten,
but eventually
Carl's cards stopped,
sometimes I wondered
if he had crashed, was
wandering in the wild
woods of Lake Alqonquin

I think I asked my mother
what happened to Carl,
the other Carl,
probably eager to know
around the time
I was beginning
to question
what was happening,
had happened to this Carl,
not sure if perhaps he too
had crashed in the dense woods
of northern Ontario,
even though I was still
a kid on the west coast
of Newfoundland

In my autobiographical poems,
I am learning how to live with wellness in the world.
I am learning that the backyard

> *is always present and always lost,*
> *writing the longing in belonging,*
> *even in being.*

Frederick Buechner (1999) asks

if there are any of us who do not feel the sadness and loneliness and lostness of
being separated from where we know in our hearts we truly belong, even if
we're not sure either where it is to be found or how to get there, if there are any
of us who do not yearn, more than for anything else, to go home. (p. 76)

RHIZOME

Newfoundland is faraway
and Lynch's Lane lingers

in imagination and poetry
bulldozed daisies, redevelopment

but last night my mother called
with more stories

Cindy Mercer, my third or fourth cousin perhaps,
but definitely a Mercer like my grandmother and mother

met a man through the Internet
moved to Australia and married him

Cindy Mercer's father said,
Nice as you could meet anywhere

like there was some doubt, some
need to defend Australian niceness

and Sal Mercer was on her way
to the new Wal-Mart in the late winter

afternoon when spring can almost be tasted
and collapsed on the sidewalk,

dead before the ambulance,
gone at 86, one of the few left,

except there are Mercers everywhere

married in Australia
on their way to Wal-Mart
seeking poems in British Columbia

like holograms, the part in the whole
rhizome connections in the earth

the sheer certitude of lives
spelling out in fractal inevitability

Re-Rumbles of Rumination

Ursula Kelly (1997) writes:

> A notion of auto/biography as readings of selves positioned within a larger
> textuality insists that this larger textuality be interrogated for ways in which we
> read and are (culturally) read to, for the ways in which we have learned to look
> and the ways in which we are looked at…. Such an approach to auto/biography
> *decenters* the subject, focusing attention, instead, on how the subject is
> constituted within a dynamics of power across a wide array of textual and
> discursive practices. (pp. 65–66)

And so in closing
I return to the year
of my birth
and a text
written recently
out of the traces
of a text
written almost
a century ago.

1953
***THE ENCYCLOPEDIA BRITANNICA YEARBOOK*:**
RANDOM HIGHLIGHTS

*

Red Buttons told jokes on T.V.

*

Albert Einstein published
Generalization of Gravitation Theory

*

President Dwight D. Eisenhower
proposed an international agency
to pool atomic energy
for peaceful purposes

*

Mexico granted the vote to women

*

world tunnelling activity increased significantly

*

image amplification apparatus
became commercially available

*

a process was perfected
which turns oranges
into a powder which may be reconstituted
into highly palatable orange juice

*

Dylan Thomas died

*

the first *TV Guide* was published
with a picture of Lucy's baby
Desiderio Alberto Arnaz IV

*

and even though
The Encyclopedia Britannica Yearbook
for 1953 fails
to mention it
I, too, was born

*In my autobiographical poems,
I am learning how to live with wellness in the world.*

References

Buechner, F. (1999). *The eyes of the heart: A memoir of the lost and found*. New York: HarperCollins Publishers.

Casati, R., and Varzi, C. A. (1994). *Holes and other superficialities*. Cambridge: MIT Press.

Freire, P. (1997). *Pedagogy of the heart* (D. Macedo and A. Oliveira, Trans.). New York: Continuum.

Keefer, J. K. (1998). *Honey and ashes: A story of family*. Toronto: HarperCollins.

Kelly, U. A. (1997). *Schooling desire: Literacy, cultural politics, and pedagogy*. New York: Routledge.

Leggo, C. (1994). *Growing up perpendicular on the side of a hill*. St. John's, Newfoundland, Canada: Killick Press.

Leggo, C. (1999). *View from my mother's house*. St. John's, Newfoundland, Canada: Killick Press.

Rieu, E. V. (1975). Night thought of a tortoise suffering from insomnia on a lawn. In R. Charlesworth (Ed.), *Imagine seeing you here: A world of poetry, lively and lyrical* (p. 209). Toronto: Oxford UP.

Rule, J. (1986). *A hot-eyed moderate*. Toronto: Lester & Orpen Dennys.

Sullivan, R. (1995). *Shadow maker: The life of Gwendolyn MacEwen*. Toronto: HarperCollins.

Vanier, J. (1998). *Becoming human*. Toronto: House of Anansi Press.

❯ By the Oldman River I Remembered[1]

Erika Hasebe-Ludt

These past few months, I have been thinking a great deal about the tricky notion of knowing and the what and how of it, but in particular the *where*: where we—myself in relation to my students, my colleagues, my friends, and my family—situate ourselves in the face of other knowledge, other traditions, and other communities, and whose knowledge we draw on, whose we challenge, in order to become wiser, more informed, more inclusive, more able to effect change...these are big questions for me right now in my geographical re- and dis-location. Traveling and living away from home, moving from Europe to Canada, moving to a different place to work, living in the tensioned space of cultural and geographic displacement, my interest is to investigate how this positioning of self in relation to other cultures and locations can be/come a generative place. So what do you think? What do you think is possible? David Smith reminds me:

> The most basic purpose of going on a journey, then, is the very ordinary one of learning to be at home in a more creative way, a good way, a healthy way, a way tuned to the deepest truth of things....What is involved is learning to understand one's own tradition with greater insight and creativity, one's cultural heritage linguistically and ritually mediated. (Smith, 1999, p. 2)

Elternhaus

Lines from a Leslie Marmon Silko (1997) poem running through my head:

---

[1] Originally presented as part of a performance session titled "Autobiography as an Ethos for Our Time: Living Well With Each Other" at the American Educational Research Association annual conference held in Seattle, USA, on April 14, 2001.

> long ago   long ago
>   remembering the lost one
>   remembering the love.

The German writer Luise Rinser remembers her family home as a mosaic composed of small fragments of memories (Pörtner, 1986).

The memory of my own *Elternhaus* conjures up an image of fragile stones crushed by bombs long ago, reassembled to make life go on. The house stands next to the one my mother was born in, in the small town of Saarbrücken in Southwest Germany, in 1911, three years before the First World War started. My parents were married in 1934 just before the Second World War, and my grandfather had given the house I remember as my childhood home as a wedding present to my parents.

I remember my mother telling stories about the two prolonged evacuations from these two homes. The first time she had to leave with her mother and sisters and brother when she was just a little girl to live with strangers in another province in the north while my grandfather fought for the Kaiser's army somewhere in foreign lands. The second time she fled, during the Second World War, a mother herself with two young boys, and my father away at sea, a soldier in Hitler's navy.

Each time she returned to fragments of a home, the gardens destroyed by conquering armies, rooms void of family heirlooms, precious playthings, my grandfather's carpentry tools; and the horse, the chickens, the cows were no longer alive in the barn.

These fragments came alive again in the mosaic of my mother's stories, but as a child I could not imagine the hardship of these journeys, my own childhood unfolding in the resurgence of postwar prosperity and peace. I never knew my grandfather—he was killed by a bomb that dropped on his carpentry shop—and life went on in my mother's house. But the stones still bear the memory of the loss and the leaving.

> long ago   long ago
> remembering the lost one
>   remembering the love.

Ginkgo

The ginkgo tree stands in the garden of the house in Vancouver, Canada, which is my home now and where I live with my husband and daughter when I am not teaching in another province. The seed of this ancient tree was a gift to my husband's father, Yukio, from a family friend who brought it all the way from Hiroshima, the Hasebe family's ancestral home in Japan. A third generation *sansei*, Ken was born in Greenwood, just after the Second World War, in one of the Japanese Canadian internment camps in the interior of British Columbia. The tiny tree seed came into the family's possession after the parents and their five children were allowed to return to the coast where Yukio had been a fisherman before all his belongings were confiscated. Father and son planted the seed in a container where it grew over the years, a memory of a distant ancestral soil, witness to my husband's adolescence, his parents' deaths, his family's recurring disintegration in the wake of diaspora, displacement, and dispossession. When the family broke up and his parents' house and belongings had to be sold once again, Ken kept the tree, cared for it, and nurtured it in that small pot in all the places he moved and traveled to. The ginkgo found a new home when we moved into a house of our own, Ken in his late thirties and himself the father of our three-year-old daughter. Over the years, he has shaped and sculpted the tree, which has now grown to a respectable height. Seeing it framed by the kitchen window, I gaze at its beauty, the delicacy and strength of its symmetrical leaves—a work of art, and a patient witness to lives unfolding around it in the mixed-culture soil of this hybrid family, a testimony to the lives lost, dislocated by wars in other worlds.

> long ago long ago
> remembering the lost one
> remembering the love.

Stones

A while ago I received a precious gift. One of the women in the writing group I belong to gave each member of the group two special stones she and her family had collected along the shore of the Oldman River, whose waters meander through the hills and coulees of the Southwestern Alberta landscape near Lethbridge, the town where I live when I teach and write and research. On the surface of one of my two stones, with delicate brush strokes inscribed by one of Connie's Japanese students, was the *kanji* for "hybrid."

My hybrid living in between the different places I call home stares back at me in a foreign language. I see my daughter's face, with her mixed Japanese, German, and Canadian identities, and only partial knowledge of her heritage; for a school project in Grade 12, she wrote:

> It saddens me to know that I will never know the lives of my grandparents and ancestors, as all records were destroyed in Hiroshima and memory can only last so long before it forgets. It saddens me that I will probably never know much more [about] my father's and grandparents' evacuation from their home during the Second World War than I do now, as it is such a difficult subject among my family.

And yet this daughter of mine lives with such grace in her hybrid worlds.

Patti Lather's (Lather & Smithies, 1997) questions interrupt my thinking on our local and global togetherness and separations:

> What structures our capacity to "name" ourselves, to "speak" ourselves, to make a "self" in the midst of the collision of shifting identities and movement across different contexts? What inherited meanings do we draw on? And how do we make sense when inherited meanings break down? How do we come to know ourselves? How do we make ourselves knowable to others? What is revealed and what remains hidden, perhaps even to ourselves? (p. 124)

As a writer, woman, and immigrant, I now live in new languages and cultures. As a teacher, supervisor, and professor, I also live with the power and the danger of naming every day. I am often reminded of Heidegger's (1969) words about the intimate connections between "what is said" and "what is known" and the original difficulty that comes with being in language. I need to take seriously the question of whether the language(s) I live with and in can offer "other possibilities of utterance" beyond what Heidegger called "the exclusive brand of metaphysics" and the marked "onto-theo-logical" permanence of Western languages. I want to find the cracks in between the languages that have constrained so many voices in the past and find new openings, new shoots of wording and growing and living with language in different ways in order to create new connections to the worlds around me.

Late October, Lethbridge
My words these days soak up brown textures between river valley, coulee, and wind; creep into small open pockets between clouds and sunsets. My words

these days burrow in aspen leaves, sweetgrass, and sage, tumble, light and heavy, among swirls of prairie dust. My words these days trek the distance between grain elevators, moons, and constellations, locating their positions and my own between earth, and heaven, and universe—while I long for familiar voices anywhere in between.

My relationship to writing is in knots and tangles and inseparable from my life. Both are untangled in many places. Only a few places feel textured, vibrant, colourful; many others feel dark and drab and displaced—not really where I want to them to be. My relationship with writing has been one of being in the middle of words from all different languages, moving out of English and back into it, often not with ease, not wanting to write in English only—looking at *kanji*, writing again in German, trying out words in French, Spanish, Blackfoot, really wanting to mix. My relationship to writing has been mixed—mixing all kinds of words and emotions, trying to confess my love, my fears, my fragility in the midst of languages, while being challenged to speak about what I believe to be true about language and life. I do not know if I can really say it well and in what language I can say it best any more.

My relationship to writing is filled with holes, reminding me of Carl Leggo's words about holes as being necessary and not necessarily empty spaces in our autobiographical writing, reminding me in those times when I feel empty and tired and overwhelmed with the presence of holes in my life/writing, that it is alright and that I can trust, trust my relationship to writing.

I often feel that by becoming a teacher and a teacher of teachers, I have become part of a relentless busyness to implement a rigidly structured and disembodied curriculum that has left few openings for creative expression for both adults and children, for us to draw, paint, sing, dance, and write together differently. In my struggles to know my place within my dislocation—physical, cultural, and otherwise—I continue to search for new ways of living and a new discourse. I remember Thich Nhat Hanh's (1995) words:

even our spoken and written words are no more than the steps of a dance, the notes of a song, the strokes of a painting...this movement, this life, is the universal manifestation, the most commonly recognized action of knowing. We must not regard "knowing" as something from the outside which comes to breathe life into the universe. It is the life of the universe itself. The dance and the dancer are one. (pp. 48–49; p. 59)

When I enter into the creative tension of those spaces, together with my students, I know that I have much to learn as a teacher, as a student of life (and) writing. Nancy Mair, in her autobiography *Voice Lessons* (1994), reminds me of what we all need to do:

For myself, I want another model. I want to hear *this* poem by *this* person on *this* muggy August morning under the pear trees. I want to know what it is doing in the life of her work, and in my life as well. I want to give her the courage to say the next hard thing, without fear of ridicule or expulsion if she strays the borders of good taste, good sense or good judgment demarcated by a tradition she has had no part in forming. I want her to do the same for me.

This is what we can *all* do to nourish and strengthen one another; listen to one another very hard, ask hard questions, too, send one another away to work again, and laugh in all the right places. (pp. 24–25)

Canadian writer Margaret Laurence, in her struggle to unearth her own voice, wrote to a friend:

I often feel that anything I write about people here will be naïve or perhaps merely corny, and for this reason I have gone to any lengths to avoid writing about the situations which really concerned and moved me....Perhaps in the long run there is no way other than to look inwardly and personally, and take the risk. I think the important thing is to go on doing something, and not to be paralyzed by one's doubts and uncertainties. (quoted in King, 1997, p. 163)

So I continue to search for those hybrid spaces between the words and the silences, the laughter and the crying, between now and then, here and there, home and not home, loneliness and community, where lives truly live in all their messiness and imperfections—where my life is lived. I keep listening very hard to the voices that call me to enter into the pedagogical struggle with memory and life writing, aware that we can never say all that we know (Polanyi, quoted in Stinson, 2000) and aware of Wittgenstein's words that "[t]he limits of my language are the limits of my life" (quoted in Gibbons, 1991, p. 119). It is in these paradoxical spaces of difficulty where "a living universe, which is more than something known, more than something learnable, but a place where something happens to us" (Gadamer, 1992, p. 59) is born, where we can declare what Hannah Arendt (1958) has called our *amor mundis*, our "love of the world" through stories, poetry, and a compassionate interest in each others' lives. Embodied language here becomes part of the eternal return, of the retelling of tales, the recurrence of memory—yet with a difference, constituting new forms, new meanings, and new knowledge of the world. Parker J. Palmer (1983), in *To Know as We Are Known*, connects this knowing with teaching and a healing movement towards belonging:

The goal of a knowledge arising from love is the reunification and reconstruction of broken selves and worlds. A knowledge born of confession aims not at exploiting and manipulating creation but at reconciling the world to itself. The mind motivated by compassion reaches out to know as the heart reaches out to love. Here, the act of knowing *is* an act of love, the act of entering and embracing the reality of the other, of allowing the other to enter and embrace our own. In such knowing we know and are known as members of one community, and our knowing becomes a way of reweaving that community's bond. (p. 8)

Thank you, Carl Leggo, for offering light(ness) to lean on—it is a precious gift. So is your contribution exploring the alchemic possibilities in the spaces of the heart. In preparing my own paper, I came across this quote: "Your heart is your most precious soil" (Radha, 2001, p. 30). I have been working with the idea that in seeking to live truthfully and in growing toward understanding, we are connected not only to the earth that surrounds us and the physical spaces of growing up—the backyards and fields and rivers of where we grew, the places we left behind to create new homes—but also to the ground of the heart. So I am seeking to trust that the knowledge and nourishment of the heart will let me keep on learning how to live and work with wellness in the world.

References

Arendt, H. (1958). *The human condition.* Chicago: University of Chicago Press.

Gadamer, H-G. (1986). *Truth and method.* New York: Crossroad.

Gadamer, H-G. (1992). The idea of the university—yesterday, today and tomorrow. In D. Misgeld & G. Nicholson (Eds.), *Hans-Georg Gadamer on education, poetry, and history* (pp. 47–59). Frankfurt: Suhrkamp.

Gibbons, P. (1991). *Learning to learn in a second language.* Portsmouth, NH: Heinemann.

Heidegger, M. (1969). *Identity and difference* (J. Stambaugh, Trans.). New York: Harper and Row. Original work published 1957.

King, J. (1997). *The life of Margaret Laurence.* Toronto: Vintage Canada.

Lather, P., & Smithies, C. (1997). *Troubling the angels: Women living with HIV/AIDS.* Boulder, CO: Westview Press.

Mair, N. (1994). *Voice lessons: On becoming a (woman) writer.* Boston: Beacon Press.

Naht Hanh, T. (1995). *The sun my heart.* New York: Riverhead Books.

Palmer, P. J. (1983). *To know as we are known: A spirituality of education.* San Francisco: Harper & Row.

Pörtner, R. (Ed.). (1986). *Mein Elternhaus: Ein deutsches Familienalbum* [My parents' house: A German family album] (9th ed.). Munich: Deutscher Taschenbuch Verlag.

Radha, S. S. (2001). The element earth. *Ascent, 9* (Spring), 30–31.

Silko, L. M. (1997). When Sun came to Riverwoman. In J. Harjo & G. Bird (Eds.), *Reinventing the enemy's language: Contemporary Native women's writings of North America.* New York: W. W. Norton & Co.

Smith. D. G. (1999). *Pedagon: Interdisciplinary essays in the human sciences, pedagogy, and culture.* New York: Peter Lang.

Stinson, S. W. (2000). Dance as curriculum, curriculum as dance. In G. Willis & W. H. Schubert (Eds.), *Reflections from the heart of educational inquiry: Understanding curriculum and teaching through the arts* (pp. 190–196). Troy, NY: Educator's International Press.

❱ Narrative Plains of Pedagogy: A Curriculum of Difficulty

Leah Fowler

Recently I moved to Lethbridge, Alberta, where Ted Aoki once taught as a disenfranchised Japanese Canadian schoolteacher. In my effort to make this place my home, I think of him, when I find myself in fierce coulee winds, in lighted prairie horizons, with colleagues at the University of Lethbridge. I think of the important pedagogy I learned from him at the Universities of Alberta and Victoria. I began writing teaching narratives in a formal way during a life-altering master class with Dr. Aoki in 1985. Fifteen years later, after several years on the Pacific coast, I find myself returned to narrative plains in these Alberta spaces, where I am at home and not at home.

My current interest lies in the curricular spaces between the narrated difficulties of teaching and the pedagogical movement made possible by locating such difficulties at the site of the teacher. What might be addressed in the spaces between narrative theory and the practice of teaching? What is the curriculum of a lost teacher, one in difficulty? What is it we need to learn/to study/to know/to ask/to say when we locate ourselves in language-scapes of difficulty? How can narrative research lead to an aesthetic and ethical inner government of a teaching self?

In this writing, I situate myself so you know *who* is writing and from where. I invite you to re/consider narrative research in education, as I explicate seven fields of narrative analysis that have emerged from my research into difficulty in teaching, especially at the site of the teacher.

PART I: Beginning Narratively: Once Upon My Time

Before I could speak, I heard stories of Christian grand narratives of creation, fall from grace, wrath, prophecy, despair, redemption, love, cruelty, forgiveness, and revelation. Worship twice a day in our western Canadian Anglo-Saxon household consisted of reading Bible stories, before praying on bended knee. I learned to read during my fourth year of life, using the Bible as my main text. Long before I went to elementary school, I had heard most of the nursery rhymes, myths, and fairy tales written in or translated into English. Narrative knowing (Polkinghorne, 1988) became a central part of my early childhood (and consequently, lifelong) environment.

I pieced together extended family history from fragments of conversations which sometimes switched topic if I entered the room. I knew who had the best stories to tell over tea or after the evening meal; I listened for tidbits through partially closed doors, or eavesdropped through hot-air registers. Repeatedly I heard distant, generational, Irish-American stories of my paternal grandfather, and English United Empire Loyalist kinfolk stories of my grandmother. These preceded my grandparents' own growing-up narratives of terrible poverty, dis/ease,[1] and suffering on Canadian prairies during the Depression years. I learned my genealogy, history, culture, and religion in narrative form.

Narrative Was the Only Power I Had as a Child

My stories in childhood were my only true possessions, my only place of dignity and privacy, my sole place of power where I could write myself into the world as a significant character whose life had some meaning. I wrote my childish self into the adult worlds of work, romance, and purpose. As an inveterate meaning maker, I had to believe my living had some meaning—the alternative was, and still is, unthinkable.[2]

The space under the blue spruce in grandmother's yard served as my first writing studio. People never knew that under the lovely tree on Reverend Fowler's corner lot dwelled a scrawny, blond, blue-eyed girl-assassin armed with semi-automatic coat hangers and pine-cone hand

---

[1] Throughout writing I struggle neologistically with crossovers of multiple word meanings, the insufficiency of language, the need to attend to nuance and subtext, the power of punctuation, and the creative call for linguistic invention, not to annoy the reader, but to make visible the perpetual difficulty of language and thought. I believe in the genetics of language, in the sex of the text, in its potential for infinite powers of recombination to produce new, young texts which grow up, mature, and may (if not killed) become wise texts.

[2] Kerby (1991) explains: "Narratives are a primary embodiment of our understanding of the world, of experience, and ultimately of ourselves" (p. 3).

grenades. Under that tree, possibilities of being good and evil informed my early moral development. Mondays I kidnapped, and Tuesdays I rescued brave and beautiful young women and men. I operated on Nobel Prize-winning scientists. I flew planes in war and banners in peace, climbed mountains, won Olympic medals, fell in love in the Swiss Alps, invented life-saving medicines, starred in famous movies, learned languages, performed all the composers' works—before the age of ten! I lived in my stories, understood and engaged with the world through them.

Developing a Writer's Memory and Perception
Growing up on Central Alberta's prairies, I learned a vast range of plot lines; like perennial prairie grass, I absorbed the patterns, connections, historical detail, cultural niches, and social relations from the ground of people's real and possible lives, mine among them (Kerby, 1991; Polkinghorne, 1988). Under that blue spruce, I developed a writer's memory and perception, began to cultivate a writer's memory of paying attention to detail, became attuned to the smallest particle of soil or the tiniest insect, noticed infinitesimal changes in the light waves of the late evening prairie summer sun on tree sap. A 5-degree drop in temperature or a 15-degree shift in wind direction could foreshadow so much. A baby's bonnet color being pink or blue; a chickadee with its neck broken, splayed below delphiniums under the dining room window; a smiling mouth while the eyes remained cold; a phone call hung up too quickly; a restrained outflow of breath: as a child I noticed how any of these had the power to alter story plots and change everything in the twinkling of an eye. Very early—intuitively one might say—I developed the eye of a researcher and the ear and the voice of a storyteller.

An Affair with Text
By the time I was 12 I had read all the books in our town library's children and youth sections, so I obtained permission to sign out books from the adult section. I needed those books because as I struggled through reading, almost beyond my ability, I began to uncover and understand my own being and emergent knowing. Reading made life more bearable somehow. By reading, I seemed to unlearn loneliness and

start to learn myself, to be bearable as a self, long before I considered the realms of inner dialectics and the ethics of inner government.[3]

At 15 I began to work in the school library and I learned cataloguing systems and the care, repair, and binding of broken books.[4] I also began to work as a Saturday cleaning woman for the head school librarian, using my earnings to buy flowers for her assistant, on whom I had developed an adolescent crush because we could laugh while we worked, play literary jokes, and give clues to each other about passages in books to be read. All history's weighty tomes served as currency in our restrained, platonic, *heady* affair with text.

Most of my adolescent reading was fiction, which I then naïvely understood as neither *real* nor *factual*, yet in which I recognized the human truths of relationship, understanding, affect, pattern, motivation, and power. Narrative truth became a kind of measuring stick for me about what really was going on in the world, in my own life, in the lives of those I knew, and in the lives of more public figures. As Weil writes:

> There is something else which has the power to awaken us to the truth. It is the works of writers of genius….They give us, in the guise of fiction, something equivalent to the actual density of the real, that density which life offers us every day but which we are unable to grasp because we are amusing ourselves with lies. (quoted in Zwicky, 1992, p. 79)

Whenever I heard, read, or wrote narratives, meaning took shape. I could understand why people did what they did, that what happened to people made them the way they were. I learned that narratives were places where people had the freedom and responsibility to tell the truth, however difficult. And I have subsequently seen how the power of good narrative lends itself to the contextual, complex, and chaotic matrices of educational research.

---

[3] Pablo Neruda imagines that heaven is a kind of library. Judging from the inordinate amount of time I still spend in libraries, perhaps already I have had the privilege of tasting the textual afterlife of eternity.

[4] Even now, to open a new book, press it wide, smell the new ink, and anticipate the pleasure of reading therein is to maintain the enduring physical bond I have developed with text.

Resisting Coming to Teaching

Before coming to teaching I performed many jobs, all of them roads less taken than those of my peers: bookstore clerk, Canada Post mail sorter, waitress, driving instructor, house-painter, gardener. At the same time, at university, I studied literature, drama, linguistics, languages, organic and inorganic sciences, and physical education. After obtaining a biology degree, I worked for a year on radiation genetics research with resistant strains of bacteria and super-antibiotics. All of these separate lives, deep with multiple narratives of self, subject disciplines, and other(s), are enfolded beneath the narratives I bring to my teaching work.

Being Thrown into Education

At the age of 26 after a tragi-comedy of errors in applying to medical school, I found myself catapulted into teaching, and into learning more about myself, my assumptions, and my commitments. These insights drew my attention to the need to be *present* in teaching, a lifelong enterprise of both self-understanding and self-forgetting.

My first teaching post was at a new high school in a small, rural, prairie area, where to my surprise, I discovered I was good at teaching science and English and began to invest my whole being in educational work. I left after four years there, to teach at a community college for eight years, returning to the public school system in 1989. In my first year back in the school system, the students were all nonacademic, the courses new to me. In the second year there, I became the head of an English department containing 16 teachers, and in the third year I served as curriculum coordinator developing programs for "kids at risk" and beginning "Advanced Placement" and "Staying in School" programs.

Although by external standards these endeavors were successful, I noticed that difficulties were glossed over in the rhetoric we fashioned for the reports we were encouraged to submit as the school basked in its ameliorative work. I was in the classroom less and less. The swaggering discourse was a sharp contrast to the reality as gaps between practice and theory began to widen, and I began to feel like a guest speaker in my own classroom.

One icy January morning, as my woolen mitten stuck to the metal handle on the front door of the school and my teaching became "unready to hand" (as Heidegger might say), I quietly decided that that would be my last winter with the school board. Later that year I won a provincial excellence-in-teaching award. I formally resigned the following year, and used accrued teachers' retirement money toward paying for more education in curriculum studies at the University of Victoria.

Coming to Teach Student Teachers

Perhaps the main reason for my resigning was the widening chasm between what I experienced in the daily broken world of a large inner-city school and the public rhetoric about our amazing successes. We used language to construct a tolerable reality but I kept falling through the linguistic cracks into the abyss below. The possibility of meaningful existence, truth, ethics, and beauty trickled away from my work/life into a life-threatening fissure between my outer role as a successful public educator, and my inner role as a distressed, private, mortal human being. The inconsistencies and paradoxes began to erode my (teaching) self. For the good of both myself and my students, I withdrew from teaching, in extreme difficulty, having lost any understanding of how to work generatively amid chaos, and not knowing how to go on living and teaching.

However, I found a mentor, returned to "school" (University of Victoria), and began to write again, to read extensively, and to think deeply more than ever before. Stories tumbled from my pen before I achieved awareness of what might lie beneath their surfaces. I began at the beginning again, thrown back to first experiences and naïve, inchoate writings. Following Rilke's advice to a young poet, I practiced learning to love the questions as well as live into them. What I learned through these five years of intensive narrative (writing) research is embedded in my method of narrative analysis.

PART II: A Perpetual Hermeneut:
Making Sense of Teaching and Difficulty

Wherever difficulty exists, there is a story behind it, often "whole, bright, deep with understanding" (Pinar, 1981, pp. 173–188). In teaching life where sempiternal difficulty abounds, where subtextual underpinnings and hidden curricula dwell beneath teaching and learning relationships, I require narrative method to draw out and clarify my research interest in questions of difficulty in education. Although "stories, including those told by teachers, are *constructions* that give meaning to events and convey a particular sense of experience" (Carter, 1993, p. 8), these stories often explain reasons enough to go on in life, however uncertainly, to dwell in difficulty without giving up, and to give significance to actions and people (Kerby, 1991).

As a result of my "regressive, progressive, analytical, synthetical" narrative work (Pinar, 1994), I have revolutionized my own teaching practices, and experienced a "coming home" to myself that allows me a sense of human entitlement: a quiet celebration of living an extraordinary ordinary life with loving relationships, hard work, social and ethical responsibility, and creative problem-solving amid the difficulties a (teaching) life presents in this new century.

Some of my narratives explore the underside of teaching, and some are "counter-narratives" (Giroux, Lankshear, McLaren, & Peters, 1996), which the teaching community of readers may find difficult to hear or accept, and which they may prefer to leave untold. Other stories of mine are memories of originary, often preconceptual, difficulty as I try to retrace my own epistemologies. Some are deliberate products of literary craft meant to create openings for more study, multiple tellings, and diverse interpretations.[5] All have their roots in some form of autobiography, although they may blossom into fiction. Through my "working from within" (Pinar, 1994), the truths uncovered in these narratives are much more than factual reports. Multiple resonances occur, because *story* appears to be the DNA, the genetic code of human consciousness. In this way narratives serve as force-field containers (in the Greek sense of *temenos*, or crucible) holding shards and images of difficulty long enough to examine them.

Researching difficulty through narrative is self-work; the narratives constitute a kind of daily, practical, if lyric (Zwicky, 1992), philosophy. They ground the reflective practitioner, who is able to call her *shadow* (in Jungian interpretations of that term) to "heel," to leave practices of

---

[5] Pinar's "Method of *Currere*" (1994), written in 1975, continues to influence me. Actually doing the kind of work he advocates requires a confrontation with all of one's minotaurs in labyrinths of ever-revealing consciousness, soul, and being. It is not for the faint of heart and requires lionhearted courage. Researcher's caveat: Don't do this at home alone! You will certainly need wise mentors, a rich community of scholars both in text and in person, and perhaps thoroughgoing psychotherapy while on such research journeys. Nonetheless, I think it is a worthy curriculum journey for every teacher.

unhealthy transference outside the door,[6] and to dwell in embodied action with students.

Our entire education system is in deep difficulty, but I only have the right to govern myself and I must do this, reconstituting my theory which is my practice. Only then can I work with others in difficulty, with a durable, intelligent, wise, humble, generative, compassionate self. Experienced teachers straddling fault-lines at the borders of self and system in their professional lives ask questions that call for a radical hermeneutics (Caputo, 1987). They ask: *"Who* in the world am I by now?" *"Where* am I and how did I get here?" *"How* do I go on from here?" *"What* interpretations can I make of my professional being and practice?"

My best engagements with such inquiry locate my curricular theory, praxis, and research in strong, valid narrative research (Fowler, 2001a). But I do want to problematize a traditional certainty of definition and assumption about narrative understanding and narrative research work, especially in the domain of education and curriculum theory.

I have done this by developing a method of narrative analysis as antidote to the plethora of naïve teaching stories, stories without analysis posing as narrative research.[7] I call into question naïve, "cheerful," unproblematized frames for narrative research. I suggest instead seven interpretive fields, as both seed and plough of analysis on the plains of narrative research.

PART III: Seven Interpretive Fields of Narrative Analysis

From my fictional, autobiographical, and educational experience, I recognize at least seven interconnected, recursive, interpretive *fields* of narrative analysis. These fields (meptaphors of both magnetics and prairie) could be useful to education researchers using stories, counter-narratives, narrative interviews, or critical incidents in their qualitative work. They are as follows:

---

[6] For example, see Anna Freud, Alice Miller, and, more recently, Deborah Britzman.

[7] This concern has arisen in a number of collegial encounters. Two recent and notable examples: Janet Miller referred to the too many "cheerful" stories of teaching that abound in the literature (in conversation, April 2000, Baton Rouge); Jean Clandinin also expressed concern to me about stories of teaching passing as educational research (in conversation, University of Lethbridge, 2000).

Naïve storying requires breaking silence, finding language and voice to (pre)consciously tell an experience, image, event, conflict, or puzzlement about a difficulty that exists either in the common world or the private world. Something happened: what is being told at the elemental story level? When I write a (naïve) story about teaching, perhaps around issues of anger in a critical incident with a student or colleagues, such as in my story "The Anger in Our Miss Maple" (Fowler, 2001b), I peel back layers of my teaching self that startle me enough to notice a particular difficulty in teaching, to pay attention to its underside, 'neath, ground. I write the story, read it again, consider the story again, first as a writer and reader. This first phase is the setting down of the significant, often troubling, stories from our lives as teachers. For me, this is only the first step of narrative research, not the stopping point. Writing the story develops one's roots of understanding, but it does not go far enough regarding other meanings and one's professional practice. Research begins here, though, where I aim to understand what happened. What *was* the meaning of that incident, encounter, difficulty? How do I tell this story to myself and to others? I want to say *who* and *what* and *when* and *where* and *how* in those early drafts of a story, to do out-loud, early readings. In this phase, I know I write out of confusion and trouble, difficulty and puzzlement, and I give myself permission to write badly. Once the story is written down, even sometimes before the first draft is complete, there is startlement at seeing "it" externalized, its storied *temenos*, held in a narrative field long enough to study a text of lived experience.

In naïve storying, I concentrate on getting the words out, writing down my "facts" as re/membered. I evaluate the story and am startled that there is a different sense and meaning than I thought, so I reach for my pen again, to learn what I think and feel more deeply. I have discovered that my student teachers can benefit in similar ways when they write their own teaching stories. And then, I ask them to take a deeper look and see what is called for in themselves to understand and to change.

Psychological construction, which includes *affect* and *cognition*, examines the knots in the narrative, and the inextricably linked cognitive process of making sense. At this second analytical layer, the narrative researcher asks about the emotions in the story and in the reader; it asks how one can think about the story. What emotions are evinced? What cognitive work is called for?

Psychotherapeutic ethics asks the researcher to engage in issues surrounding professional ethics and morality, as each of us confronts our own potential for harm in teaching and research. Here we recall our shadows, admitting our capacity for projection and transference, and doing honest work on our own psyche (spirit/soul/self). Auto-narrative provokes a deeper awareness of one's own potential for projection, control, and harm to students and involves a mindful examination of self. As a reflective teacher, I have a desire for understanding and for developing moral agency and ethical responsibility in my teaching. Perhaps this narrative work and analysis is one way of grappling with interior issues of difficulty, identity, and pedagogy. Part of the work of ethics has to do with research on my own inner government and how I colonize myself. Often I am startled by how each story reveals more than I intend about the legislative, executive and judicial branches in the country of my own (teaching) consciousness.

I reread teaching stories that I and my student teachers have written, but each time, a desire emerges to improve the way the psyche relates to others in a more self-aware way, particularly between teachers and students. Reflective practitioners need to become knowledgeable about the possibilities of transference, projection, and shadowy behaviors in times of the unexpected or of deep stress. Questions must be asked about whose interests are being served, what the relations of power are, what ethics are being challenged, what is being revealed that requires work on the self. Startled by this phase of thinking about personal teaching stories, I reach for the pen again and move back to the safety of writerly concerns, before I consider how to shift to more generative pedagogy.

Narrative craft refocuses the author on those elements of convention, structure, and craft which constitute the safe container (*temenos*) of story. Narrative safely holds everything in one place—people, events, relationships, settings, and difficulty or conflict—long enough to study it. *Hermeneutic philosophy* concerns itself with what messages might lie beneath the surface text as one moves toward opening deeper meaning. Careful interpretive exploration of what is "uncovering" and "revealing" returns the reflective practitioner to original difficulties of Being and self. The reader asks what other interpretations of the story in question can be provided and what the story can mean. What is too difficult to talk about and what is too difficult to hold is of critical interest, as we open ourselves to mystery and play in a community of mortals (Caputo, 1987).

Curriculum pedagogy asks what the story text offers in terms of insightful implications for teachers, for teaching, and for all the contingent relational networks. Auto-narrative startles the pedagogic self and educates the imagination into better ways of teaching student teachers. This pedagogic phase of research is the site of careful thought about the implications that arise for one's own practice. One examines possible explanations and ways of thinking differently about difficulty in teaching. The goal is to find generative lessons from those difficulties. This is the point: to pay attention to how one is thinking about the issues in a story in terms of the foundations, theory, and practice of teaching. Here, one discovers even more about what it means to teach, to be human, to learn.

Autobiographical narrative research (student) teacher stories startle the pedagogue, artist, poet, philosopher, and friend in each of us. With a narrative worked and reworked, studied and researched at multiple phases, one can notice the parts of teaching that have to do with truth, meaning, beauty; this makes possible the fresh, startling, poetic, reframed vision and understanding of teaching that begins to emerge and form. The possibility opens for renewal of practice with a lighter, durable, quantum (professional) teaching self that is brought to a new, co-constructed curriculum, away from old malignant and ineffective or habitual pedagogic practices held onto for far too long.

Poetics of teaching is a conscious reconstitution of our selves toward beauty, truth, justice, wisdom, art, and meaning while we mindfully dwell in the *present* on this planet.

I believe narrative codes serve to bridge figurative understanding across differences, borders, and ruptures. They give us a way to explore the qualities of auto-historical and allo-historical curricula that make possible understanding and generative co-dwelling on our shared lands and languages of being. But stories themselves are not enough. We need analysis of stories to make narrative research an authentic mode of educational inquiry. Perhaps we also need to reconsider Hayakawa's legendary claim that the map is not the territory. What if the map *is* part of the territory? What curriculum studies, research, and theoretical maps *do* we draw from the narrative research we construct, and into which new territories and plains must we dwell? Through narrative research we can ask how we re/construct understanding of self and not-self, in community, especially in uncomfortable places.

Startled and breathing mortal that I am, I come now to teaching with more attunement, humility, and care. Narrative analysis is not for the faint of heart and certainly not for those seeking escape from quantitative research. Unfamiliar horizons will emerge, some daunting, some redemptive. A choice to engage in narrative research should arise out of authentic research questions, from the difficulty revealed in emerging narrative, which leads to deeper study, luring the teacherly and writerly mind to inner landscapes of the self and profession.

With a narrative worked and reworked, studied and researched in multiple fields, I do believe one notices the parts of teaching that have to do with truth, meaning, and beauty, which make possible fresh, startling, poetic, reframed vision and understanding of teaching. The possibility opens for practice with a lighter, more durable teaching self.

Selected References for the Narratively Inclined

Aoki, T. (1981). *Inspiriting curriculum and pedagogy: Talks to teachers.* Edmonton, Alberta, Canada: University of Alberta, Faculty of Education.

Aoki, T. (Ed). (1985). *Understanding curriculum as lived: Curriculum Canada VII.* Vancouver, British Columbia, Canada: University of British Columbia, Faculty of Education, Centre for the Study of Curriculum and Instruction.

Aoki, T. (1986, April/May). Teaching as in-dwelling between two curriculum worlds. *The B.C. Teacher,* 8–10.

Aoki, T. (1992a). Layered understandings of teaching: The uncannily correct and the elusively true. In W. I. Pinar & W. M. Reynolds (Eds.), *Understanding curriculum as phenomenological and deconstructed text* (pp. 1–27). New York: Teachers College Press.

Aoki, T. (1992b). *Teachers narrating/narratives teaching.* Victoria, British Columbia, Canada: Ministry of Education and Ministry Responsible for Multiculturalism and Human Rights, Province of British Columbia.

Britzman, D. (1991). *Practice makes practice: A critical study of learning to teach.* Albany, NY: State University of New York Press.

Britzman, D. (1992). The terrible problem of knowing thyself: Toward a poststructural account of teacher identity. *Journal of Curriculum Theorizing, 9*(3), 23–46.

Britzman, D. (1993). Slips that show and tell: Fashioning multiculture as a problem of representation. In C. McCarthy & W. Crichlow (Eds.), *Race, identity, and representation in education* (pp. 188–200). New York: Routledge.

Caputo, J. D. (1987). *Radical hermeneutics: Repetition, deconstruction, and the hermeneutic project.* Bloomington: Indiana University Press.

Carter, K. (1993). The place of story in the study of teaching and teacher education. *Educational Researcher, 22*(1), 5–12, 18.

Clandinin, J., & Connelly, M. (1990). Narrative, experience and the study of curriculum. *Cambridge Journal of Education, 20*(3), 241–254.

Clandinin, J., & Connelly, M. (1991). Narrative and story in practice and research. In D. Schön (Ed.), *The reflective turn: Case studies in and on educational practice* (pp. 258–281). New York: Teachers College Press.

Connelly, M., & Clandinin, J. (1990). Stories of experience and narrative inquiry. *Educational Researcher, 19*(5), 2–14.

Fowler, L. (1989). *Gifts from the tribe: The writing and teaching of five Canadian authors.* Unpublished master's of education thesis, University of Alberta, Edmonton, Alberta, Canada.

Fowler, L. (1999). Home run. *Language and Literacy, 1*(2). Available: http://educ.queensu.ca/~landl/.

Fowler, L. (2001a). *A curriculum of difficulty: Stories and narrative analysis in educational research.* Unpublished manuscript.

Fowler, L. (2001b). The anger in our Miss Maple. *Language and Literacy, 3(2).* Available: http://educ.queensu.ca/~landl/.

Giroux, H., Lankshear, C., McLaren, P., and Peters, M. (1996). *Counternarratives: Cultural studies and critical pedagogies in post-modern spaces.* New York and London: Routledge.

Hayakawa, S. (1939). *Language in thought and action.* New York: Harcourt Brace Jovanovich.

Heidegger, M. (1962). *Being and time* (J. Macquarrie and E. Robinson, Trans.). New York: Harper and Row. Original work published in 1927.

Kerby, P. (1991). *Narrative and the self.* Bloomington: Indiana University Press.

Kirby, S., and McKenna, K. (1989). *Experience, research, social change: Methods from the margins.* Toronto: Garamond Press.

Miller, A. (1983). *For your own good: Hidden cruelty in child-rearing and the roots of violence.* New York: Farrar Straus.

Miller, A. (1988). *Banished knowledge.* Frankfurt: Suhrkamp.

Miller, J. (Winter 1986). Women as teachers: Enlarging conversations on issues of gender and self-concept, *Journal of Curriculum and Supervision,* 111–21.

Miller, J. L. (2000). What's left in the field: A curriculum memoir. *Journal of Curriculum Studies, 32*(2), 253–266.

Pinar, W. F. (1981). "Whole, bright, deep with understanding": Issues in autobiographical method and qualitative research. *Journal of Curriculum Studies, 13*(3), 173–188.

Pinar, W. F. (1994). The method of currere. In *Autobiography, politics, and sexuality: Essays in curriculum theory, 1972–1992.* New York: Peter Lang.

Pinar, W. F., and Reynolds, W. (1992). *Understanding curriculum as phenomenological and deconstructed text.* New York: Teachers College Press.

Pinar, W. F., Reynolds, W. M., Slattery, P., & Taubman, P. (1995). *Understanding curriculum: An introduction to the study of historical and contemporary curriculum discourses.* New York: Peter Lang.

Polkinghorne, D. (1988). *Narrative knowing and the human sciences.* Albany: State University of New York Press.

Zwicky, J. (1992). *Lyric philosophy.* Toronto: University of Toronto Press.

Performance, Place, and Possibility: Curricular Landscapes, Curricular Songs

Lynn Fels

> *Singing the space*
> *there are meetings*
> *and I am transformed...*
> —Eugenio Barba, *The Paper Canoe*

Singing the Space

On the edge of the sea, i wait, wind-caressed, standing against the horizon. Footsteps, traces of my presence, momentary signatures on sand. A turbulent sky is a scrim of cloud and sun playing light through light. In the distance, white winged boats map the ocean landscape; angel vessels in ponderous movement, seeking knowledge through wind-cries. What crew hauls on sheets in fevered response to an absent captain's command? Do i sail pregnant-bellied, white against blue? The cool touch of brass, the wheel turning beneath flesh—is it i that sets the compass reading? Whose voices sculpt sand responses in the failing tide? How does this moment perform?

My work investigates curricular places of possibility, absence, and disruption realized through performance. *Performance not as process nor as product, but as breath, intermingling, unexpected journey landscapes reeling against the sky in a sudden moment of recognition.* I am curious about the spaces that we breathe into being through imaginative play and exploration, curricular spaces that open to us with invitation.

> ...the role of imagination is not to resolve, not to point the way, not to improve. It is to awaken, to disclose the ordinarily unseen, unheard, and unexpected. (Greene, 1995, p. 28)

Performative inquiry is my vessel of investigation. Performative inquiry is a research methodology which explores possible journey-landscapes, charting space-moments of learning that are realized through performance (Fels, 1998). Performative inquiry draws, in part, from enactivism (e.g., Varela, Thompson & Rosch, 1993; Davis, Kieren & Sumara, 1996) through which learning is a "laying down in walking" of "new possible worlds." An ecological reading of the interplay between voice, imagination, and body, performative inquiry embraces intercourse, fortuitous interminglings of embodied presence and as yet to be imagined absence that breathe new possible curricular worlds into being.

> *within pools of echoes and silence*
> *a lover awakes*
> *madness touches her skin*
> *drenched in phosphorous kisses*
> *she arises translucent in moonlight*

Performance studies theorist Peggy Phelan (1993) states that:

> Like a rackety bridge swaying under too much weight, performance keeps one anchor on the side of the corporal (the body Real) and one on the side of the psychic Real. Performance boldly and precariously declares that Being is performed (and made temporarily visible) in that suspended in-between. (p. 167)

It is Phelan's rackety bridge that I want to suspend between the tensionality[1] of the known and the not-yet-known world(s) of being; I want to lean from precarious heights, to create the bridge's presence in the very swinging of our embodied imaginations. And in the moment between the height and fall of our swing, what curricular opportunities await?

Performance plays on "the edge of chaos" where patterns of interrelations and interconnections are continually created and recreated through an "endless dance of co-emergence" (Waldrop, 1992, p. 12). It is not the dance but the interplay that is our research and space of curricular inquiry. To entertain performative inquiry as a research vehicle and curricular place of learning is to recognize risk, the unexpected embodied

---

[1] See Aoki (1991, p. 8) for his reading of *tensionality*.

in performative action and interaction that opens us to possibility and impossibility.[2]

A playful etymological reading[3] of the word *performance* brings us to *form* as structure and *ance* as action, as in (d)ance. Performance, then, is both form and action. It is the duplicity and complicity of the prefix *per* in the word *performance* that gives us pause. A momentary stop. *Per* prescribes the adjacent *form* and brings with it the meaning of "utterly, throughout and through," but also, "to do away, away entirely or to (the) destruction of." So we may read performance as meaning that *simultaneously through form and through the destruction of form we come to action*. Understanding that action is "knowing, doing, being, creating" (Fels, 1995), we recognize the learning that happens through performance.

> *performance is the heartbreath that dances*
> *possibility and interstanding into presence* [4]

Performance is realized on the fine edge of chaos, a space where possibilities seduce and life dances into being. Performative inquiry is an ecological interstanding that invites the coevolving world(s) of performance, interpretation, complexity, and cognition into a transformative dance of possibility.

In the Wind Clothes Dance on a Line

> *Hand over hand hauling in the netted light,*
> *the holes in the representational,*
> *the holes in the visible* (Phelan, 1993, p. 177).

---

[2] In conversation with Dr. Ted Aoki, in which he inquires about the "impossible," that which is not yet possible to imagine into being, that which remains beyond our grasp like the force that moves the tides, unseen yet present in all our innocence and ignorance of movement.

[3] See Barnhart (1988, pp. 398, 775).

[4] Taylor and Saarinen (1994, *Interstanding* 2). The authors propose that "understanding has become impossible because nothing stands under. Interstanding has become unavoidable because everything stands between." I chose the word "interstanding" because it is through the interplay between the "known world(s)" and the "not-yet known world(s)" that performance breathes learning into presence.

Mario is hamming it up in the dory. I recruited him as my crew for early morning cod-jigging in the bay, a decision I am now regretting. Indifferent to my dramatic struggle to create a coastal outport in lecture room 210, he halfheartedly pulls at imaginary oars. Unknown to me, he sneaks copious gulps of screech from a flask and slyly winks at the audience—a circle of his peers who, like Mario, are reluctant to migrate from the solidity of the classroom to the elusive space of dramatic imagining. Outside, the January evening spills winter rain against the windows.

"Look, Mario." I sweep a generous hand across the horizon of blackboards. "The village looks like the broken grin of an old man's smile. Boarded up windows. Fallen fences. How many people live here now?"

Mario shrugs. Coughs. Tugs haphazardly at an oar.

"Remember that signpost outside of town, just where the road bends?" I am sweating under the layers of fisherman's sweater, life jacket, and overalls, trying to kickstart our role drama on the fishing industry in Newfoundland. The outport refuses to take shape. *Why isn't this working?*

"Never seen it," says Mario with another swallow of screech.

You're wrecking the logic of the drama. Of course you've seen it! You've lived here all your life! Can't you just pretend?

"You know the sign." I jab him in the ribs and point emphatically at a sign that I had taped before class on the blackboard: Come by Chance—Pop. 157.[5] I am silently cursing him under my breath, *Come on, Mario, work with me on this.* But he refuses to play along with my paper props. He refuses to follow the expected script.

"Nope. Never laid eyes on it. But," he says suddenly rocking the boat with unexpected enthusiasm. "I know how we can figure out the population."

"How?" I am suspicious. *Is he going to swamp the boat?* The class eagerly leans forward on their seats—sea vultures waiting for us to capsize.

"Count the clotheslines!" He stands triumphantly in the dory, pointing to the blackboard. "One, two, three..."

And to my amazement, clotheslines magically appear—diapers, workmen's overalls, cotton dresses, woolen socks, sheets dancing in the wind. The entire population of the outport leaps into being.

Within that single moment, Mario captures the very heart soul body of the outport and gifts us life. Realized in the choreography geography of cloth limbs

---

[5] I am aware that the real Come by Chance, in Newfoundland, has a significantly larger population, and is not the isolated outport we imagined in our role drama. I am, however, captivated by the town's name, reflective of our attempts to create imaginary landscapes through performative exploration.

dancing on lines in the wind, the outport unknown becomes known. Within a moment, the not-yet-real[6] is realized and possibilities open to exploration.[7]

Here we are. In this moment. What if? What happens? What matters? Who cares? What is possible? How will we respond? Through performative explorations we realize a curriculum of possibility.

We engage in our momentary world of clotheslines and, in role, explore what happens when the local fish processing plant is closed. How are families affected by the closure? What action will the outport take in response? When we discover that the plant manager has absconded with all the plant's profits, will our anger be contained within the town hall meeting, or will it spill out into the imaginary streets? Will we, as a mob, advance with shouts and raised fists to the manager's home? What letters to the editor will be written in the local newspaper? How will the editorial read? What personal complicity may be read in the accountant's subdued announcement that the manager's body was found hanging from a basement beam in his home?

And what eloquence of silence/resistance/welcome will speak when the fisherman's sweater belonging to a grandfather drowned at sea—

> *Sometimes I imagine that he will return, standing at the wheel of his fishing boat. And dancing in the waves, aft and at the bow of his boat, will be the cod, thousands and thousands of codfish. He'll be shouting, Give me back my sweater, boy! It's damn cold out here! And he'll be bringing the cod, and all our wealth, home to Newfoundland.*[8]

is handed to an entrepreneur from "away" who promises a resort and jobs for everyone, exchanged for a lost fisherman's dreams?

Our role drama, embodied through clothes on a line dancing in the wind, plays curricular possibilities into presence, within which questions are asked, and possible answers set windchimes to singing. Through debriefing, we listen to the learning that happens through performance: within the role drama, in connection to life experiences, to seeing the world darkly through other lenses, other perspectives.

Unexpectedly clotheslines of our Newfoundland outport give birth to memories of clotheslines from our childhood

---

[6] "Not-yet-known" describes the unknown that may become known through performance.

[7] A version of this dramatic incident is published in Fels (1998), p. 27.

[8] Excerpt from monologue in Newfoundland role drama.

  cotton limbs
    frozen on a february line

      clotheslines strung between apartment buildings
        backdropped by jets in a Hong Kong sky

        a birdcage swinging empty on a line.

Each clothesline is a story, a poem, a family album, a lost trace; within these stories are invitations to curricular exploration, remembrance, and shared recognition. Performative inquiry explores and maps unfolding journey-landscapes that twist in sudden gusts of recognition like clothes on a line. And through our bodymind mapping, curricular possibility enters our language of embodied action and interaction.

Dislocation

Close your eyes. Breathe deep. Listen to my voice. You are going on a journey.
 Imagine this. We live in a time of war, of terror, of mistrust. You are hiding in a dark room; you are waiting for someone to come. Your neighbors have already escaped this place of madness. You have been abandoned by all you know, by your colleagues, by your friends, your family. Before the war, what was your work? Were you a journalist? A banker? A politician? A shopkeeper? Before the war, did you live a life of wealth? Or one of poverty? The city has been under siege for several weeks. Look around your room. What room are you in? A bedroom? The kitchen? A one-room flat? What kind of furnishings are in your room? The windows are shattered from the force of the bombs that have fallen in the streets several blocks away. The noise of a gun battle interrupts your restless sleep. Your safety could be betrayed by candlelight, by the smell of soup simmering on the stove. There is no turning back. You are alone. Listen. Do you hear that noise? Don't move. Don't let them hear you. Your heart is pounding, your breath loud in the empty room. Shhhhhh. There? Again. Oh god! Footsteps. And voices. Outside. There

now. They're banging on doors. Shouting. Coming closer. How many? You must leave. You have time. You must leave the country. Cross the border tonight. But wait. There is something you must take with you. Something that you cannot leave behind. What is it? A letter? A picture? A diary? Incriminating evidence? A family heirloom? A child's forgotten toy? An address book? You can bring only one thing with you. What will you choose? Quickly now. Wrap it up safely. Do you have anything to put it in? To keep it safe? A box? A rag? An envelope? Careful. You must leave. Now. Quickly, they are close to you! How do you escape?

You are in the streets now, running. How do you find your way to the border crossing? Do you walk? Have you found passage in a truck? Now, you are at the border. You can hear the officers talking, checking visas, looking at passports. They are carrying flashlights. Can you see them? Will they see you? Are you hidden? Do they take your papers, and write down your name? Don't be afraid. They won't discover your secret. They won't arrest you. It is late. They are tired. There now, another moment. Be patient. Yes. You have crossed the border, into a new place, a place that welcomes you, that holds you safe. Soon you will have a job, you will build again your lost life. Wait a moment. Do you still have what you took from your room? Is it safe? You will keep this with you all your life. This is a remembrance of your journey, your border crossing. What is it? What have you brought with you into this new land of hope and exile?

When you are ready, take a breath. One, two. You may open your eyes. Welcome.

And in opening my eyes, I see reflected, in startling tears traced on cheeks, an awakening of other journeys, places, moments of songs yet to be heard within the curricular space of our being/becoming. In our sharing of multiple border crossings that we experienced during the visualization, we speak of past lives imagined, the dark rooms in which we hid, and the objects we chose to bring with us into the new land. A woman speaks of smuggling a baby across the border. Another brought a precious Ukrainian egg. Another brought a diary, and yet another describes a photograph. And, breathlessly, one tells of a stone that she had gathered from the beach, a remembered site of joy and pleasure, carried over the ocean to Canada, which now rests on her desk, a reminder of a lost landscape, a witness to her current life and success in her chosen land. Some participants wove their visualization experience around their personal lives, integrating fragments of memory, family, experience. During debriefing, they share with us stories of emigration, loss, and new beginnings.

The learning is one of surprise—freefalling through moments of crisis and recognition of possibility.

We discover that many of the named objects are of cultural, linguistic and/or family memory or significance. As imagined exiles, participants imported foundation stones on which to build a new relationship of interaction with the landscape. And so we stumble upon the transplanting of cultural presence; an unplanned curriculum of multiculturalism. Our collection of objects and the stories that accompany our border crossings open a curriculum of intercultural conversations. How do we choose to map our presence in landscapes that are simultaneously places of home and exile?

What stories within stories are revealed within the embodied performance of our visualization? This is unexpected curriculum, curriculum that coevolves through performative inquiry; participants opening curricular landscapes in shared tellings and retellings.

Honoring Landscapes

we cannot know what country will
emerge in the moment of our meeting
as yet unmapped
bearing witness to the interstices of our journey
between dawn's early light and
the beating of an eagle's wing against a darkening sky
we shall find ourselves new explorers
in the terrible first moments of our awakening

Here then, on the edge of the sea, at the foot of the mountains, I dismantle cardboard boxes, and voices cry out, "Stop! Don't destroy our forests! Who are you to reap profits from our mountains?" And I am stopped.

In curricular exploration, if we are truly listening, body aware, the learner so often is the teacher, arrested by a voice crying out, "Listen! Hear me!" *Voice of a child. Voice of a moment. Voice of a forgotten presence. Voice of absence.* To empower our children through embodied imagining is to learn yet again the mystery and terrible wonder that is performance.

It is within the stop that the possibility of absence springs to presence. And so we come to a place of curricular recognition and possibility. What not-yet-known stories will we perform?

A role drama is presented.[9]
There are modest ambitions.
How does community come into being?
Can we create a place of shared relationship
within a space with our
voices, bodies, imaginations, experiences,
a jumble of cardboard boxes
a white sheet
a blue sheet for the sea?

In a circle we tell stories of emigration
yet again dislocation
each of us choosing a direction from which we travelled
an imagined history of past experience and connection.
We play our arrival to this space,
tell tales of our voyage,
some crossing the ocean,
others fording the prairies,
some have come willingly,
others are in exile.
Together we gather to create community.

Now, I tell them, imagine a space on the edge of the sea
in the shelter of the mountains—
it is here on this fine line between that our community
is to be located.

I assemble the boxes, and with the group,
create mountains.
A participant drapes the white sheet over
snow peaks
while another spells the ocean on a concrete floor
through the laying down
of a blue sheet.

---

[9] *Finding Ourselves on the Map.* Role drama performed at "Imagining a Pacific Community: Representation and Education Conference," Vancouver, BC, April 23–26, 1995. A longer version of this role drama is published in Fels (1998, pp. 31–33).

I bend and give the sheet a tug. *It's too close to the boxes*, I think.
Hey, put that back! A woman shouts. The mountain comes down to the edge of
the sea!
Tectonic response. Quickly I replace the ocean.
*How is it that she inhales the presence of the sea, and runs bare-footed along
the waves*
while I see only sheets and boxes and
hear the low hum of the
air conditioner?
Already the land and sea are in relationship
swelling one against the other
in melodic response
to our presence.

Let us build our houses, I command, seizing a box.
Each box can be a house.
Stop! Don't destroy our forests! Who are you to reap profits from our
mountains?

*How is it I suddenly discover myself an unfriendly giant disrupting the contours
of the land? My intentions are good.*

My hands burn with the broken piece of a mountain
that I in my uncaring
have ripped from the landscape
to sculpt new ownership—

Clearcutting. Parking lots. Tracts of suburban housing.

Resonance of another time, another people, another community
retold within a space-moment of recognition
weave through the telling of this performance.
ancient injuries
swirl around my naked feet cold to the touch
drawing me backwards with the tide
relentless pull of the moon

In my haste to create community I betray community
only now recognizing in the moment of the stop
that community is
relationship to the mountains
                                        the ocean
the edge between.

Quickly I repair the territory

which does not heal but remembers
mourned in the laments of seagulls sailing against
an empty sky and in the silent scars
that map our presence.

I am stopped.
And within a space moment of learning,
hope sings
on the edge of the sea in the shelter of the mountains.

re-imagining curriculum

Curricular moments of possibility are realized within the elusive space of Phelan's "rackety bridge" of performance.

Through space moments of learning—
counting clotheslines,
     dismantling mountains,
          carrying a treasured object across borders

—new landscapes are revealed, relationships illuminated, journeys anticipated. These are curricular opportunities embodied through performance which simultaneously become possible spaces of interstanding and curricular exploration.

Not a Narrowing Down But an Opening Up

Mario's counting of the clotheslines invites our outport into being, and we, in turn, breathe our presence through improvisation, tableau, writing-in-role. Our outport is fragmentary, elusive; closing the door at the end of class leaves behind an empty space that sings of traces. For a suspended moment, our outport demands our attention, our actions produce a particular anguish and joy of participation, and in our leaving, within our absence clothes dance on a line. The curricular song that becomes the telling of our experience is a celebration of our journey-landscape. Multiple lines, shadowed absences; linen echoes, dancing briefs resonate, enrich our telling, and bring forth new possible curricular worlds to explore.

hope
splash ascends

wavebillows of light
whisperblue

At the edge of the sea, in the shelter of the mountains, issues of environmentalism, native rights, ownership, birth, and community are spelled out in the embodied interactions that are our momentary presence. And when the cardboard boxes are dismantled and the sheets folded, the embodied memory of our shared landscape writes its presence in our conversations about clear-cutting, in our revisiting of treaty negotiations, in our attempts to build community within our own dwelling places. The tide spells our learning in the sand, retracing our curricular encounters. Within performance we are performed.

you lay down a path in walking.
in walking you lay down a path...

and in turning around...
wanderer, path there is none,
only tracks on ocean foam.[10]

In the visualization that is an exploration of exile and homecoming, the border-crossing is a metaphor that we hang on a line. Opening our eyes, welcoming again the present space, we speak of border crossings: those of immigration, of changing careers, of abandoned marriages, stepping across a line that is at once a barrier and an opening.

when flight is
danced into presence
on a line between

Three landscapes—each welcomes an unexpected entry into curricular spaces of exploration. Curricular possibilities open and we are engaged.

Three landscapes unfold within the performance that is us. We can locate our explorations, identifying the props and supplies of our immediate presence: our experience, our identity, our cultural and intercultural locations and imaginative interplay. Our presence matters.

---

[10] Poem by Antonio Machado, from *Proverbios y Cantares* (1930) as translated by F. Varela (1987, p. 63).

Our absence sounds loudly. We shape our worlds of exploration through the intertext of our embodied imagining, performing possibility. Curriculum as realized through performance is a tidal exploration, subject to the nuances of light, position of moon, and presence of a second pair of dry socks. Space-moments of learning are elusive in the hopeful intermingling[11] of place, inquiry, and participants, and yet, in that joyful cry of "Aha!"[12] we are recognized.

What learning is possible on the edge of the sea in the shelter of mountains? How is it that through the counting of clotheslines an outport leaps into presence? Mario's clotheslines become the line dance of our own laundered childhood memories. And in the crossings that are the intermingling of exile and homecoming, objects carried across the line bring intercultural presence to our landscape.

Our performative intertext(s) invite a reimagining of curriculum. These new interstandings lead to changes in our practices of teaching, research, curriculum development and learning as defined and sought. Our curricular dance on the "edge of chaos" through performative inquiry resonates. How can I now, having watched the clothes dance on a line, return to the structured texts that are the voice and expectations of my community? How can I write in the language of the oppressor when the song of my heart catches the flight of winged gulls? What happens when we trust the freefall that is performance, and, in reaching out, are arrested in mid-flight? How do we write our learning that is in the border crossings of our shared journey-landscapes? How is it that light spills between our fingers, and mountains are born?

---

[11] The term "intermingling" is found in an unpublished essay, "Phosphorescent Creatures, Earthly Features, Luminous Things," April 2000, by Susan Hass, a doctoral student writing in the field of planning.

[12] Aha! moments are moments of transcognition—space-moments of learning that come into being in the interstices between the real world(s) and the not-yet-real world(s) of performance. The aha! moment realizes unexpected connections for us, illuminating the not yet known in the brilliant light of the dance. An aha! moment is not an end point in learning (or research), but a landmark or signpost in a coevolving journey-landscape that welcomes further exploration and contemplation. Aha! moments come from a place of trust, where a momentary imbalance sends us scrambling to secure our footing on unfamiliar ground. An aha! moment happens when participants knowingly or innocently throw themselves into freefall, and are momentarily arrested in flight.

On the edge of the sea, i wait, wind-caressed, standing against the horizon. I catch the jib sheet and pull, weight of the wind in my hands. A curricular space of possibility. Beneath my feet, the sea spells our story, intermingling flesh and wind, vessel and water. And a song is born on a breath of wind...

References

Aoki, T. (1991). Teaching as in-dwelling between two curriculum worlds. In *Inspiriting curriculum and pedagogy: Talks to teachers* (pp. 7–10). Alberta: University of Alberta Press.

Barba, E. (1995). *The paper canoe: A guide to theatre anthropology* (R. Fowler, Trans.). London: Routledge.

Barnhart, R. D. (Ed.). (1988). *The Barnhart dictionary of etymology*. New York: H. W. Wilson.

Davis, B., Kieren, T., & Sumara, D. (1996). Cognition, co-emergence, curriculum. *Journal of Curriculum Studies, 28*(2), 151–169.

Fels, L. (1995). Cross-country with Grumet: Erasing the line. *Educational Insights*. http://www.lane.educ.ubc.ca/insights/home.html.

Fels, L. (1998). In the wind clothes dance on a line. *jct: Journal of Curriculum Theorizing, 14*(1), 27–36.

Greene, M. (1995). *Releasing the imagination: Essays on education, the arts, and social change*. San Francisco: Jossey-Bass.

Phelan, P. (1993). *Unmarked: The politics of performance*. London: Routledge.

Taylor, M., & Saarinen, E. (1994). *Imagologies: Media philosophy*. London: Routledge.

Varela, F. (1987). Laying down a path in walking. In W. I. Thompson (Ed.), *GAIA: A way of knowing—Political implications of the new biology* (pp. 48–64). Hudson, NY: Lindisfarne.

Varela, F., Thompson, E., & Rosch, E. (1993). *The embodied mind: Cognitive science and human experience*. Cambridge, MA: MIT Press.

Waldrop, M. (1992). *Complexity: The emerging science at the edge of order and chaos*. New York: Simon & Schuster.

❱ Cultural Politics, Film Narratives, and Adult Education: Changing Identities in a Postmodern World

Aristides Gazetas

Introduction

The motive behind this essay is to appraise the special ways personal or cultural identities are constructed through an analysis of a film narrative that calls to our attention the politics at play in certain classical myths such as Sophocles' tragedy *Antigone*. The reasons for this narrative revival originated in the late 1960s in Europe and the United States as a challenge to the hierarchical orthodoxies of governments whose representatives proposed that they spoke for and on behalf of others. In Margaretha von Trotta's film *Marianne and Juliane* (1981) we can easily locate a modernized translation of the Antigone—Creon confrontation. Von Trotta's updating of this legend for today's audiences considers the acts of terrorism committed by the Red Army Faction (RAF) in the Germany of the 1970s. It is personalized through a rewriting of the life and death of Gudrun Ensslin. In this transformation, von Trotta, as playwright and director, brings together three important contemporary discourses relating to adult education. They focus on an examination of the Lacanian formation of identity in the complexities of female bonding with the Other; the impact of power relations and knowledge from a Foucauldian viewpoint; and the concept of empowerment toward a discourse on human rights as advocated by Paolo Freire. This paper will contend that cultural identities are locally and historically specific, and that they become available for human understanding only within certain "language games," "paradigms," and "discursive formations." In a textual analysis of von Trotta's film narrative, I discuss how the fanatical-ascetic Marianne uses her newly honed terrorist tactics to provoke a debate on the "regimes of truth" that mask the totalitarian state. In her attacks upon fascist police state and its enforcement policies, she demonstrates ways to deconstruct the binary, linear logic of Western rationality and to foreground it in the open-ended nature of knowledge claims through the play of contingencies, ambiguities, and ironies. Her acts put into question the benevolent images that fascist governments present in the formation of modern forms of governance and its attacks against "terrorist" protesters seeking justice.

By targeting the "already always given," this film narrative deconstructs the "regime of truth" existing between the presence/absence of Self and Other, between justice and the law. In entering the spaces of a cinematic world, the viewer is placed within a political struggle between the imaginary and the symbolic. Here the boundaries of identities are firmly set at the beginning of the narrative, but are challenged by a series of metonymic activities that generate new possibilities for viewers to locate "the language games" of a repressive logic used by a totalitarian police state. These deconstructions also allow both viewer and educator opportunities to disengage and disrupt the narrative codes, cultural values, and ideological goals found in the imposition of (ir)rational laws. In today's world such anti-terrorist laws are being written to include detention without charge and suspension of the right of silence. Thus with such draconian measures an irony emerges which neither attacks nor mocks but irritates "because it denies us certainties by unmasking the world as *ambiguity*" (Kundera, 1986, p. 134).

It is a major assumption of this essay that all film narratives have several basic functions. First, they are a means of symbolizing events that situate the viewer in different space/time perspectives. Second, they become "experiences of experience," giving expression to different cultural identities or representations of the "Other." However, some film/video narratives provide situational learning experiences in which to develop new ways of seeing the world and new frameworks to understand differences among other cultures in the world. They encourage an open mindedness toward value systems other than one's own. Also, they can be interpreted as important ideological weapons for the dissemination of propaganda by the state for the maintenance and/or subversion of the dominant political order.

Today, the profusion of images produced through film/video/television inform and persuade us about our "imaginary" selves in multiple forms of representation. This new hyper-space world of electronic-video transmission becomes directly linked to how motion pictures mediate information about the world out there while advancing discourses about postwar political alliances toward Western globalization. In television, every broadcast makes a connection between the "reality" of the image and the cultural constructs operating within any given society. Therefore, each narrative contains within its illusionistic framework a cultural power to mediate reality based upon actual historical happenings or events. The purpose of this paper is to analyze one recent film narrative, *Marianne and Juliane,* to see how a Western democracy reacted to the political actions of a terrorist gang taking state officials hostage and killing them.

When asked why some people believe in the power of cinema, the producer in Peter Weir's film *The Truman Show* (1998) responded, "We accept the reality of the world as it is presented to us. It is as simple as that." The implication of this cinematic situation hopefully forces the viewer/spectator to realize that illusions are part of our reality. This becomes the political condition of our lives, as the German playwright and essayist Bertolt Brecht declared during the 1920s (Wright, 1989, p. 21).

Cultural Politics and the Representation of Women

As part of the new historicism of today, a new mode of cultural politics has emerged, grounded in the belief that "history" is not a set of fixed and unchangeable objective facts but is, like literature, a text that interacts and re-presents "reality" as "ideological products" or "cultural constructs" of a particular time and place. Thus, contemporary film narratives, based upon historical events, require analytical study both as an apparent representation and reflection of a "reality," and as a cinematic construct by filmmakers, in most cases serving as a personalized political text about society consciously re-formed into a powerful narrative discourse.

By gaining an awareness of the cinematic structures and genres used by most filmmakers, educators can gain a new understanding of several key concepts such as culture, ideology, ethics, and aesthetics, as filmmakers re-present and reinterpret events and people in their film narratives. Educators then can question why film directors choose particular myths or stories to recount and contest "the already given" in a postmodern society. Moreover, they can interrogate these meta-narratives of the past as representations of "historical truths." Thus, while adhering to a time chronology, today's postmodern films engage the viewer with a fusion of the past and the present by reconstructing the ways in which memory and imagination can validate their own narrative films. This revisioning of the past into the present becomes a significant strategy for today's political feminists like Sunera Thobani, a University of British Columbia professor of sociology, whose speech to a women's conference on the subject of violence against women generated much public controversy in news reports, including "vicious" personal attacks upon her. In brief, she said in rebuttal that "in the aftermath of the terrible attacks of September 11 [on the World Trade Center in New York City] I argued that the U.S. response of launching 'America's new war' would increase violence against women" (Thobani, 2001).

The learning process with respect to political speeches and pedagogical practices requires an identification of the social/political discourses in which the formative ideological frameworks are placed to characterize the power/knowledge structures representing both aspects of Western society. This is also applicable to institutions of learning which are structured as major mechanisms for the transmission and reproduction of the dominant culture. In the 1980s, schools were challenged as cultural and political sites that disregarded the relation between the knowledge/power nexus and domination. Like film narratives, schools are politically structured as agencies for cultural propagation and reproduction. The reason radical educational critics and feminists have sought to raise questions regarding the curriculum is to "unmask" the hidden ideological constructs operating within the schools and to reflect upon the assumption that most "cultural constructs" operate in Western society as a way of assigning meaning to predetermined social/political discourses over time. As stated by Bill Nichols, "Ideology uses the fabrications of images and the processes of representation to persuade us that how things are is how they ought to be and that the place provided for us is the place we ought to have" (Nichols, 1981, p. 1).

Thus, educational critics such as Henry Giroux and Peter McLaren (1989) have struggled to deconstruct the logic of the traditional pedagogy found in different school sites. As Giroux states,

> Far from being neutral, the dominant culture of the school was characterized by a selective ordering and legitimating of privileged language forms, modes of reasoning, social relations and lived experiences. In this view, culture was linked to power and to the imposition of a specific set of ruling-class codes and experiences. (Giroux & McLaren, 1989, p. 129)

But not until these same radical pedagogues became concerned with acting as "transformative intellectuals" were they able "to help students acquire critical knowledge about the basic societal structures, such as the economy, the state, the workplace and mass culture, so that such institutions could be open to potential transformation" (Giroux & McLaren, 1989, pp. 138–139).

This new position, which carried both political and moral authority, was achieved at the beginning of the 1990s. For some, it meant that as transformative teachers they had "to be concerned about issues of social justice and political action" (Giroux & McLaren, 1989, p. 139). The pedagogical rationale behind this new position was the notion of a "commitment grounded in an affirmative view of liberation which acknowledges that the notion of 'truth' does not reside in abstract definitions of principle, but is, in part, the outcome of particular power struggles that cannot be removed from either history or existing networks of social and political control" (p. 139). Thus the stage was set for pedagogues to test their beliefs in a deconstructive analysis, one that recognized how their own perspectives could also be "both challenged and transformed." Their own pedagogical practices thus would be critiqued in a manner similar to judges who are required to reinterpret the law anew in each situation with respect to the liberating notion of justice, since "justice is the relation of one to the other" (Levinas, cited in Caputo, 1997, p. 17). Yet would their own recognition of schooling as a form of cultural politics cultivate a "reality" that would be productive of greater knowledge, meaning, and life-supporting values? Here, the postmodern condition of our times promotes critiques of modernism, offering alternate definitions on the role of intertextuality in all cultural constructs. In any deconstruction of these constructs, it discloses not only the dominant ideology but also the subversive forces at play in such texts. This dramatic relationship is clearly demonstrated in film narratives that are in conflict with the dominant politics and ideology. These films attempt to uncover the power struggles arising between the cultural groups that play a role in molding contemporary society.

Cultural Politics

In philosophical terms, the key discourses of postmodernism examine concepts on the relationship of knowledge to power (Foucault), interpretations of subjectivity (Lacan), and empowerment toward a liberatory discourse in education (Freire), as well as a rethinking of Marxist models of society (Jameson). In all of these discourses, reason, objectivity, and certainty are displaced by a focus on "regimes of truth," a deconstruction of the binary, linear logic of Western rationality (Derrida), and a foregrounding of ambiguity, plurality, and contingency.

Further, people as diverse as Wittgenstein, Kuhn, and Foucault argue that objects of knowledge are locally and historically specific, and that they become available for human understanding only within certain "language games," "paradigm shifts," and "discursive formations." From these different positions, postmodernist texts provide multiple histories that attempt to "distance" and "estrange" the reader from the illusions of a humanistic idealism based upon modern Western thought. In doing so, these texts search for the "discontinuities, breaks, and ruptures" between the past and the present. The sense of repositioning our subjectivities suggests that our identities, beliefs, and practices are culturally "contingent" upon the construction of paradigms or models, subject to revisions or paradigm shifts, but not connected to any historical determinism. Foucault (1977) calls these measures part of a "disciplinary society" where all future conflicts appear already won in advance by Western society since the exercise of power and the forces policing this power are no longer visible. They are now hidden, diversified, and strong enough to avoid battle.

Henry Giroux reiterates this argument in his powerful foreword to David Trend's text, *Cultural Pedagogy: Art/Education/Politics* (1992). Giroux states that "the new work on pedagogy…as a form of political and cultural production is deeply implicated in the construction of knowledge, subjectivities and social relations" (p. vii). While computer information systems enhance the electronic transmission of knowledge and skills, the older concepts of pedagogy are shifting away from the transmission of information to a form of cultural politics. For Giroux, the practice of the new pedagogy begins in the production and representation of meaning through "the link between education and cultural work…in the light of recent developments in feminism, cultural studies, postcolonialism, deconstruction and the new historicism" (p. vii).

Such pedagogical shifts toward a new cultural politics are central to film narratives when they serve as sources of history in relationship to postmodernist reforms in pedagogy. By implicating the cinematic representation of any subversive discourse, educators can approach contemporary concerns illustrating the relation of the "Self" to the "Other" in the dynamics of Western hegemonic thought. Some film narratives of the late 1970s and 1980s, now broadcast on television, are international in scope, including Coppola's *Apocalypse Now* (1979), Fassbinder's *Ali: Fear Enters the Soul* (1972), Bertolucci's *The Conformist* (1970), David Lynch's *Elephant Man* (1980), Antonioni's *The Passenger* (1975), von Trotta's *Marianne and Juliane* (1982), and Kurosawa's *The Shadow Warrior Kamemusha* (1980).

In the 1990s Hollywood produced a number of films that attempted to deconstruct the power of cinema to "construct a reality" for viewers. First on the scene was Lawrence McTiernan's *Last Action Hero* (1993), starring Arnold Schwarzenegger as a super-hero who willingly deconstructs his own film persona. Then there was James Cameron's *True Lies* (1994), also starring Schwarzenegger, in a Bond-like action-adventure that deconstructs the hero when the narrative doubles as a romantic comedy. *The Truman Show* (1998), directed by Peter Weir, attempts to convince the viewer that a television show can house a real-life community. Director Barry Levinson's *Wag the Dog* (1997) satirizes the powers in the White House who resort to television replays to create a war with Albania in order to divert media attention from a serious presidential indiscretion with a young woman.

In a more serious manner, von Trotta's *Marianne and Juliane* depicts the personal struggle of two sisters fighting against the secret police in West Germany as the police combat terrorist bombings and hostage takings. While this film is based upon the real-life terrorist acts of the Baader-Meinhof Group the director only hints at those historical events to construct this personal memoir of two German sisters. The questions arising from the analysis of such a film narrative are as follows: What political power informs such "terrorist actions" carried out both by the state and by the insurgent terrorist agents within this narrative? How believable are the causes of these actions in relationship to the rise of Western democracies? How is justice served by such cultural representations? Further, how do such personal cinematic depictions deconstruct the political justice system and foreshadow future political actions that would implicate education?

Germany in Autumn: An Omnibus Film

The political situation in West Germany was severely shaken by the continued rise of urban terrorism during the early 1970s led by the Red Army Faction, also known as the Baader-Meinhof Group. In April 1975, members of this terrorist group invaded the West German embassy in Stockholm and took a number of German diplomats as hostages in an attempt to secure the release of their leaders, Baader and Meinhof, who were already imprisoned. But the German government refused to release them. Two of the hostages were killed before the other gang members were captured. After these members were put on trial, the two leaders committed suicide (or were murdered) in prison in 1977.

In reaction to the violence and the political motives of this small group of terrorists, the Federal Republic instituted legislation to restrict the liberties of all citizens. Like the Canadian War Measures Act, imposed by Pierre Trudeau in October 1970 to counteract the Front de Libération du Québec crisis in Montreal, it sought to protect the public and to ensure that such terrorist acts would be stopped since they posed a serious threat to civil law and order. By claiming that terrorists were jeopardizing the civil liberties and rights of other citizens, the government created a political atmosphere in which it curtailed the freedoms of citizens by using strong-arm military tactics on some suspects, thus imposing a neo-fascist state.

In response to the cultural politics of this specific situation, a group of leading German filmmakers, including Werner Fassbinder, Volker Schlöndorff, and Alexander Kluge, assembled several short documentaries and interwove them with fictional narratives to protest the government's strict laws in reaction to terrorism. Under the leadership of Kluge, who used voice over narration to tie the documentaries together into a film, the filmmakers compared the government's police state with the Nazi past and its military mentality.

The final sequence of the film, written by Heinrich Böll and directed by Volker Schlöndorff, concerns the refusal by a West German television programming committee to broadcast a production of Sophocles' *Antigone*. The ban reveals their fear of being sympathetic to terrorists. Further, the suicides of Haemon and Antigone in the play are all too similar to the actual suicides of members of the Baader-Meinhof gang whose bombings, killings, and kidnappings openly defied the authority of the state. The implications of censorship and political correctness come to the fore. In its own way, *Germany in Autumn,* with Kluge's ironic commentary on the search for justice in the present based upon the past, achieves its goal by using the Brechtian device of "distanciation" to produce a critical awareness of the current situation (Sandford, 1980, p. 148).

Foucault's Theater of Discipline and Surveillance

However, the "great, tragic theater" of the past no longer survives. As Foucault shows in *Discipline and Punish* (1977), the theater of public torture and execution allowed the public to act as participants in the public ritual where the execution could be resisted and possibly reversed. Foucault states that this public theater where power was seen face-to-face has been displaced by the theater of discipline and surveillance. Now, any intervention by the public is neutralized and, as if they are watching the event unfold on the TV screen, members of the public are only spectators of the interrogations, and are silenced by being kept in their own place. Contact in public space is now prevented. All that remain in the theater of surveillance and discipline are "thousands of tiny theaters of punishment" that provide a regulating form of interrogation designed to produce "docile bodies" (Foucault, 1977, p. 113). Power and authority remain invisible, masked by various discourses in education, knowledge, humanist ideology, judicial reform, etc., as is the case with various TV programs on law and order. This is "serious theater with its multiple and persuasive scenes" which is more absolute and also more successful against public outrage.

Foucault addresses the different effects created by discourses on the power/knowledge nexus. Foucault claims that a new type of power and control came into existence in Europe at the end of the nineteenth century; he describes this as "disciplinary power." It is concerned with the regulation and surveillance of the human species and the governance of the individual and the body. It is sited in the new institutions of the modern world, from schools and hospitals to workshops and prisons, infiltrating and shaping what is said and done. Its purpose is to produce human beings as "docile bodies" through the power of administrative regimes and the expertise of professionals.

By employing Foucault's writing of history or "genealogy," von Trotta's film, *Marianne and Juliane* (1982), illustrates the connection of the past with the present, from the rise of fascism in Germany in the 1930s, to the wartime atrocities of the Nazis, to the terrorism of the 1970s. In this manner, the director was able to demonstrate how a "disciplinary regime...brought individuality into the field of observation through a vast meticulous documentary apparatus" (Dreyfus & Rabinow, 1982, p. 122).

Marianne and Juliane

Von Trotta's *Marianne and Juliane* is a fictional narrative that dramatizes the public and personal rebellion of two German sisters caught in the turmoil of the West German state of the 1970s. The film was inspired by the real life and death story of Gudrun Ensslin, a member of the German Baader-Meinhof terrorist group. However, von Trotta's film articulates the emotional bond experienced by two sisters when one, Marianne, is incarcerated by the police and dies or commits suicide in prison.

Throughout this film, the historical developments are analyzed and understood from the point of view of the older sister, Juliane, who attends to the needs of her younger sister, Marianne. The younger sister is shown learning her terrorist tactics to provoke her debate on the "regimes of truth." These "truths" mask the totalitarian state and act as an excuse to destroy terrorists. In her attacks upon the state's surveillance policies, Marianne demonstrates how "rituals of power" are brought into the public space in order to counteract and deconstruct the binary logic of Western rationality. Her terrorist activities thus become symbolic forms of retribution to combat the repressive acts of this neo-conservative postwar German government and its implementation of draconian laws. In the film, however, these terrorist attacks are not depicted. Paradoxically, what is depicted throughout this narrative is the way such "disciplinary powers" of a police state operate on the body of the "self," upon Marianne. Here, von Trotta reveals, in many ways, the disguises worn by the police, whose punitive actions against Marianne are legitimized by the authority of the state and its martial laws.

Most of the film is a reconstruction of the rebellious natures of the two sisters; Juliane, the older sister, is a journalist working for a small anti-abortionist newspaper. Marianne, the younger rebel, disowns her role as a mother and adopts a new identity by becoming a member of a terrorist group. She learns to place bombs in public places to demonstrate how terrorist tactics can disrupt and destroy Western institutions in the play of power politics.

In particular, von Trotta's *Marianne and Juliane* is important since it takes a classical Greek tragedy, Sophocles' *Antigone,* and reshapes it into a postmodern film interpretation of this dramatic conflict. Here, however, in the retelling of the story, the central conflict is between the political tactics of an "urban terrorist" and the hidden powers of a police state. Unlike the Sophoclean play, in which the two central characters, Antigone and Creon, are caught within a tragic vision, von Trotta's film becomes, in part, a narrative on the knowledge/power nexus in relation to the use of the law against the rise of terrorism in Germany. Moreover, the film also presents a powerful feminist critique of the struggle for justice by women caught within a dominant patriarchal society.

More in keeping with the Sophoclean play, in which the situation illuminates the tragedy of Creon rather than the passionate death of the heroine, von Trotta's dramatization of a local and historically specific series of events shows the effects of unreasonable power on the body of its female victim in episode after episode, and declines to represent the powerful leaders that inflict such punishment in return for her "crime." The film narrative, then, doubles both as a critique of the roles of women and a critique of the surveillance and identification of a subversive group of people in relationship to a growing resistance to the postwar policies of the West German government and its "disciplinary" society. The major issue, as in *Antigone,* is the question of justice, in deference to martial law, in affording human beings the right to receive a public burial regardless of whether they are deemed enemies of the state.

The film is designed in a Brechtian fashion using episodic flashbacks to bring the past into close comparison with the present. Most of these flashbacks reveal the psychological traumas experienced by the two sisters when, as high school students, they first learned about past Nazi terror and violence through viewing an Alain Resnais documentary film (*Night and Fog,* 1956) on the Holocaust. Further, their father is a Lutheran pastor whose weekly sermons portray the wrath of God. Their home prominently displays Grünewald's painting of the bloody crucifixion of Christ, with its stoic images of Mary and John confronting Christ's agony on the cross. These images run through the narrative as a comparison to the horrors faced by Marianne after she is captured by the police. Over a long period of time Marianne undergoes torture and dehumanizing experiences that end in her death.

Von Trotta spends the major portion of the film on the revealing ways Juliane attempts to protect and defend her sister, Marianne, against the pervasive influence of the police as well as the public. Throughout the narrative, each sister exchanges her mental identity with the "Other," and Juliane, who opposes the role of motherhood, adopts Marianne's son, Jan, and serves as his surrogate mother in the end. Yet, ironically, this ending reminds the viewer that Juliane is the narrator of the film. In response to Jan's tearing up his mother's photograph, Juliane decides to tell the young boy about his mother, "all that I know, but it is not everything." This ending brings us full circle to the opening sequence when we were introduced to Juliane and Jan. The entire film then becomes the recollection by Juliane of the events that brought imprisonment, suffering, and death to her sister, Marianne, at the hands of prison officials.

Feminism and the Patriarchal Society
Von Trotta's film offers two important approaches to feminism as part of the cultural politics of the time. On the one hand, feminism is regarded mainly as an Anglo-American attempt to recover and revalue literary works by women as subjects of a minority culture. Within this critical perspective, the major goal is to seek out the "discontinuities" within the narrative that challenge the patriarchal culture of a society in which "woman" is defined by the maternal role she plays. On the other hand, a more aggressive French perspective focuses on Lacanian psychoanalysis, the unconscious, and the symbolic role language plays in de-centering the sociological subject of woman (Fowler, 1973, p. 92). Based on Lacanian psychoanalysis and Derridean deconstruction, Julia Kristeva provides a critique of the patriarchal society by unmasking the means through which linguistic strategies form and produce the feminine as a gendered subject. Kristeva's feminist readings reveal how cultural politics process the identity and subjectivity of men/women, sons/daughters, and mothers/fathers. The importance of an independent, imagined self is registered as a political challenge in these life histories. Film narratives like *Marianne and Juliane* thus become a retelling or telling of self and other as they seek to subvert patriarchal authority.

Instead of being reduced to silent acceptance of societal roles, the women depicted in this film seek a place for the "melancholic imagination." The term "melancholic imagination" comes from Kristeva's psychoanalytical exploration of a subject's affective experience of loss or despair. As a disciple of Lacan, she echoes Lacan's point about the signifier/signified as a distinction between the semiotic and the symbolic. Lacan claimed that the signifier preceded all verbal representations. Kristeva uses the term "semiotic" to explain the mental representations of the senses as they are informed by the primary Freudian processes of unconscious displacement and condensation. To this notion, she identifies the semiotic with the material, maternal body or *khora*: "the psychic receptacle—archaic, mobile, unstable, prior to the One, to the father." Like a "floating signifier" it cannot be defined in the language system since it is a desire proceeding from a need or "lack" within a person. Kristeva equates the symbolic with language formation—or the signifier—and with the paternal hegemony of grammar, syntax, and the law (Kristeva, cited in Silverman and Welton, 1988, pp. 22–23). Like Lacan, Kristeva reveals that the "subject" of a discourse becomes a "split subject," a woman (Marianne/Juliane) divided but also a woman belonging both to the semiotic *khora* and to the symbolic order. Her reaction is seen as a despair created by a melancholic imagination in which the "self" attempts to unite with the Other.

I place *Marianne and Juliane* within this French perspective. In many ways, Juliane seeks justice in terms of deconstructing the law that brought about her sister's death and seeks for the place of the *khora* as she gathers information on the death of her sister to illustrate the repressive patriarchic system and its effects upon women. In both instances the call for justice and the *khora* give Juliane "the impulse, the drive and the movement to improve the law, that is, to deconstruct the law" (Derrida, quoted in Caputo, 1997, p. 16). Juliane becomes the storyteller for von Trotta as she attempts to expose the audience to the conditions that bring revolution, ethics, and morality into cultural politics, and as she deconstructs the identity and subjectivity of women. Von Trotta's film serves as a cultural text, as part of a postmodern society, to show that the "condition of possibility of deconstruction is a call for justice" (p. 16). Thus, as part of a pedagogical *discourse,* the film illustrates the tragic political struggles of women caught within an oppressive and destructive patriarchal system.

References

Buñuel, L. (1962, July). Cinema: An instrument of poetry. *Theatre Arts,* July 1962.

Caputo, J. H. (1997). *Deconstruction in a nutshell: A conversation with Jacques Derrida.* New York: Fordham University Press.

Dreyfus, H., & Rabinow, P. (1982). *Michel Foucault: Beyond structuralism and hermeneutics.* Brighton, England: The Harvester Press.

Foucault, M. (1977). *Discipline and punish: The birth of the prison* (A. Sheridan, Trans.). New York: Pantheon.

Fowler, R. (Ed.). (1973). *A dictionary of modern critical terms.* London: Routledge & Kegan Paul. Revised 1990, 1991.

Giroux, H. A., & McLaren, P. (Eds.). (1989). *Critical pedagogy, the state, and cultural struggle.* Albany: State University of New York Press.

Kundera, M. (1986). *The art of the novel.* New York: Grove Press.

Nichols, B. (1981). *Ideology and the image.* Bloomington: Indiana University Press.

Sandford, J. (1980). *The new German cinema.* New York: DaCapo Press.

Silverman, H., & Welton, D. (Eds.). (1988). *Postmodernism and continental philosophy.* Albany: State University of New York Press.

Thobani, S. (2001). *War frenzy.* Available: http://www.print.indymedia.org (22 October).

Trend, D. (1992). *Cultural pedagogy: Art/education/politics.* New York, London: Bergin & Garvey.

Wright, E. (1989). *Postmodern Brecht.* London: Routledge

❭ Teaching Tracks

Tasha Henry

Sitting on the steps of the Vancouver Art Gallery
having teaching anxiety
too many buildings to get through
to people
crude faces amid strained landscapes
between bodies travelling north east south
inwards
towards me
I review the lessons—
my life-lessons
to be learned
for tomorrow
plans built by me
to be shaped by children
I map out my life—
in units
by grading passages
and moving passed points of love
into moments of art
imprints
small handprints
making tracks

❯ The Pedagogy of Technological Replacement

David Blades

In aiming for virtual (technical) immortality and ensuring its exclusive perpetuation by a projection into artifacts, the human species is precisely losing its own immunity and specificity and becoming immortalized *as an inhuman species.*

—Jean Baudrillard, *The illusion of the end*

The End of History

A metallic hand slowly opens the door to the Historian's room. Quietly, the caregiver android looks in on his charge. The Historian is slumped over at the desk as usual, but the posture strikes the caregiver as odd. Gently touching the Historian's neck, the android discovers no pulse in the carotid artery: the human has finally died. With reverent care, the android picks up the ancient figure and carries the body to the facility specially prepared for this important event. The android communicates with an attendant android along the way that the last human being is now gone. The attendant acknowledges the gravity of the moment and sends the information to the Collective.

After arranging for the preparation of the corpse, the caregiver decides to return to the Historian's room. Despite established protocols for dismantling the quarters, some supervision and guidance would be needed, especially to preserve any relics produced by the Historian and, of course, to return the many items taken from the museum. With characteristic android efficiency, the caregiver forms a plan for dealing with these remains of humanity, moving into the Historian's room with purpose and determination.

The room, however, is a mess. A half-eaten supper and an unmade bed mean the Historian has once again been writing into the early morning. Not that it is easy to find the bed. Random piles of papers are everywhere but worse still are the books, borrowed, of course, from the museum. Almost every available space is occupied by piles of books, in no pattern obvious to the caregiver. The android had asked the Historian once about the chaos, but the last human gave the enigmatic response, "This is what historians do." Looking around now, the caregiver is not certain where to begin.

The android starts with the Historian's desk, by far the tidiest area of the room. The large desk is surprisingly well organized. Books in piles, often with papers stuck in them, line the back. Around the edges lies the museum's entire collection of ballpoint pens. A stack of quaintly hand-written papers lies off to one side: The Historian's life work. Pulling up a chair, the caregiver sits in human fashion at the desk, picks up the pile of papers, and begins to read.

After only a few pages the caregiver realizes that the Historian was attempting to write a historical account of the twenty-first century. The last organic human very nearly succeeded: The final chapter of the historical narrative catalogues the rather uneventful decade since the dedication of the Museum of Humanity in the latter part of the century. The historical account is clearly more than a record, however; the Historian has selected events to construct the argument that the replacement of human body systems with artificial counterparts coupled with the genetic engineering of human DNA led to the demise of humanity.

The Historian's point bothers the caregiver; it's not that humans no longer exist, the android counters. Humans simply evolved into their machines, achieving the immortality through technology prophesied in 1994 by Marvin Minsky, at that time Director of the Artificial Intelligence Laboratory at MIT:

> To lengthen our lives, and improve our minds, in the future we will need to change our bodies and brains. To that end, we first must consider how normal Darwinian evolution brought us to where we are. Then we must imagine ways in which future replacements for worn body parts might solve most problems of failing health. We must then invent strategies to augment our brains and gain greater wisdom. Eventually we will entirely replace our brains—using nanotechnology. Once delivered from the limitations of biology, we will be

able to decide the length of our lives—with the option of immortality—and choose among other, unimagined capabilities as well. (p. 1)

In the margins of the historical narrative the caretaker finds the Historian has scribbled two comments: *seduced* and *Heidegger was right.* Intrigued, the caretaker decides to try and unravel the meaning of these messages.

The comments lie alongside a discussion about events at the end of the twentieth century. The Historian duly catalogues the spectacular inventions of the late twentieth century, including the remarkable developments in medicine, the developments in computer technology, and the rise of the Internet. These achievements should have been a source of great pride and satisfaction for humanity, yet the Historian records that some people were deeply concerned at that time about the direction of technological innovation. Ellwood (1996) suggests that these concerns arise from the human experience that "technology is *never* neutral. Even seemingly benign technologies can have earth-shaking, unintended, social consequences" (p. 8). Tenner (1997) calls these the "revenge effects" of technology. He notes a historical pattern in the way technological innovation "bites back" with increasing difficulty:

> The nineteenth and twentieth centuries were an age of crisis, a time when people were awed by technological scale and intensity...the combination of scale and the complexity of technological systems guaranteed that catastrophes happened far more often than they had in previous centuries...but something else was happening as disasters were coming under control in the West. The very means of preventing them sometimes created the risk of even larger ones in the future. (p. 30)

Yet technological change accelerated unabated by such concerns during the first decade of the twenty-first century. As early as 1984 philosopher Robert Burch predicted this possibility due to the self-deceptive nature of the relationship of humans to their technology. In a passage surprising the android, Burch points out that most humans are charmed by technology, adding that with technological innovation "the tendency is to search for 'reasons' to justify on other grounds what is a simple enchantment with the evident power of the machine...it [technology] serves as a kind of *pharmakon*, a drug that both poisons and cures" (pp. 6–7).

These assessments and the Historian's comment that technology is seductive do not impress the android. Certainly all technologies have potential for harm, admits the caregiver, but the promise of technology is the ability to master nature and thus find a better existence, of which the android Collective is a prime example. Reading on, the caregiver agrees with Noble (1997) that modern technology is "essentially a religious endeavor" (p. 5) in its belief that salvation from the demands of nature is possible. The android notes that such faith was not misplaced since humans were able to find a new place free from the material constraints of their organic existence—a "re-place-ment" into technology. Given the way the twenty-first century turned out, the caregiver is slightly amused by Noble's concerns over a century ago that the religious nature of human relation to technology "has become a threat to our survival" (p. 208).

How was this a threat and not a promise? Glancing over to the books on the desk, the android finds a copy of Heidegger's *The Question Concerning Technology* (1954/1977). The caretaker opens the book and glances over the contents, stopping at a series of underlined passages. The Historian was clearly drawn to Heidegger's argument that technology "is a way of revealing" (p. 294) in the way that technology brings forth a fundamental challenging. Heidegger points out that in this challenging,

> everywhere everything is ordered to stand by, to be immediately on hand, indeed to stand there just that it may be on call for a further ordering. Whatever is ordered about in this way has its own standing. We call it standing-reserve. (p. 298)

Heidegger builds on this idea, emphasizing that the view of everything as a standing-reserve enframes modern society, thus limiting the horizon of possibility for thinking in any other ways, a kind of "destining" to technological ways of being in the world. The result, claims Heidegger, is that in the second half of the twentieth century humanity will necessarily find itself in danger.

Heidegger's warning of danger was short-sighted or misguided—depending on the interpretation—since he did not foresee in 1954 that the years ahead would witness such rapid developments in genetic engineering. The Historian identifies 1978 as the pivotal year in the evolution of humankind, although the Historian also calls it the "beginning of the end for humanity." In that year the first child produced through in vitro fertilization was born and scientists successfully transferred DNA from one species into a bacterium's genome, creating the first transgenic organism. The ability to manipulate genetic combinations in bacteria, plants, and animals progressed rapidly in the years that followed and the subsequent culturing of human embryos prior to implantation led to the therapeutic replacement of genes in humans by the end of the century. The Historian argues that from a human perspective, one of the most significant events in the twentieth century was the cloning of the first mammal, the sheep "Dolly." Quoting the editor of the popular magazine *Shift*, the Historian notes that with the birth of Dolly "the last bastion of our individualism, our chromosomes, has been breached. And that's science's ultimate goal: to learn our primary language, the language beneath language, the unspoken grammar of the universe. Learn it, then put it to work" (Solomon, 1997, p. 14).

This is precisely what happened in the first decades of the twenty-first century. The same year that the first human clone was born, scientists successfully added a gene from a plant species to human DNA, creating a transgenic human that developed to the 64-cell stage. This feat laid the groundwork for twenty-first century eugenics, demonstrating Burch's (1986) point that the intrinsic impulse of modern technology is to "encompass all aspects of life and to render all things in terms of the instrumental will to power" (p. 9), including humanity itself. As Krell (1977) observes, this is the essence of technology: "an ordering of, or setting upon, both nature and man [*sic*], a defiant challenging of beings that aims at total and exclusive mastery" (p. 285). Agreeing with this view of technology, the android finds one reason for this instrumentality of Being in the strange notation scribbled in the margins of the historical narrative: *I Cor. 15:26.*

A linkage to the android Collective is required to decipher the meaning of the reference, which turns out to be a verse from the Christian Bible: "The last enemy that will be abolished is death" (Creation House, 1973, p. 272). The android nods approval; this was indeed the great technological achievement of twenty-first century technology: defeating death. Investing in the standing-reserve of human genetics, the Historian records how disease became less and less common by the mid-century. The caregiver finds this narrative in complete agreement with android lore, which also reaches the Historian's conclusion that the end of disease became an impetus for science and technology to find ways to extend those body systems that simply wear out. This technological urge was fueled, argues the Historian, by a deep human desire for immortality. As DeLillo observes in his novel *White Noise* (1985), human technology "is lust removed from nature....It's what we invented to conceal the terrible secret of our decaying bodies" (p. 285); except by the mid-twenty-first century, instead of decay, human bodies became the subject of replacement technologies.

The Historian provides an overview of how this replacement began in earnest in the century before, although humans did not realize it at the time. A sense of familiarity sweeps over the caregiver as the narrative outlines the evolution of androids. As in android lore, the Historian records that android technology reached a milestone in 1998 with the creation of WABIAN, one of the first human-sized bipedal robots capable of "normal dynamic biped[al] walking forward and backward with its arm fixed to its own body, dynamic dancing and dynamic carrying of a load with both arms" (Yamaguchi, Inoue, Nishino, & Takanishi, 1998, p. 96). That same year the Honda Motor Company announced the designation of an entire division of their company devoted to the creation of personal robots. This followed their famous announcement in 1986 of the goal of developing a mobile, intelligent humanoid robot that could "coexist and co-operate with human beings, by doing what a person cannot do and cultivating a new dimension in mobility both of which would result in value added to society" (Honda Motor Company, 1999). Every android knows of the famous Honda P3 that was completed in 1997, since this self-contained, ambulatory robot is considered in android lore to be the ancestor, at least in basic architecture, of all androids.

The Asian economic recovery of 2012, mainly stimulated by breakthroughs in android production, would not have been possible without great strides in the development of artificial intelligence in the United States. Just as the problems of duplicating human movement were being worked out at the end of the twentieth century in Japan, researchers at MIT were working on "Cog," the first android capable of interacting with humans "in the same way that a baby learns from its mother" (Kaku, 1997, p. 88; Williamson, 1998). Fueled by ideas shared at international meetings and Internet forums, combined with the use of increasingly powerful microcomputers and tool production techniques, some researchers at the end of the twenthieth century confidently declared the goal of creating a team of androids capable of beating the World Cup champions by 2050 (Kitano & Asada, 1998). They were close; an all-android team won the trophy in 2061.

This victory became possible through breakthroughs in computer artificial intelligence. The demands of the famous Turing Test of intelligence—where computer responses cannot be distinguished from human responses—began to be met with the defeat in 1997 of the reigning chess champion Gary Kasparov by the computer "Deep Blue," in the year the Historian was born. From this point the development of artificial intelligence was stimulated by the demand for reliable machines capable of analysis and of working within complex systems, such as stock market investment strategizing, weather forecasting, and car manufacturing. Already by the end of the twentieth century billions of dollars were being spent on computer systems constructed along the lines of the architecture of the human brain, the so-called "neural nets" (Kurzweil, 1999). These sophisticated analytical machines paved the way for the development of miniature electronic "brains" which began to appear in 2039, about a decade later than predicted by many twentieth century futurists (Kaku, 1997; Kurzweil, 1999; Mander, 1991; Noble 1997). The futurists were correct, however, that nanotechnology—engineering at the atomic level—would accelerate the development of machines analogous in function to the human brain, but few predicted the important role androids would play in the evolution of artificial intelligence.

Android lore also points to 2039 as a significant moment in android history. In that year human engineers first allowed androids to be responsible for the management of android manufacturing. What was not predicted was the extent to which these managers would take the initiative in directing the evolution of androids, including improving their electronic brains. As this self-evolution was allowed and even encouraged by manufacturers, android development fulfilled in only three years the prediction by science fiction writer Isaac Asimov (1977) of a future where robots, "in their particular province of collecting and analyzing a nearly infinite number of data and relationships thereof, in nearly infinitesimal time, have progressed beyond the possibility of detailed human control" (p. 175).

In a classic understatement, the Historian suggests that the ability to copy human brain patterns into the neural nets of artificial brains, beginning in 2045, complicated android development while laying the foundation for the extinction of organic humans. The caretaker is surprised by this negative view, universally rejected in android lore. The interpretation that prevailed among androids is aligned more with the views of artificial intelligence specialist Hans Moravec, who in 1988 envisioned a "post-biological" future for humanity where humans would eventually pass their consciousness into sophisticated androids and thus achieve immortality (Moravec, 1988). While such a merger began to be possible in 2045, in a very limited way, the years ahead proved that replacing human organic existence with analogous machinery would not go smoothly.

As Noble (1997) predicted, the production of androids complex enough to merge with human consciousness required the prior manufacturing of androids that were already conscious, in essence a new species: *Machina sapiens* (p. 163). By 2055, most homes had android companions and a debate raged about whether such synthetic humans should enjoy the same civil rights as their organic counterparts. This reached a crisis when the Dutch human, Melog van Tobor, married her android lover Robbie in an unofficial ceremony. The outpouring of public support—human and android alike—led the country of Holland to declare androids full citizens in 2057, with most countries following this example over the next three years.

In a way, notes the Historian, citizenship was becoming moot since in the decades that followed, the boundary separating humans from analogous mechanical technology became blurred. In the early sixties more and more humans were electing to replace body parts with durable synthetics. This led to a brief cyborg movement, a loose social development where some individuals proclaimed the superiority of their synthetic and bio-engineered combinations over "normal" humans and even androids. The prosthetics fashion mania that swept the wealthy nations in the late sixties briefly stimulated the development of cyborgs, but by the mid-seventies the technical ability to place the entire consciousness of a human into a new, mechanically equivalent body totally immune from disease led most people to choose the android alternative; very few cyborg combinations existed by 2080. Over the next two decades the term "android" came to be used both for those machines of artificial intelligence and those with similar bodies containing the analogues of human consciousness. Finally, during the first two decades of the twenty-second century the two types of androids completely merged, forming the android Collective. Those that held to their organic existence due to nostalgia, religious beliefs, or poverty began the curious process of dying in the last decade of the twenty-first century, either from old age or during the Great Plague of '98–'99. The rest of humanity, safe from the failings of flesh, entered the twenty-second century pondering their immortality.

The Pedagogy of Replacement

The end of the Historian's work degenerates into scattered reports of a few major historical events, such as the dissolution of national entities and the Collective's declaration in 2099 at the dedication of the new Museum of Creation that it would take care of the remaining organic humans. It is clear the Historian had lost interest in the narrative before dying, except for the sudden flurry of writing comprising the final pages. These begin with a comment that strikes the caregiver as almost sacrilegious: *It's OK to die.*

According to the discussion that follows, the Historian was reacting to a comment made at the start of the twenty-first century in a keynote address at a teachers' convention:

> We are in danger as a species of inventing ourselves to death. We have at the most one or two generations to gain public control over the direction of technological change. The children about to start school next year, our little ones—certainly their children—will face a radically different world than humanity has ever known. Indeed, these changes have already begun and the time is short in beginning the public discussions and action needed to direct the evolution of our technology. (Blades, 2001, p. 1)

While this educator was right about the extent of the changes that would take place in the twenty-first century, the history of events revealed a key flaw in the educator's thinking: The danger to humanity was not in the possibility of inventing to death, but in the act of inventing *away* from death.

The android is deeply disturbed by this point and the argument that follows. Android ontology was formed on the assumption that androids re-present humanity; in fact, androids *are* humanity in an evolved form. The Historian seemed to be developing a counter argument that the act of cheating death through technology essentially robbed humanity of its Being. Once again, the Historian turns to Heidegger, this time the philosopher's sketch in *Being and Time* (1962a) of the existential-ontological structure of death in relation to "Dasein"—the existential and ontological possibilities of Being.

Heidegger begins his discussion of death by reminding readers that "death is a possibility-of-Being which Dasein itself has to take over in every case" (p. 294). This is clearly true since death is the possibility of no longer Being-in-the-world. In other words, understanding what it means to live in the world begins by confronting the possibility of death. According to Heidegger humans are thrown into this position: Every organic human has to face the real event of death. Thus far the android has little argument. But Heidegger takes this obvious point much further. After discussing inauthentic responses to death, he suggests Being-towards-death can be seen as *"Being towards a possibility*—indeed, towards a distinctive possibility of Dasein itself"* (p. 305). He explains that this possibility arises by *"waiting for that actualization"* (p. 306); that is, the anticipation of this actual event "turns out to be the possibility of understanding one's *ownmost* and uttermost potentiality-for-Being—that is to say, the possibility of *authentic existence"* (p. 307). So claimed by death, one becomes

> liberated from one's lostness in those possibilities which may accidentally thrust themselves upon one; and one is liberated in such a way that for the first time one can authentically understand and choose among the factical possibilities lying ahead. (p. 308)

The android puts down the Historian's notes, shaken. Heidegger is making a radical suggestion: Rather than something to overcome, the authentic anticipation of death leads to freedom from being lost, revealing the possibility that is life itself. Authentic Being-in-the-world *requires* death; the ontology of humanness begins, argues Heidegger, with the "impassioned freedom towards death" (p. 311). And, realizes the android, this essential anticipation is not logically possible if you are immortal.

What does the technological replacement of humanity teach? In *White Noise*, DeLillo (1985) points out the importance of death in understanding life:

> I think it's a mistake to lose one's sense of death, even one's fear of death. Isn't death the boundary we need? Doesn't it give a precious texture to life, a sense of definition? You have to ask yourself whether anything you do in this life would have beauty and meaning without the knowledge you carry of a final line, a border or limit. (pp. 228–229)

The Historian expands on this point, citing the experience of the character Fosca in Simone de Beauvoir's novel *All Men Are Mortal* (1946/1995). Frustrated by the death and decay he faces daily, Fosca chooses to drink from a potion that guarantees immortality. But through this character, de Beauvoir shows that immortality is a terrible curse. Living forever eventually leads to a bland experience of boring predictability. Fosca explains:

> It was a fine morning, but the peasants, bent over the land, did not look at the sky. As for me, I was weary of seeing it day in and day out for two hundred years, always the same....Endlessly! Will I never awake in another world where even the air will taste different? (pp. 138–139)

Before drinking the potion Fosca neglected to consider the consequence immortality might have for relationships. As his friends and companions grow old his retention of the same age separates him from the essential, normal human experience of aging. In response to his proposal of marriage and in full knowledge of his immortality, Beatrice responds, "You're not a man....You're a corpse" (p. 153). But even a corpse has a future, returning through decay to the fabric of the natural world; Fosca is even denied this possibility. Eventually he comes to realize that as an immortal he is

> a man from nowhere, without a past, without a future, without a present. I wanted nothing; I was no one. My hands were forever empty: an outsider, a dead man. They were men, they were alive. I was not one of them. I had nothing to hope for. (p. 400)

In the end, Fosca finds immortality to be "a terrible curse. I'm alive and yet I'm lifeless. I shall never die and I have no future. I am no one. I've no past and no face" (p. 29).

Fosca shows us, suggests the Historian, that by achieving immortality through technology humanity moved away from the very sequences of time that defined being human. These sequences are linked to a much larger pattern of life over billions of years. In her novel about a family that by accident became immortal, Babbitt (1975) uses a conversation between the mortal Winnie and the immortal Tuck to explain how living involves being part of a larger pattern. When Winnie tells Tuck that she does not want to die, Tuck replies,

> Not now. Your time's not now. But dying's part of the wheel, right there next to being born. You can't pick out the pieces you like and leave the rest. Being part of the whole thing, that's the blessing. But it's passing us by, us Tucks. Living's heavy work, but off to one side, the way *we* are, it's useless, too. It don't make sense. If I knowed how to climb back on the wheel, I'd do it in a minute. You can't have living without dying. So you can't call it living, what we got. We just *are*, we just *be*, like rocks beside the road. (pp. 63–64)

Like rocks beside the road—the android ponders these words—and then: Am I alive? Stretching out an arm, the caregiver adopts a critical stance. Is this arm, so much like the Historian's arm in shape and function, *actually* an arm, or just an artifact, part of an interconnected collection of parts that amounts to no more than a sophisticated "rock on the road"?

The Paradox and the Potential

Despite having only two more pages to read, the android gets up and walks around the room, struck by the Historian's argument. Looking around, the caregiver sees ample evidence of the differences between organic humans and their android progeny. No android, for example, would allow a room to degenerate into such systematic chaos. Androids also keep regular schedules; the idea of impulsively getting up in the middle of the night to write a history—by hand no less—is totally foreign to them. In the new world, androids-as-humans-as-androids ensure that every system of interaction is kind, predictable, and efficient. Because of this, the caregivers found their organic human charges enigmatic at best, sadly mortal and inefficient at worst; in every case androids interacted with the remaining organic humans with careful pity.

After reading the Historian's views and ideas, however, the caregiver is no longer certain who should be pitied.

Examining the half-eaten supper, the android wonders what it would be like to be born, eat, sleep, know love, become sick, age, and die. It seems a dreadful, short existence. Bothered, but unsure why, the caretaker moves purposefully back to the desk to finish at least one task this afternoon: reading the final pages of the Historian's work.

The Historian begins the final two pages of the incomplete history with the words, "Somehow we became paralyzed in relation to the inevitability of annihilation because of our paradoxical relationship to technology." To the caretaker, this comment is a bleak but understandable confession of the inability of organic humans to redirect or even stop the evolution of humankind into artificial forms. Yet by including the word "somehow" the Historian seems to suggest that what became the history of the twenty-first century was not destiny but a concession to a problematic relationship.

Immediately the Historian's writing starts to change, as if during the last hours before dying the Historian seized upon an idea. Comments are quickly scribbled, often in note form and all over the page. In some cases the caregiver cannot make out the words, a sharp deviation from the Historian's usual careful script. The Historian placed numbers in red at certain points on the page and the android realizes these represent the logic of a developing argument.

The first number is beside a shorthand reference: "Krist. 14." This turns out to be a page marked in a small book amidst the others on the Historian's desk, Krishnamurti's *Education and the Significance of Life* (1981). The choice is not lost on the android; the Historian's choice demonstrates Heidegger's point about the actualization of death opening up possibilities for life. To the question, "What is life?" the Historian finds an unusual response: "To understand life is to understand ourselves, and that is both the beginning and the end of education" (p. 14).

The second number links to another cryptic reference: "Hope! The Vision—Levin." This takes a lot of work to track down, but eventually the android finds this passage:

> With an understanding awareness of our suffering, we can struggle to separate ourselves from the metaphysics of the moderns; but our inseparability is a more powerful fact and holds us in the vice of the between: between the old vision of

> modernity, now steered by death, and an altogether different vision, already perhaps implicate, but which has in any case not yet unfolded. (Levin, 1988, pp. 384–385)

An arrow joins this quote to another in the margin of the page, where Burch (1986) argues that even though "we are *irretrievably* committed to high levels of technology, we need to be more self-conscious and self-critical of the standpoint from which we judge its value" (p. 11). The Historian, as far as the android can make out, uses these quotes to make the case that through the education of children humanity could have developed a different vision from the functionalist metaphysics of modernity. Finding this new vision, suggests the Historian, would have required a different educational system, one that would have helped children separate the ideology of technological innovation from notions of human progress. To counter such modern thinking and the subsequent capitulation to the inevitability of technological innovation, not only would education have had to provide children with the skills to direct technological innovation, but children would have needed educational experiences that allowed them to discover the value, characteristics, and depth of their humanity.

After reading such a scholarly, well-thought-out history, the caretaker was disappointed to see the Historian approach the end with such naïveté. A student of the events of the late twentieth and the early twenty-first century, the Historian was well aware of the social and political structures hindering fundamental change in education. As if in response to the android, the third number on the page is linked to a series of quotations and references to a number of educators concerned about the technicality of education. This paradigm borrows much from the patterns of industry and technological functionalism; during the last half of the twentieth century, features such as timetables, fractionated knowledge, and final exams represented the highly technical nature of public education. Aoki (1988) argues that "this technological orientation, strongly instrumentalist in orientation, is rooted in the human interest of intellectual and technical control of the world" (p. 409); thus education at the start of the twenty-first century was not only historically technological in organization, but philosophically committed to the agenda of modernity, which was to master nature. Finding a new vision would thus involve finding freedom from the destining of modernity (Blades, 1997); this means that a complete revolution in the system would have been needed to lead humankind away from extinction by technology.

Moving to the fourth number, the android suddenly realizes that these numbers were probably the last marks added by the Historian and thus have a pedagogical intent: The Historian is trying to teach the android that a revolution in education was not a naïve hope but a lost opportunity.

The caregiver turns to the remaining points with anticipation. The number four is written beside one word: "Rebellion." A circle has been drawn around this word with a line leading to the next page.

The last page is a mess of notes and references, but numbers continue to guide the android. The page begins with a quote from educational philosopher Maxine Greene: "In the classroom opened to possibility and at once concerned with inquiry, critiques must be developed that uncover what masquerade as neutral frameworks" (Greene, 1988, p. 134). This critique begins, suggests Greene, when teachers and students "learn to love the questions" (p. 134). Beside this quote the Historian writes, in large letters, "ASK WHY" and a large number five.

The android bristles a bit at this, since questions that ask why are regularly used among androids for systematic diagnosis. As for general speculation, however, the question seems so impractical and pointless. Anticipating this response, the Historian argues that it is fundamentally human to ask ontological questions arising from the question why. As Heidegger (1962b) points out, to ask why is to make "a daring attempt to fathom this unfathomable question by disclosing what it summons us to ask, to push our questioning to the very end" (p. 221). Questions open the possibility of challenge to the social structures that bind and define us, but Heidegger also points out that the questions brought forth by asking why are sources of revelation about the human condition.

Questions are thus crucial to the survival of humanness. Androids may inherit the ability to ask why, but the question shifts in meaning and purpose when death is not part of the equation and individuality is absent. When every part is replaceable and consciousness is linked to a Collective, asking why as an individual is meaningless. The corporate existence of androids robs them of the ability to ask with any meaning the questions that naturally rise from the human experience. For this reason, argues the Historian, every school should have embraced a curriculum of questioning since through questions children could more deeply understand their situation and Being.

In their seduction by the superficial, however, schools historically avoided the deep questions that can be brought forth by asking why. Instead, notes the Historian, schools in the late twentieth century and early twenty-first century encouraged students to leap to the sanctioned right answer, effectively policed by a testing mania that seemed to grip public education. This call to the correct answer considerably narrowed the vision of what else might be, limited what other questions might be posed, and failed to explore what opportunities might exist. As a technology of answers, the system failed most woefully by not teaching children to pose the difficult questions.

What was needed, argues the Historian, was a system-wide rebellion initiated by brave teachers who encouraged children to ask questions, including questions about the nature, direction, and role of technological innovations. Drawing from several leading twentieth century critics of technology (Ellwood, 1996; Mander, 1991; Postman, 1993), the Historian had sketched out several questions children, along with teachers and adult mentors, might learn to ask in order to uncover the political and social issues presented by existing and emerging technologies, such as: Does the technology

1. provide benefits for the majority or a few?
2. promote social and economic justice?
3. influence the protection of fundamental human and civil liberties, including the rights of minorities?
4. respect cultural diversity? What will be the quality of interactions with this technology across a variety of cultures?
5. allow a reasonable balance between time alone and time interacting with others?
6. humanize living? Help people act with kindness and respect to others?
7. respect the natural world? Favor conservation or waste?
8. have social effects that can never be reversed?

The hope animating the last page of the historical account turns sour, however, with an underlined comment that appears halfway down the page. The caregiver senses the frustration in the statement: "We squandered the opportunity." It is true that the education system was not able to change enough to help children deal with the technologies that emerged in the twenty-first century. The seductive, almost sexy promise of a better life with each new invention was embraced by a generation of students who in large part accepted and internalized the corporate mantra that happiness is equated with material possessions. The invasion of consumerism into homes via television led that generation to be passive—or even welcoming—toward *any* technological change (Mander, 1991), accepting these innovations just as inevitable as the sunrise.

It was not surprising, then, that when androids first became available it was the children entering school at the start of the twenty-first century who proved to be the largest group of purchasers. Their children grew up never knowing a world without androids. But it was a vastly different society than even 40 years earlier. The broad functionality of androids meant the end of public education since androids were able to provide in-home tutoring. Leisure time increased for most humans as androids took on such daily tasks as shopping, cleaning, cooking, and transporting children to various clubs. Relationships changed as second and third generation androids became able to fully interact with humans; indeed, the only surprise of the first marriage to an android in 2056 was that it took so long to legalize such increasingly common partnerships.

What remained unchecked was the critical rebellion through questioning that would have halted the merger of humans with their machinery. Instead, schools on the threshold of the twenty-first century continued to offer a moribund curriculum blissfully out of step with emerging technology and unaware of the impending doom of public education systems.

Number seven, the final number on the page, brings the android to a chilling comment: "We could have done it." The caretaker knows exactly what the Historian means. The numbers of educational theorists critical of the existing system grew during the first years of the twenty-first century and a few new programs designed to at least acquaint students with some of the ethical issues presented by technology had begun to appear as early as the 1980s. This was not a case of too little, too late. The Historian notes widespread discontent with schooling at the end of the twentieth century, from curriculum developers to teachers to children and their families. Everyone knew the system needed changing, yet despite this impetus, the changes did not occur. Why?

The final words of the Historian provide a clue. It was not that issues were poorly understood or philosophical perspectives unclear. In the end, what was absent from all the talk about education was direct, determined, and sustained social action.

As the twenty-first century began to unfold, teachers increasingly complained about the side effects of individualization of instruction through computer integration in schools, but no teacher association went on strike over this issue. People talked about how technological systems modified human activity too much or damaged the environment, but hardly anyone bothered to stop using a car. There was general horror and public outcry at the birth of the first transgenic human, but no one withheld taxes to demand laws against this technology. Rebellion by asking questions was not enough to ensure social change; what was needed was an active discourse on the ethics of technology and then the courage to act on decisions, even if this meant life would be somewhat less comfortable.

This discourse could have begun in schools, notes the Historian, but history reveals that the engine of change would have needed to involve the public domain to bring talk to action. This idea of the movement of a conversation of change from schools to the public reflects philosopher Jana Thompson's concept of "collectivist ethics" (1998). Collectivist ethics rejects the idea that an individual is all that is needed to discover what is true and what is false or what action is moral and what is immoral. Instead, ethics are determined through rational inquiry, which depends on a *group* process assuming that "aspects of reality can only be discovered collectively" (p. 3). Through a series of steps, ethics is built in a "bottom-up" direction through critical dialogue, critique, proposal, rejection, and finally construction of a conclusion. This is *not* a process of compromise or consensus but a group-directed, rational inquiry towards actions the group will come to deem valid.

Schools could have been the agency to develop the public collectivist ethics to determine what is morally right in the evolution of a technology. As the twenty-first century began, notes the Historian, children almost everywhere on the planet could be found attending schools. Before the rapid developments in individualized instruction, a brief window appeared in which one generation of children had a common experience of public education. It was a unique opportunity to begin a deep, worldwide public questioning of technology and the functionalism that allowed technological innovation to remain mainly under corporate control. A new discourse could have emerged, leading to the vigilance and political action required to ensure that technological innovation never threatened the survival of humanity.

But this potential was never realized. Humans, far too comfortable with their inventions, slid into the twenty-first century in an almost comatose state, missing the opportunity to discover with children the humanizing potential of asking the important questions. The final words of the Historian served as an epitaph for humankind: "Seeking immortality, we neglected to ask why."

The Burial

The responsibility for dealing with the Historian's corpse falls naturally to the caretaker, although the Historian had made particular requests in this regard. The instructions, given to the caretaker by the Historian during a late-night conversation a year ago, were quite peculiar. Unlike most of the remaining humans, the Historian insisted on not being cremated, instead asking the caretaker to arrange for a burial, complete with instructions for a service. Since this was the last organic human, the Collective agrees to the request.

The Historian is clothed and wrapped in the particular garments made for the occasion and then laid in a simple box made of pine, as requested. The burial site is located near the museum on a spot that encourages reflection.

After one last look at the person who was so much a part of the caretaker's existence these past 13 years, the casket is secured and an honor guard of seven androids gently begins the journey to the gravesite. The pallbearers stop seven times to place the casket on the ground along the way, again in accordance with the Historian's wishes although the reasons still seem mysterious. Finally, the casket is lowered into the grave.

Standing at the mouth of the grave, the caretaker recites the words requested by the Historian and then picks up a shovel and drops some dirt onto the casket. Other androids join in and soon the casket is completely covered, signaling the end of the funeral. Maintenance androids will complete the task, so all the androids except the caregiver leave.

Gazing down at the half-filled grave, the caregiver is moved by the tentative nature of history. If children had learned to critique the evolution of technological innovation, if humanity had come to understand the importance of its essence, this last funeral for an organic human would have been unlikely.

But humanity did not seize the vision of a different relation to technology and now the last of its kind has disappeared. The consciousness of the Historian could have been downloaded into an android body at any time, but instead the Historian chose to participate in the natural order of life which included a return to the natural world through death and decay. In the choice of the final place to be, either a grave or a machine, the Historian chose the earth.

No such fate awaits the caretaker. Turning to face an uncertain and never-ending future, the caretaker walks away from the grave, wondering what to do now.

References

Aoki, T. T. (1988). Toward a dialectic between the conceptual world and the lived world: Transcending instrumentalism in curriculum orientation. In W. Pinar (Ed.), *Contemporary curriculum discourses* (pp. 402–416). Scottsdale, AZ: Gorsuch Scarisbrick.

Asimov, I. (1977). *I, robot.* New York: Ballantine Books.

Babbitt, N. (1975). *Tuck everlasting.* New York: Farrar, Straus and Giroux.

Baudrillard, J. (1994). *The illusion of the end* (C. Turner, Trans.). New York: Verso. (Original work published 1992)

Blades, D. (1997). *Procedures of power and curriculum change.* New York: Peter Lang.

Blades, D. (2001, February). *Education for a hopeful future: Opportunities amidst rapid technological change.* Keynote presentation to the Alberta North Central Teachers' Association, Edmonton, Alberta.

Burch, R. (1984). Technology and curriculum: Toward a philosophical perspective. *Department of Secondary Education Occasional Paper No. 27.* Edmonton, Alberta: University of Alberta.

Burch, R. (1986). Confronting technophobia: A topology. *Phenomenology and Pedagogy, 4*(2), 3–21.

Creation House. (1973). *New American standard Bible.* Carol Stream, IL: Creation House.

de Beauvoir, S. (1995). *All men are mortal* (E. Cameron, Trans.). London: Virago Press. (Original work published 1946)

DeLillo, D. (1985). *White noise.* Toronto: Penguin Books.

Ellwood, W. (1996). Seduced by technology. *New Internationalist, 286,* 7–10.

Greene, M. (1988). *The dialectic of freedom.* New York: Teachers College Press.

Guenther, C. J., Jr. (2000). Coopting ethics education: Ethically challenged ethics lessons. *Bulletin of Science, Technology and Society, 20* (6), 441–444.

Heidegger, M. (1962a). *Being and time* (J. Macquarrie & E. Robinson, Trans.). San Francisco: HarperSanFrancisco. (Original work published 1926)

Heidegger, M. (1962b). The fundamental question of metaphysics. In W. Barrett & H. D. Aiken (Eds.), *Philosophy in the twentieth century* (pp. 219–250). New York: Random House. (Original work published 1959)

Heidegger, M. (1977). The question concerning technology. In D. Krell (Ed. & Trans.), *Martin Heidegger: Basic writings* (pp. 287–317). London: Harper & Row. (Original work published 1954)

Honda Motor Company. (1999). *Humanoid robot.* Available: http://www.honda.co.jp/english.technology/robot.concept1.html.

Kaku, M. (1997). *Visions.* Toronto: Anchor Books.

Kitano, H., & Asada, M. (1998). RoboCup humanoid challenge: That's one small step for a robot, one giant leap for mankind. *Proceedings of the 1998 IEEE/RSJ International Conference on Intelligent Robots and Systems,* Victoria, BC. NJ: Institute of Electrical and Electronic Engineers.

Krell, D. F. (1977). Introduction to the question concerning technology. In D. Krell (Ed. & Trans.), *Martin Heidegger: Basic writings* (pp. 284–286). London: Harper & Row.

Krishnamurti, J. (1981). *Education and the significance of life.* San Francisco: HarperSanFrancisco.

Kurzweil, R. (1999). *The age of spiritual machines.* New York: Viking.

Levin, D. (1988). *The opening of vision.* New York: Routledge.

Mander, J. (1991). *In the absence of the sacred.* San Francisco: Sierra Books.

Marcel, G. (1962). On the ontological mystery. In W. Barrett & H. D. Aiken (Eds.), *Philosophy in the twentieth century* (pp. 364–386). New York: Random House.

Minsky, M. (1994). *Will robots inherit the earth?* Available: http://www.ai.mit.edu/people/minksy/papers/sciam.inherit.html.

Moravec, H. (1988). *Mind children: The future of robot and human intelligence.* Cambridge, MA: Harvard University Press.

Noble, D. F. (1997). *The religion of technology.* Toronto: Penguin.

Postman, N. (1993). *Technopoly.* New York: Vintage Books.

Shelley, M. (1988). *Frankenstein.* New York: Dilithium Press.

Solomon, E. (1997, May). Hello Dolly. *Shift Magazine,* 14.

Tenner, E. (1997). *Why things bite back.* New York: Random House.

Thompson, J. (1998). *Discourse and knowledge.* New York: Routledge.

Williamson, M. E. (1998). Rhythmic robot arm control using oscillators. *Proceedings of the 1998 IEEE/RSJ International Conference on Intelligent Robots and Systems,* Victoria, BC. NJ: Institute of Electrical and Electronic Engineers.

Yamaguchi, J., Inoue, S., Nishino, D., & Takanishi, A. (1998). Development of a bipedal humanoid robot having antagonistic driven joints and three DOF trunks. *Proceedings of the 1998 IEEE/RSJ International Conference on Intelligent Robots and Systems,* Victoria, BC. NJ: Institute of Electrical and Electronic Engineers.

❭ Reading and Resisting Silent Spaces of Whiteness in School Literature

Ingrid Johnston

A far-reaching danger of whiteness coded as "no culture" is that it leaves in place whiteness as defining a set of normative cultural practices against which all are measured and into which all are expected to fit. This normativity has underwritten oppression from the beginning of colonial expansion and has had impact in multiple ways.
    —Ruth Frankenberg, *White women, race matters: The social construction of whiteness*

When I first became a teacher, in apartheid South Africa, I taught in an all-white, segregated high school. My students, although living in an ethnoculturally diverse society, were encouraged both by the government and by the school to see themselves as privileged and set apart by their whiteness. Nothing in the curriculum contradicted such expectations. Their school textbooks and the literature curriculum offered a particular view of a world dominated and framed by whiteness. As their teacher, I was complicit in such framing. Nothing in my own life experience had prepared me to challenge my own or my students' assumptions about whiteness as the cultural and racial norm. I had grown up and attended schools in Britain with a homogenous white student population and I attended a segregated South African university with an all-white teacher education program. My stance in the classroom was one of cultural silence born of oblivion.

Now, many years later, I am a teacher educator in a faculty of education where more than 90% of the student teachers are of European descent, but many are preparing to teach in urban schools that are characterized by increasingly large numbers of students from diverse ethnocultural backgrounds. Some of these teacher education students who have grown up in rural or suburban schools have had little personal experience of cultural diversity in their own schooling; others have grown up in classrooms with peers from a variety of ethnocultural backgrounds but claim that cultural diversity is not an issue they have thought about very much in relation to becoming a teacher. As a co-investigator with Dr. Terry Carson in the Culture and Teaching Project at the University of Alberta (see Carson, Johnston, Chana, Leard, & Wiltse, 1998), I conducted surveys and interviews with our student teachers about their understanding and experience of ethnocultural diversity and the development of their professional teaching identities. The results of these surveys and interviews suggest that very few of our teacher education students have been challenged to consider their own privileged positioning as white, middle-class citizens in a multicultural society and very few have received any preparation for teaching in ethnoculturally diverse settings. In failing to address questions of cultural difference and whiteness with our teacher education students, we, as teacher educators, have also selected a stance of cultural silence.

My involvement in this research project has helped to make me conscious of the need to begin to take risks in my teacher education classes. As Giroux (1992) suggests, teachers need to "envision the possibility of an education grounded in an ethic of risk that is unafraid to expose the mutations of racism and the ways in which such social forms work to undermine the democratic impulse in postmodern life" (p. 2). What I believe this means for my teaching is that I need to become more self-conscious and reflective about my own cultural and political sense of location. I need to rethink the politics of liberal multiculturalism, to move beyond simply acknowledging "others" and examining stereotypes, toward recognizing how self-representation is constituted in relationship with others. This recognition is linked with postmodern perspectives of identity formation, with the need to acknowledge that, as Stuart Hall (1991) explains,

> [t]he Other is not outside, but also inside the Self, the identity. So identity is a process, identity is split. Identity is not a fixed point, but an ambivalent point. Identity is also the relationship of the Other to oneself. (pp. 15–16)

Such attempts to explore questions of identity and difference with my students relate to hooks' (1994) notion of an "engaged pedagogy" that does not seek simply to empower students but requires that professors are also willing to take the risk of sharing their own experiences and challenging their own assumptions in the context of a classroom. As hooks (1994) suggests, "professors must practice being vulnerable in the classroom, being wholly present in mind, body and spirit" (p. 21).

As a white, middle-class woman who teaches student teachers, the majority of whom are also white, I feel I should be addressing and challenging the perceived norms of whiteness. In seeking to explore how whiteness can be addressed within the context of power relations, I am also conscious of Giroux's (1997) caution that I must allow my student teachers "to go beyond the paralysis inspired by guilt or the racism fueled by anxiety and the fear of difference" (p. 299). Giroux explains:

> Educators need to connect Whiteness with a new language of ethnicity, one that provides a space for White students to imagine how Whiteness as an ideology and a location can be progressively appropriated as part of a broader politics of social reform. (p. 315)

One attempt to address issues of whiteness and cultural difference focused around a class I taught for undergraduate students in the teacher education program who are secondary English language arts majors. I met with them every day for six weeks in preparation for their eight-week student teaching experience. Students came to this class with varied backgrounds in the subject area—some were students with an arts degree or an Honours BA, while others were fourth-year Bachelor of Education English majors. In the class, we explored the current curriculum and various possibilities for teaching English language arts. I attempted to help students to see resonances between theory and practice in their subject specialization and, as Britzman (1991) suggests, to address the negotiatory character of professional identity formation that takes place during their formal teacher education and their initial teaching experiences.

In teaching this class, I also attempted to combine Giroux's imperatives about the location of whiteness with suggestions by Ghosh (1996) that those educating multicultural educators must be willing to reflect on their own attitudes, seeking ways to improve the preparation of teachers for culturally diverse classrooms. I decided to challenge my students and my own understandings of race, culture, and whiteness through a reading, viewing, and discussion activity that focused on issues of racism, prejudice, and intolerance. The activity was built around a novel, Harper Lee's *To Kill a Mockingbird* (1960/1962), which has become a staple in North American schools and which many of my students would be expected to teach during their field experience or early years of teaching.

Lee's novel, highly praised for its literary merits and antiracist perspective, offers a liberal humanist stance on questions of race and intolerance. Filtered through the perspective of Scout, a young white girl, the story centers around Atticus, her lawyer father, who exposes the racism of Maycomb, a small southern U.S. town, and saves the life of Tom Robinson, a black man wrongly accused of rape. In a survey of literature titles most commonly authorized or recommended by Ministries of Education in all Canadian provinces in 1980 (Gambell, 1982), *To Kill a Mockingbird* was the number one novel cited. In a survey of titles taught in Grade 10 in Edmonton schools in 1996 (Altmann, Johnston, & Mackey, 1998), *To Kill a Mockingbird* was by far the most popular novel taught. There is little doubt about the entrenched nature of this novel in North American classrooms and about its continuing popularity as a supposedly "antiracist" text. Even the most recent edition of Nilsen and Donelson's respected *Literature for Today's Young Adults* (2001) gives pride of place to Lee's novel on its cover photo of book titles and discusses the novel in six different places in the text. The American authors speak highly of the ability of the novel to withstand constant attempts at censorship and explain that *To Kill a Mockingbird* ranks as one of the five "most widely used titles" in school and district curricula (p. 373). English education students graduating from the Faculty of Education at the University of Alberta will undoubtedly also encounter the novel in school storerooms in Canada and be asked to teach it in their secondary school classrooms.

In an effort to show that the story is told from a white middle-class perspective, I asked my student teachers to read (or reread) Harper Lee's novel in conjunction with *Roll of Thunder, Hear My Cry* (1976/1991), a Newberry award winning book by the African American writer Mildred Taylor. In this novel, which is set in a time and place similar to Lee's book, racism and intolerance in the American South are portrayed through the eyes of Cassie, a young black girl. I also asked students to view the film *A Time to Kill*, a late 1990s Hollywood version of John Grisham's novel depicting the trial of a black man accused of killing the white men who raped his daughter. Students kept a reading and viewing log of the ideas, reflections, and memories that the three texts evoked and then brought these to class for whole class and small group discussions.

I introduced this activity by discussing with the teacher education class my own experiences of living and teaching in apartheid South Africa. I explained how my positioning as a white reader had never been challenged by the books I read as a young adult or by the books I taught to my South African students. I shared with the class the results of an earlier research project in which students from diverse ethnocultural backgrounds in a Canadian high school had read both Harper Lee's and Mildred Taylor's novels and had discussed their varied responses to the texts with me. In this study, several African Canadian students had pointed to the importance for them of hearing a story of discrimination told through the voice of an African American narrator, rather than a white narrator. As one young woman had commented, "Usually, we only read *about* black people (like in *To Kill a Mockingbird*). But in *Roll of Thunder, Hear My Cry*, Cassie tells her own story."

I hoped that my student teachers would bring to their discussions some insights and reflections about the limited point of view on racism and power relations presented in *To Kill a Mockingbird*. I wanted them to critique the novel for its modernist ideals and liberal humanist stance; I hoped they would see limitations in Lee's portrayal of strong, rounded white characters compared with the shadowy, one-dimensional portrayal of the black characters in the novel. I was concerned that they should begin to understand how Lee's novel and the Hollywood film version of Grisham's novel are constructed through a vision of righteous white lawyers "saving" voiceless and marginalized black characters. Underlying my activity was the hope that students would begin to recognize how texts work to construct audiences, and to begin to expose and critique the ideology of these texts. As Pirie (1997) explains:

> For any text, we can ask students what kind of ideal audience is being constructed. Who does this story think its readers are? Who would it like them to be? What does it assume about the reader's attitudes, values, and prejudices, and about the best ways of trying to change those attitudes? Or *is* it trying to change the reader at all? We can then compare our responses as actual audience: Do we willingly allow the text to construct us in the shape of its ideal reader, or do we find ourselves resisting at some points? (p. 30)

Very few of my students offered any resistance to being constructed as the "ideal reader" of Lee's novel and very few of the insights I had hoped for actually emerged. I realize now that I was naïve in expecting them to read the novel critically rather than empathetically. A majority of my student teachers loved the novel, identified effortlessly with the novel's strong white characters, felt angry at the racist views held by many of the town's citizens, and expressed empathy for the weak black characters who were so unjustly treated in the story. Similarly, they saw only the "rightness" of the white lawyer in *A Time to Kill* bringing about justice for the oppressed African Americans. My students' responses reminded me of Pearl Rosenberg's (1997) discussion about the "risks of empathy." Rosenberg suggests that the model of "social imagination" that is seen as helping white students imagine themselves in the shoes of "others" allows them to indulge in nothing more than a "harmonious experience of reversibility and the pleasure of identification" (p. 83).

Many of my students' comments resonated with those of Dennis, a young white man who had attended Christian Reformed schools in Canada. He explained:

> This was the first time I read the book, *To Kill a Mockingbird*. I thoroughly enjoyed it. Lee has created some believable, real characters. Because of this, I found it easy to empathize with them and their situation. In much of the novel, I could see my own childhood. My father was much like Atticus; he possessed the same wisdom, compassion, and understanding.[1]

I had hoped that reading Mildred Taylor's novel in conjunction with Harper Lee's book might cause students to question their identification with the white characters in *To Kill a Mockingbird*, but this was not the case. Many of them found Mildred Taylor's book less engaging. The majority of students explained that her book was less interesting for them and they could not see any advantage of teaching it alongside (or instead of) *To Kill a Mockingbird*. Daniel, for example, who had attended a small rural high school, wrote:

> I really, really enjoyed *To Kill a Mockingbird*. I remember reading it in Grade 10 and I didn't like it. I guess I've learned to appreciate good literature. I didn't

---

[1] I am grateful to the undergraduate students in this English Majors class who gave their signed permission for me to quote their written comments on this class activity.

like *Roll of Thunder, Hear My Cry.* To be honest, I only read the first chapter and I was too uninterested to continue.

Only a few students commented on differences in the characterization of African American characters in the two novels. One of these, Tom, commented that

> I enjoyed *Roll of Thunder, Hear My Cry* a little more than *Mockingbird* because it drew me into Cassie's life more so than I was drawn into Scout's. I felt more sympathy for Cassie and the Logans as their character seemed to be explored beneath the surface level more than the black characters in *Mockingbird.*

Students also demonstrated little resistance to the ways in which they were constructed as "ideal viewers" of the film *A Time to Kill.* Most considered that the film had potential for exploring contemporary perspectives on racism and addressing ethical questions of justice and human rights and would provide a contemporary counterpart to the issues of racism dealt with in *To Kill a Mockingbird.* Those students who criticized the film did so because they found it "too Hollywood" and "rather graphic." Hardly anyone commented on how the narrative is focalized through a white perspective.

Of the 21 students in this class, only three students raised insightful questions about how each writer/producer had filtered experiences of racism in particular ways and how each text dealt with characterization. Two of these students were immigrants to Canada. One student, a mature woman from Lebanon, commented on the "limited perspective" on racial matters offered by Lee's novel. She felt that it was important to read the book in conjunction with Taylor's novel in order to offer both a white and a black perspective on racial discrimination. The other, a student with an Iranian background who had herself experienced racism both in the United States and in Canada, commented on the power of Mildred Taylor's book to "make the experiences of racism come alive." She felt the novel would be a valuable addition to teaching *To Kill a Mockingbird* but remained convinced of the value of Lee's text because "it takes a valuable stand against racism."

Roxanne, a white student with a background in postcolonial studies, argued against *To Kill a Mockingbird* with a passion that was almost unique in the class. She wrote:

> Am I the only one here who didn't like *To Kill a Mockingbird*? I find the ways
> in which Lee negotiates racial tension and class conflict are highly problematic.
> Lee's approach to Tom Robinson's trial reveals some of her biases, as well as
> some of the novel's weaknesses. Throughout the trial, Atticus Finch...comes
> across as the voice of reason and justice. This is a dangerous and controversial
> authorial manoeuvre because it undermines the voices of African Americans
> and women (represented in the text by Tom Robinson and Mayella Ewell
> respectively), without interrogating, or even acknowledging Atticus's
> privileged status as an educated, middle-class, white male. In effect, Lee
> displaces the racism inherent in the dominant ideology onto women, the
> economically disadvantaged, and the children, drunks and "crazies" with whom
> these two minorities are allied.

Although few students agreed with Roxanne's views, in their group
discussions they did begin to interrogate how the three texts provoked
and evoked issues of racism and social justice, and a number of students
raised questions about how such literary texts might be presented and be
received by students from different cultural and racial backgrounds in
their classrooms. For many of my student teachers, these discussions
raised issues and opinions not previously debated or disclosed in their
teacher education classes. In a small way, they were being challenged to
consider their own positionings about race, culture, and power, and to
realize for the first time how much the "norm of whiteness" has been a
source of power and discrimination. For a few of my students, these
discussions also brought uncomfortable realizations of the prejudices that
lurked beneath the surface of the "tolerant" faces of their peers. For
example, Joan, a thoughtful, quiet student, explained in her response to
the activity:

> The discussion I was involved with in my small group frightened me. I felt that
> many of my peers do not have a very good understanding of racial problems,
> discrimination, prejudice and what should/has to be done. I feel very uneasy
> that these people will be spreading their ignorance to others.

In retrospect, I realize I was not particularly successful in these first
attempts to move beyond cultural silence in my classroom. I had hoped
that students would become more aware of themselves as readers and
would begin to acknowledge what Pirie (1997) calls a "personal
platform" of reading that consists of "our personal history and values" (p.
44). He explains:

To be aware of ourselves as readers, we must acknowledge these personal platforms. That does not mean surrendering to subjectivity. Once we recognize how our values shape our readings, we are in a position to criticize those values, measure them against the values of others, guard against our prejudices, and celebrate or revise our values as appropriate. To engage students in this kind of thinking means inviting them to position themselves in relation to the values in the text, so that they are ultimately not merely reading the text, but also reading the world and reading themselves. (p. 44)

It seems that for the majority of the white students in the class, Lee's novel affirmed rather than challenged their personal platforms, by inviting them to identify with the white heroes of the text. Of course, not all students responded to this invitation in the same consensual way. Charles Sarland (1999) points out that "readers take up a range of positions of greater and lesser involvement, and of varied focalisation" (p. 49). Some students appeared to take a more detached and evaluative stance toward Lee's text, affirming its value for the classroom more on the grounds of its "literary merit" than on the grounds of their personal involvement with the story's characters or themes.

After teaching this curriculum class, I read more studies that highlight some of the complexities of reading and responding to Lee's novel in multiethnic classes. Carol Ricker-Wilson (1998), who was teaching Lee's novel in her high-school class, affirmed that most of her white students appeared comfortable with the way Lee positioned them as readers. In her article, she explains that for many of the white students in class, "their experiential identification with the wise and kindly Atticus and feisty Scout enabled them to close the covers, angered by injustice, but with their racial identities unscathed" (p. 70). In contrast, despite her efforts to frame and mediate the text, her black students reacted very negatively to the novel. Written comments from black students suggested that it was the very act of reading, through their identification with the black characters in the novel, that caused them to feel demoralized. One student wrote, "I began to think of being black as an inequity." Another wrote, "It's bad enough hearing racist views about black people on the news...but having to read the book...I don't want any part of it." A third explained, "It was disgusting, embarrassing and depressing to read a book...where blacks were constantly being called 'niggers' or treated the worst" (p. 69).

Ricker-Wilson points out that, although her black students had been willing to speak about issues of black identity and slavery during discussions in which "they were the subjects of their own carefully framed depictions" they still felt demoralized by their reading experience of a book which they perceived had "positioned them as objects of a lesson on racism for white students" (p. 70). She surmises that even though the author's intent might have been to critique marginalization and racism, the novel still positions black readers as "others" while it invites white readers to share in the pleasurable experience of identification with the main characters of the text:

> Is it possible that catharsis and the subsequent pleasure experienced when Jem is saved, Boo redeemed, Bob Ewell dispatched—the loose ends all neatly tucked away for the *white* characters in the novel—is most readily available to its white readers? Is any reading pleasure gleaned from the text more accessible for them? (p. 69)

James Ryan (1999), in his study of literature taught in a multiethnic school, points to similarly contrasting reactions to Lee's novel by adolescent white readers and African Canadian readers in a Grade 9 classroom. Many African Canadian students "were almost unanimous in their condemnation of the book" and found "the experience of taking up *To Kill a Mockingbird* in class a troubling one" (p. 134). These students, James explains, were "more likely to identify with the people in the novel who are the objects of racism and the derision associated with it" (p. 135). White students in the class (and their white teacher), in contrast, more often claimed to have "really loved" the novel. James explains:

> While some White readers may not approve of the treatment Blacks receive in the book, they may nevertheless take comfort in the fact that the central characters also disapprove of it. It is quite easy, then, for them to see an antiracist message in the book. It is also easy for White readers to distance themselves from the racist attitudes displayed in the novel. (p. 134)

James concludes that at the root of these different responses is "the strategy of the author to write for a particular audience" (p. 135). Harper Lee, white herself, was clearly writing for a white audience and anticipated that the values that emerged from the novel, filtered through a child's naïve view, would be acceptable to white readers. She was probably less aware of and less concerned with the stereotyping and exoticizing of African American characters in the book that so many students of color find offensive in classrooms today.

These studies of students' responses to Lee's novel in school classrooms have helped me to understand my own student teachers' responses to the book. I had hoped that their reading of *To Kill a Mockingbird* and *Roll of Thunder, Hear My Cry* and their viewing of the film *A Time to Kill* would make them more reflective about their own cultural positions and personal reading platforms. But I paid insufficient attention to Lee's ability to construct them as "ideal readers" of her text, and I failed to take account of their lack of experience of or preparation for dealing with issues surrounding cultural difference. As Ricker-Wilson (1998) suggests, "White students are rarely required to consider what it means to possess white skin...they tend to see racial identity as something troublesomely possessed by other people and are unaware of how their own privileges them" (p. 72).

In future education curriculum classes, I would foreground the novel reading and film viewing activities with a discussion of the historically privileged positions of power conferred by "whiteness." I would help students to see how writers construct "ideal readers" of a text and how a text is focalized through a particular narrative voice. I would present student teachers with the diverse responses of Ricker-Wilson's and Ryan's students to Lee's novel, so they might understand how the novel can be read through varying lenses of racial identifications and historically constructed frameworks of marginalization and power relations. This foregrounding might enable student teachers to become aware of the contrasting voices of the texts and to be more critical of their own reading positions. This activity might help these prospective teachers to more coherently challenge and resist discourses that privilege or marginalize readers in particular ways in their own classrooms of the future.

References

Altmann, A., Johnston, I., and Mackey, G. (1998). Curricular decisions about literature in contemporary classrooms: A preliminary analysis of a survey of materials used in Edmonton grade 10 English courses. *Alberta Journal of Educational Research, 44*(2), 208–220.

Britzman, D. (1991). *Practice makes practice: A critical study of learning to teach.* Albany: State University of New York Press.

Carson, T., Johnston, I., Chana, T. K., Leard, D., and Wiltse, L. (1998). Cultural difference and teaching: Exploring the complexities and ambivalences of multicultural education. *International multiculturalism 1998: Preparing together for the 21ˢᵗ century,* (pp. 147–158). Edmonton, Canada: Kanata Learning.

Frankenberg, R. (1993). *White women, race matters: The social construction of whiteness.* Minneapolis: University of Minnesota.

Gambell, T. (1982). *Canadian learning materials in elementary and secondary education.* Toronto: Association of Canadian Publishers; Ottawa: Canadian School Trustees Association.

Ghosh, R. (1996). *Redefining multicultural education.* Toronto: Harcourt, Brace & Co.

Giroux, H. (1992). *Border crossings: Cultural workers and the politics of education.* New York: Routledge.

Giroux, H. (1997). Rewriting the discourse of racial identity: Towards a pedagogy and politics of whiteness. *Harvard Educational Review, 67*(2), 285–320.

Hall, S. (1991). Ethnicity: Identity and difference. *Radical America, 13*(4), 9–20.

hooks, b. (1994). *Teaching to transgress: Education as the practice of freedom.* New York: Routledge,

Lee, H. (1960/1962). *To kill a mockingbird.* New York: Popular Library.

Nilsen, A. P., and Donelson, K. L. (2001). *Literature for today's young adults* (6ᵗʰ ed.). New York: Longman.

Pirie, B. (1997). *Reshaping high school English.* Urbana, IL: National Council of Teachers of English.

Ricker-Wilson, C. (1998). When the mockingbird becomes an albatross: Reading and resistance in the language arts classroom. *English Journal, 87*(3), March, 67–72.

Rosenberg, P. M. (1997). Underground discourses: Exploring whiteness in teacher education. In M. Fine, L. Weis, L. C. Powell, and L. Mun Wong (Eds.), *Off white: Readings on race, power, and society* (pp. 79–89). New York: Routledge.

Ryan, J. (1999). *Race and ethnicity in multi-ethnic schools.* Clevedon, England: Multilingual Matters.

Sarland, C. (1999). The impossibility of innocence: Ideology, politics and children's literature. In P. Hunt (Ed.), *Understanding children's literature* (pp. 35–59). London and New York: Routledge.

Taylor, M. (1976/1991). *Roll of thunder, hear my cry.* New York: Penguin.

❭ Hiding in Plain Sight

Michelle Bertie-Holthe

The school day began like any other. The morning was gray and cloudy, very unspring-like weather. Sometime during the day it began to snow; it was to be the last snowfall that spring. An observer looking in would not see anything unusual that morning: kids rushing to their desks just as the bell rang out, retrieving books from lockers, and gathering outside the doors between classes, teachers taking attendance, handing back assignments, and introducing new lessons. And then, just as the final bell ended the lunch recess, the path of one young boy carrying a gun was timed in such a way as to intersect with the path of two other boys, carrying schoolbooks. The intersecting steps left one boy dead, another seriously wounded and the third—forever marked as a murderer. It was Wednesday, April 28, 1999, and the school was W. R. Myers High School in Taber, Alberta.

A fourteen-year-old former student was arrested, charged and eventually convicted of the crime. As part of the child's defense his lawyers provided evidence to show that he had suffered from constant and unrelenting abuse at school. This intimidation began during his very earliest days in the elementary grades in Ontario and continued even after the family's move to Taber when he was in Grade 6. For years, this child had apparently been marked "different" for a variety of obscure reasons, which placed him further and further in the margin.

I was a teacher at Myers during that time. The boy who was seriously wounded that day was en route to my classroom for his Grade 11 English class. The boy, Jason Lang, who died in the attack, grew up five houses from my home, and had been my son's classmate ever since their kindergarten days. The young boy who killed Jason had been in my English 9 class for a brief time.

I wanted very badly to believe that this violent act was a random and freak incident that could find no reflection in the safe enclave that I and many others considered "home." What I believed to be "home," what I believed to be my place in that "home" was shattered during this time. Erika Hasebe-Ludt, one of my committee members, suggested to me that my thesis is about writing my way home. Perhaps it is. Writing these shards and slivers of memory from that time is my way of searching for the questions to ask, questions that may lead me to a home in which home-ness means a place open to being, rather than a place that defines the "right" way of being.

It was the last time she saw Nate. He was not in class that day, had not been present for quite some time. There were perhaps ten minutes left in English 9, period 3. She noticed Kevin walk back into the classroom, heading directly for her. He was returning from the bathroom. "Mrs. Holthe, there's something strange in the boys' bathroom." A touch of anxiety blended with the uncertainty of whether he should be anxious played across his face, the expression seeming to say, "It's probably no big deal."

"What do you mean 'strange'"?

"There's like this weird kind of candle burning on top of one of the toilets."

"Show me," she says. As they leave her classroom together, David, another teacher, exits the computer room next door, where he has been working during his prep. Except for her, David and Kevin, the hall is empty. Both landings to the stairwells, which are on opposite ends of the hallway to each other, appear to be deserted as well. The stairwell closest to the boys' washroom takes students and staff toward the center of the school. The opposite stairwell provides easy access to a back door exit. She feels pulled in two directions. She asks David to go with Kevin into the boys' bathroom to check what is there. Moving in the opposite direction of the boys' bathroom, she walks toward the stairwell nearest her room. As she opens the fire door she smells it immediately. It is not so much a burning smell, but rather the pungent *sulfurous* odor that is left over after matches have been lit and extinguished.

Sulfurous: [L.] of or containing sulfur; of or suggesting the fires of hell; violently emotional, heated, fiery.[1]

---

[1] The definitions are taken from *Webster's (1984) New World Dictionary*. (2nd ed.). New York: Simon and Schuster.

The stairwell is an open design. The solid wood banister, perhaps a little higher than 80 centimeters, is not flush to the floor. Standing just inside the landing, but facing the stairs, she can look down and see through the gap between the floor and the railing to the stairs that join the hallway immediately below her. There, through the gap, perhaps halfway down the stairs she sees one runner-clad foot, frozen it seems, posed in descending mid-step. It is a foot that does not want its steps to be heard, that does not realize it can be seen. It is attached to a body that is hiding in plain sight. The stance seems to freeze her too, for a moment. Then she walks toward the railing and looks down. There is Nate, frozen in his *downward* flight.

Downward: [ME. < OE.] toward a lower position, place, state; from an earlier to a later time.

As she speaks he raises his head to her voice. "Hey Nate, whatcha doin'?"

He shrugs and mumbles, "Nothin."

"You're supposed to be in class now, aren't you?" Again he shrugs. She does not remind him that it is her class he should be in even though she would guess that he does not remember his class schedule. Nor does she mention the odor that still hangs in the air or the strange candle in the bathroom, although it seems certain to her that he is responsible for both. "You know I have to report you for being truant, right?" He shrugs. It seems obvious he does not care. He moves down the rest of the stairs and leaves the stairwell. She does not try to stop him. As she walks back toward the boys' bathroom, she turns into David's classroom instead and walks across the room to look out his window. She can see the boy running fast across the school grounds toward the street north of the school, his dark coat tight around his body.

David and the principal are just leaving the bathroom as she finally approaches that end of the hallway. The homemade candle, constructed using a tin can, cardboard, wax and wick, and placed in such a way, has unsettled David enough that he has called the principal upstairs to see. On seeing, the principal kicked the candle from the toilet tank and stomped out its light with his foot, dismissing the incident as a meaningless prank. Like David, she too is unsettled. She mentions her stairwell encounter with Nate and his flight away from the school to the principal. He takes note of what she says, but does not seem particularly interested. Later, she repeats her experience to the vice-principal in charge of dealing with unexcused absences. The vice-principal does not ask for more details of the encounter, or a description of what was found in the washroom, but rather replies that the absence will be dealt with, suggesting that this latest truancy will probably be the last straw, adding that it is doubtful that the boy will be back.

She does not see Nate again.

It is only many months later that she learns that Nate was taught to construct this type of homemade candle in his Boy *Scout* troop, as part of camping survival training.

Scout: [ME. < OFr., to hear < L., to listen] a soldier, ship, etc. sent to spy out the strength, movements, etc. of the enemy; a person sent out to observe the tactics of an opponent; a member of the Boy Scouts or Girl Scouts; the act of reconnoitering; to go in search of something, hunt.

❱ Whispers among Places: Teaching and Writing In-Between Past, Present, Future

Renee Norman

In considering place and curriculum, I must first place myself in the present, caught up as I am in the autobiographical, what much of my writing/being is about.

And it strikes me that my place does not seem as if it ever changes, if you consider that I have lived in the same house and suburb for 15 years, completed my undergraduate and graduate work at the same university where I now teach sessionally, and still mother three school-aged, growing daughters. Yet with/in that seeming stability and constancy I feel as if I am constantly moving, blown from place to place with/in present place like a pink cherry blossom in the wind. Place is not necessarily a physical space, but a mental and emotional and intellectual state of being that resides in the head.

Having completed my PhD, I agreed to teach a graduate curriculum course billed as a foundations course. I was excited about sharing with peers and colleagues what I felt I had learned so far on my journey. The term seemed full of possibility. I felt strong connections to the people in the course, as we began to live and relearn curriculum together, as I offered what excited me in curriculum and what I hoped to subvert in curriculum.

CURRICULUM AS DREAM

curriculum is a dream
I teach dreams
learn them too

days pass

filled with steps
bringing me closer
closer to the dream
never quite there
always the dream
is in front of me
in the distance
just a thought away

days pass
filled with plans
filled helping others
see their dreams
like a fiddler
I play on
wanting them
to hear the music
not the pied piper
I want them dancing
to their dreams
want the caves
that imprison them
empty

alienated and bereft
we seek the dream
seek the awe
and tasting it
change forever

if curriculum is a dream
I am the dreamer
(Norman, 1995, p. 3)

But there is always a subtext, fissures fracturing present place. My excitement was complicated by tension, too. Wife, mother, teacher, woman, daughter, sister, Jew, feminist, scholar, writer...we are never only teacher. And it is all these parts of our lives that we constantly juggle. I am torn to pieces, a student I taught in a drama course wrote, a student who is also a teacher, a mother, a dancer. Her words resonated with me. I knew exactly what she meant. I remember words I heard Ted Aoki speak: "the tension in teaching, in living, at home. If you're alive, there's tension. If you're dead, no tension" (Aoki, 1994).

Alive, I sometimes feel torn about whether and how much to teach. Returning to graduate school in mid-life was a renaissance of sorts for me. I began writing in earnest at long last and discovered a writing life as well as a life of the mind. "I am a writer, I am a writer"—the two lines with which I ended an early piece of writing that details my coming to writing. There is incredulity in those lines as well as the force of repetition which emphasizes a discovery that is joyful. The lines are a strong voice in the wind, the same wind that carries all those loose cherry blossoms from place to place. But nagging doubts remain: Am I good enough? Who wants to read what I write? What else can I possibly write about? My dissertation was my tour de force, and is my oeuvre over? Dry? And most grating of all, am I teaching so I'm not writing?

Belenky, Clinchy, Goldberger, and Tarule (1986) write of many bright, competent women who suffer from an astonishing lack of confidence. I've seen it in some of my women friends. I've noticed it in the classes I teach. And I feel it on occasion as strongly as the joy I felt when the chancellor bopped me on the head with my new diploma.

What surfaces and resurfaces when juggling teaching and writing in the air is this: when you're teaching, you're not writing. Teaching is a giving art. The preparation, the energy of being in performance mode, the marking, the conversations, the students' needs and hopes and requests. Like having more children, children who stay for a while, then move on. Teaching drains me. I seek ways to renew myself and begin anew: the next group, a new subject, some different strategies. I want to begin anew. Hope and possibility. Fresh starts after satisfying conclusions. But all this takes its toll in time as well as energy. When you're teaching, you're not writing.

Nagging doubts nag more: Will I forget how to write? Lose the desire? When's the last time I wrote something new, instead of drawing (again) on what I already wrote, especially the dissertation? A long year's work that places me somewhere, fixed, even if I want/hope/need to move on.

Yet having written all this, I remember how bereft I felt after the birth of my third child when an insensitive and overbearing personnel officer forced me to consider resigning from the school district in which I taught. My sense of loss was palpable. I did not resign. At the prospect of not teaching, I know I want to teach. (At the prospect of not writing, I know I want to write.)

One day, as I was carrying bags of masks and mirrors to the drama class I was about to teach, a professor in our department cruised by me and commented: "You look like a teacher."

"I AM a teacher," I replied without hesitation.

At convocation, a woman taking my graduate curriculum course introduced me to her son, saying: "This is my teacher." Powerful words. How those words move me, how they place me in the wor(l)d in ways that feel sound and good and right, despite the tensions and difficulties.

Yes, the graduate curriculum course was an exciting prospect. Time for writing would wait.

SEARCHING

the squirrels and i are scurrying
from building to building
them in search of more food
me in search of rooms
filled with people

i love campus in the fall
the unfulfilled promise of summer
heating the pavement with September's gift
twice i give directions to lost students
from Nairobi and North Van
certain of where they should be headed
and wondering about me

when at last i enter the right room
i see wariness in my students' eyes
they are searching too
it's then i know
where i am
(Norman, 2001, p. 97)

Course Description

This course, an introduction to the field of curriculum, examines its history and development, relevant themes and issues.

Historical and contemporary curriculum discourses will be explored by focusing on an understanding of curriculum historically, politically, autobiographically, and from feminist and postmodern perspectives, with attention to the way in which texts are interrelated.

During the course we will engage in individual and collaborative activities/projects that assist us in reflecting upon questions such as: What is curriculum? How do curriculum discourses function? What does it mean to educate? To be educated? How do you interpret the lines of curriculum in relation to your individual, specific situation?

Topics will include:
Mapping the History of Curriculum
—from Bobbitt to Dewey; the Progressive Movement; Tyler and Taba; Sputnik; Bloom; Goodlad; the Reform Movement (1960s); Mastery Learning; Schwab; Reconceptualization—a Paradigm Shift (1970s); Eisner; Greene; Pinar; Miller; Aoki; Grumet; Apple; Giroux.

The Politics of Curriculum
—the Hidden Curriculum; Hegemony; Critical Theory; Feminist Theory.
—McLaren; Freire; Lather; Ellsworth; Lewis; Willinsky; Carson.

Phenomenological Inquiry
—van Manen; Aoki; Greene; Grumet; Jardine; Smith.

Poststructuralism, Deconstruction, and Postmodernism

Autobiography

The Arts Stream

Research Possibilities on the Edge and Beyond

This course outline is dizzying with its words, but if we look long enough, words have spaces between them for possibility and creativity and artistry, despite their seeming to be set in stone. I am mystical about curriculum, and how it catches us in its grip, pulling us from present place into past place and future too, and back and forth between them. Each place whispers of the one that we left, the one we move to next. Our lives in these places are interconnected...

First day of class, 1999. Text set, readings and assignments to work through, and Ted Aoki lined up as a guest speaker towards the end of the course when we would reach phenomenological and postmodern curriculum text. We set about finding out about one another.

But this is not really the beginning. There are whispers...

First day of class, 1994. Ted Aoki is already in the classroom, and I am eager to hear him speak after reading some of his writings (Aoki, 1991; 1992). What draws me to Ted's work is hope and goodness and vision. He asks us, students in a narrative/curriculum course, to introduce ourselves. I speak about the profound effect his words have had on me philosophically, about the crossroads I feel I have reached in my work, and how I intuitively sense that I am in need of Ted's wisdom and poetry in order to proceed. Humble, always humble, Ted responds that his earlier work is largely essentialist, that he has in many ways moved to a more poststructural consideration of curriculum, though he slides back and forth between the two. I feel immediate relief that this eminent scholar openly admits to movement and change, and admiration that Ted seems constantly in motion: reading, re-reading, re-learning, re-considering. The re at work, Ted would say.

Place is also a mental and emotional and intellectual state of being that resides in the head...

1999

Place was brought home to me full force in the course of the graduate curriculum course, as we ran the course (currere) together, teacher and students. We spanned the globe: the people called so many places home—Hong Kong, China, Korea, St. Vincent's, Trinidad, South Africa, Québec—truly an international group. Several of these students were completing their studies away from their immediate families as well as their homeland. They brought bright photographs of wives and daughters dressed in finery for family weddings the students could not attend. They spoke of preschoolers who were beginning to forget a parent and did not feel like talking when Mom phoned. They wrote in their autobiographical course journals about their hopes for their children, for what they would bring back to these wor(l)ds. If we were to study and make sense of North American curriculum, a requirement of this required course, we would place it in contexts that included all these places and spaces. It felt somehow colonial that this introductory course centred on North America, when the people with whom I was working knew additional languages, experienced ways of life that differed considerably from American ways, and viewed curriculum in terms of education in their own countries. I felt a bit like Nathan Price in *The Poisonwood Bible*, proselytizing the Curriculum Bible in a veritable Congo of cultures, languages, meanings. In *The Poisonwood Bible*, author Barbara Kingsolver explains that many of the Kikongo words have double (if not multiple) meanings. So when Nathan Price would call out, "Tata Jesus is bangala" in prayer, he could have been saying Jesus is beloved, or Jesus is the poisonwood tree! It seemed to me, as we proceeded with the study of curriculum, that many concepts doubled and tripled their meanings as we engaged in discourse about discourse that was always against a complex international and personal backdrop...

1994

In Ted's course I believe I lived for a time in what he calls a middle place for culture, a place where people of varying backgrounds and opinions, Eastern and Western, could meet, study, discuss, share, and laugh. Through the course we investigated narrative (story) as a research strategy in a Pacific Rim context. We wrote and re-wrote out lived experiences against the texture of an intercultural landscape. We also examined and interrogated identity in terms of the multiplicity of beliefs we discovered in ourselves and others. The course drew people whose homelands were Canada, the United States, Asia, Europe, people who spoke several languages, people who had lived in several cultural settings, people knowledgeable about other cultures...

1999

Early in the term, one student came to me, puzzled by our discussion of Bobbitt and Dewey, supplemented by text readings, articles from other sources, and a newspaper article I had written on my own beliefs in response to a political furor over educational testing results in British

Columbia (Norman, 1996). This student asked: Could you not just lecture us on Bobbitt? Many times our class conversations had included the differences between education in the West and the very structured and rigid expectations that featured in some of the students' educational upbringing. I was not about to resort to a lecture format in order to satisfy anyone's longing for more order, less chaotic learning. No, I would not be like Nathan Price, arrogantly provide the Word, the ultimate gospel, the absolute truth about Bobbitt and Dewey. Learning involves necessary tensions, the working out of what we read and hear, compared to what we believe or aspire to. What puzzles us also inspires us, what challenges us keeps us questioning and searching for the many meanings in any one word or concept. Tata Bobbitt is bangala!

But I learned that we cannot assume that discussing is necessarily understanding. I became conscious of drawing more and more of the quieter students into the conversations. I invited students to speak more about education and curriculum in their countries of origin. I began to temporarily interrupt our discussion for clarification if I thought some term or reference needed explanation.

And I felt more and more surreal at times as I moved between this course and the others I was teaching. The graduate students and I explored curriculum-as-live(d); pre-service teachers and I in language education courses coped with curriculum-as-plan. As we opened up the resource packages of curriculum materials in order to make ourselves familiar with them, I not only knew that those plans were subject to the political whims of a government that could change direction, I also knew that no matter how much the pre-service teachers wanted to rely on the packages, they would also need to learn to fly without them. At this time, one of my daughters came home with the story of the boy in the back of her French class who was crying because he had no one to work with. Their teacher did nothing, and in relating this story to my pre-service teachers, I appealed to them to learn to deal with children's loneliness and pain, and claimed such learning does not necessarily come from curriculum packages. I moved between the obligations of preparing prospective teachers using the ministry curriculum and the freedom of creating a place for seasoned teachers to call into question our assumptions about curriculum. Living with curriculum as school materials and curriculum as live(d) and all the places in between.

1994

    Ted created an atmosphere that both evoked difference and supported it. He envisions a cultural space which is open, inclusive, and in the middle. In Ted's words, "Neither this or *that, but this* and *that." A place where cultural stereotypes are both evoked and erased, the traces remaining but the stereotypes turned inside out so that we can contemplate people in new ways.*

    How does one put such a philosophy into practice? Ted did this by honoring and respecting the diversity with/in the class, pulling out the varied backgrounds that people arrived with. He did it by insisting not only that we examine the new ideas of scholars from varying cultural backgrounds, but also that we should continually question ourselves: What do we believe? Why? How did we arrive at such a belief? What are the conditions that make possible such a belief? What are we really saying? What are others saying?

    There was no invisibility in this class, and Ted ensured that each person was introduced into the cultural fabric of the classroom. Sometimes he did this when he returned a journal, chatting to everyone about the journal-writer's interesting stories. Sometimes he drew a silent face out from the crowd, asking a pertinent question that he intuited would relate to a person's lived experiences. At other times he commented on someone's comment made during earlier discussions of what we were reading. He asked those who spoke and wrote other languages to share their knowledge with the class. Dissenting views were accepted and, through this acceptance, became important considerations. Once people knew such diversity was tolerated, differing views were entered into discussions with care, more consideration, deeper analysis. Confusion and questioning were more often the states of our being. Dogmatic views and pretence faded, replaced by a still listening silence, a loud thinking clamour, a place where East and West flourished in shared thought, traded language, variant philosophies, common laughter.

    There were many highlights in such a cultural meeting place. Sometimes we examined only a word, seeing it in new ways as we all deconstructed and reconstructed it through our varied understanding and experience. Sometimes we "heard" how another language looks, sounds, means: Chinese or Japanese characters and calligraphy. We discussed our names, our schooling, our heritage arising out of Eastern or Western traditions. The classroom life which Ted hoped to stir up evolved out of the lives of all the people living the course. Books changed hands, people chatted over coffee, and a convivial, amiable atmosphere replete with joking and laughter filled the air...

1999

Last night L. quietly and privately asked me: "What are the three R's"? I showed S. how to use the index in *Understanding Curriculum* to look up names or issues or topics to aid him with the readings. I asked N. to speak to the group about the curriculum material he had sent for from St. Vincent's. I wondered if C. would lead the Freire discussion as she had lived in South America for a while. Would V. share her expertise about the Frankfurt School with the group? I learned when to talk and when to be silent and listen.

I brought my set of drama masks to class and we looked at curriculum as mask.

MASK

orange
three grey tears hand-painted
on the hardened felt
of a small mask on the table
like a flat oval pumpkin
with sockets
a skeletal shape
beckons

she molds the mask to her face
folds of cheek & chin
a perimeter of disregarded flesh

to lose herself she gazes deeply
in the ornamental mirror on the table
looking for the character hidden
in the rigid form

the glass absorbs the felt
the trace of grey
reveals another face
but when she turns around
only eyes return my stare

when she turns away
peels the mask from skin and bone
the tears transform
orange too

for once i felt beautiful
she says
in another face
imagining it anew
(Norman, 1997, p. 119)

I also brought a piece of mask art that one of my daughters had completed at school, although I did not divulge the identity of the artist until later. At the centre of the work is a mask of a girl's face, eyes shut and tears dripping down the cheeks. A jungle of green leaves and vines surrounds this face. I asked the students to write/speak of what reading the work conjured up for them and why. They linked it to Michael Apple and the institutional, to the inherent goodness of the child, to Maxine Greene and the possibilities in the arts, to Elizabeth Ellsworth and oppression. They saw a mother crying tears of joy over her children. They saw the sadness and sorrow of having to relinquish a child to the system and wanting to bring her home again. They saw a child who did not cope well with the curriculum-as-plan aspect of the school system.

Every week I moved the lectern off the table to create less distance between myself and the students. Our classroom was a place with nailed down tables and a view of concrete in amongst more concrete. For those of us who are trying to teach differently in the academy, to bring the many voices of our students into the chorus, desks and locks and curtained windows and immovable tables—the whole ecology of the classroom—need to be deconstructed if we hope to change power structures. As R. I. Simon and Elizabeth Ellsworth remind us, "The task of the critical educator thus becomes finding ways of working with students that enable the full expression of multiple voices engaged in dialogic encounter" (Ellsworth, 1989, p. 101). At the end of term, the geography of physical place remained the same. Chalkboard, screen, audiovisual cupboard, lectern. But I like to think the geography of self was somehow changed. I like to think that our voices remained in the walls, in the windows, wafting out onto concrete, the everpresent whirring fan circulating through the whispers of past conversations, sucking up sound.

1994

MIDDLE PLACE
(for Ted Aoki)

Dwelling with Ted
in the and
where the teacher disappears
the I's dissolve
and in their place:

a word seen again
spun into the air
like a juggler's plates

a silent face drawn
out from the crowd
beckoned to meet the stickiness
at the merest breath of movement

a voice heard
that now echoes endlessly
bouncing off the wall
splitting into atoms

a deed honoured & shared
hopeful celebration
in already knowing eyes

a dissent respected
the remnant of a whisper crying

an unformed thought
encouraged to flounder
entered into emptiness

an idea recaptured
and reflected back
hopeful dreaming
a vision

cultures felt
through language people
thoughts & laughter

and the middle place
is home to all

Hush for a moment.

Do you hear the memory singing?

1999

I wept as I read some of the students' autobiographical journals and my tears fell upon the words on the pages, an interemotional textual event, tears mixing with letters, emotions felt and received and sent again. D., full of regret for his past teaching, asking for just one more day with those students. K., full of passion for what she wants for her daughter in China. A curriculum for a daughter. W., discovering the joy of autobiographical writing and words she can give to feelings and concerns. I copied down a quote that W. included, words I wanted to hang over my desk:

> The highest good is like water.
> Water gives life to the ten thousand things and does not strive.
> It flows in places rejected and so is like the Tao.
> In dwelling, be close to the land.
> In meditation, go deep into the heart.
> In dealing with others, be gentle and kind.
> In speech, be true.
> In ruling, be just.
> In daily life, be competent.
> In action, be aware of the time and season.
> No fight; no blame. (Needlemen, 1998, p. 10)

1994

Perhaps the moment that remains for me most potent and memorable is when Ted told his story of being asked years ago where his allegiance lay when war with Japan put Canadians of Japanese descent under scrutiny. I am Canadian, Ted told us he had replied, and his quiet voice rang with dignity as he related this story. I believe his voice also resonated with the pain that can be part of cultural difference if we are insensitive to common human emotion, common human existence, regardless of religion, race, philosophy.

When Ted spoke these words, the very last day of the course, there was a palpable listening silence in the room: a silence permeated with past mistakes, present hopes, and future visions. A silence that laid open a new kind of cultural Canada. A silence that until that final day Ted had not allowed himself to fill with stories of his own experience: too much "I," Ted would say about narrating his own stories. Here was Ted's middle place for culture: learning about ourselves with and through others; living with ourselves as we live with others.

I still feel the imprint of Ted Aoki, who is committed to new paths of understanding, new ways of looking at the world.

I still hear the memory singing.

1999

A small man with big ideas, one student wrote in his journal about Ted's visit and talk. Ted first spoke autobiographically about place, the Angus Building in which we were deconstructing curriculum, the same building where he had studied commerce. And Ted told us how Henry Angus, one of his professors, had been the one person to speak up when Japanese Canadian students were asked to leave the university. All this reflection and recollection arising because we had asked Ted to come and speak to us about curriculum. Ted spoke of place, and he dis/placed us in many different spaces and locations and in-betweenesses of curriculum.

All these whispers, all these places, the movement between where we are, where we've been, where we're going, and all the many places in-between.

G. exclaimed at the end of the curriculum course: "We've come a long way since Bobbitt!"

And so we had, and so we had. I write these words retrospectively, as I once again find the time for writing, knowing that I have been many places through the writing, through the teaching, and that there are many places with/in these places yet to revisit.

POET'S SYMPHONY

above the words
the turns of the flute
under the saxophone trills
in the spaces between the keys

but the letters will not behave

up and down the scale
they turn and lift
lift and thrust
dancing on the ascent
descending into the chaos
of chorus

dry reeds crack
words burn holes
pads come loose
strings twinge
POP!
the sound is an earthquake of alphabet
silent as a deaf mute
raging
hands signing thoughts

it is enough to play
the words
(Norman, 2001, p. 46)

References

Aoki, T. (1991). Sonare and videre: Questioning the primacy of the eye in curriculum talk. In G. Willis and W. H. Schubert (Eds.), *Reflections from the heart of educational inquiry* (pp. 182–189). Albany: State University of New York Press.

Aoki, T. (1992). Layered voices of teaching: The uncannily correct and the elusively true. In W. Pinar and W. M. Reynolds (Eds.), *Understanding curriculum as phenomenological and deconstructed text* (pp. 17–27). New York: Teachers College Press.

Aoki, T. (1994, July). Course lecture. *Modern Languages 508B*. Vancouver: University of British Columbia, Canada.

Belenky, M., Clinchy, B., Goldberger, N., & Tarule, J. (1986). *Women's ways of knowing: The development of self, voice, and mind.* New York: Basic Books.

Ellsworth, E. (1989). Why doesn't this feel empowering? Working through the repressive myth of critical pedagogy. *Harvard Educational Review, 59*(3), 297–324.

Kingsolver, B. (1998). *The poisonwood bible.* New York: HarperCollins.

Needlemen, J. (Ed.). (1998). *Tao Te Ching/Lao Tsu* (G. F. Feng and J. English, Trans.). New York: Vintage.

Norman, R. (1995). Curriculum as dream. *Educational Insights, 3*(1), 3.

Norman, R. (1996). How those math and science scores add up. In *The Vancouver Sun,* Sept. 6.

Norman, R. (1997). Mask. *Canadian Woman Studies/Les cahiers de la femme, 17*(3), 119.

Norman, R. (2001). Searching. *Our Schools/Ourselves, 11*(1), 97.

Norman, R. (2001). Poet's symphony. *English Quarterly, 33*(1&2), 46.

Pinar, W. F., Reynolds, W. M., Slattery, P., and Taubman, P. M. (Eds.).(1995/1996). *Understanding curriculum: An introduction to the study of historical and contemporary curriculum discourses.* New York: Peter Lang.

❯ Uncanny Demarcations: Metonymic Writing as/in a Doubled Gesture

Patricia Palulis

Writing…already, always already, has a reading relationship
with itself, which divides its act…[1]
—Geoffrey Bennington, *Derridabase*, in *Jacques Derrida*

*It was the summer of '96. It was the second day of class. And, there, at
my place at the seminar table, was a text with a note attached. The text
was Slavoj Zizek's* Tarrying with the Negative. *The note alerted me to
attend to the introduction where I read about Zizek's notion of the hole
in the flag as a moment of sublime openness. Zizek insists that the role of
the critical intellectual is to occupy the place of this hole—to maintain a
distance from the master signifier. But in the distancing which is in itself
an im/possibility, one struggles—always already—with/in a "third"
discourse—a "third" moment—a "third" space—working out on the
slope of a "third" ground. Catching only glimpses of what might be
distancing—fleeting moments of a void—trembling within a tropological
moment—a Metonomy inhabited by an uncanny doubling of
metonymy/metaphor—an Aokian moment that keeps us mindful of our
location in the language of pedagogy. For just as language courses
through us, we are located in discourse—a doubling movement.*

---

[1] See Bennington's (1993) *Derridabase* for a reading with and against the line of
separation of signatures. Bennington engages in an exposition of Derridean thought
while Derrida, writing at the base of the text, engages in a series of periphrases as his
own *Circumfession*. I draw my opening citation from Bennington as I struggle with
readings of Aokian Metonymy—in the im/possibility of location—the demarcation in-
between writer/reader. My writing always already a divided act. As I pull citations
from contextual habitats and juxtapose my fragmented prose, who occupies the vacant
spaces? If, as Lacan contends, metonymy is the necessary condition for metaphor, let a
specter emerge as tenant. A specter leaving lively impressions—*à pied.*

assigning estrangement: a paper that is not a paper

Metonymic writing[2] evokes a messy text within an outlaw genre—both inside and outside the law of genre and yet neither inside nor outside—uncanny demarcations of a working language in what Derrida would term a "strange topography of edges."[3] A space that Trinh designates as a "third" ground. How does one respond to an Aokian invitation to write a paper that is not a paper—to write within the performative space of an oscillating syntax? How does one stage a *mise-en-page* for a double gesture—as a *bricolage*? as a *découpage?* Writing along a *via rupta*—a path cut through? How to stage a performativity that might startle itself? A text that seeks to un/do itself—that splits into fragments each working at displacing an/other—one with/in the other. Footnotes trail as detours—as drifting habitations. Citations are suspended within a cryptic domicile—unable to be still in the wake of shimmering phantoms. Hélène Cixous contends that, when we have lost all other places of habitation, we enter the country of words. In exile, we enter a diaspora of words. Diaspora is a postponement of

...as soon as genre announces itself, one must respect a norm, one must not cross a line of demarcation, one must not risk impurity, anomaly or monstrosity...

And suppose for a moment that it were impossible not to mix genres. What if there were, lodged within the heart of the law itself, a law of impurity or a principle of contamination?...

The law and the counter-law serve each other citations summoning each other to appear...perhaps someone has noticed...[t]he punctuation was slightly modified...[t]his barely noticable shift....A particularly rich combinatory of possibilities would thus ensue... (Derrida, 1993, pp. 224–227)

---

[2] Della Pollock (1998) contends that metonymic writing "takes its pulse from the *difference* rather than the *identity* between the linguistic symbol and the thing it is meant to represent" (p. 82). But the specter of identity always already haunts the empty stage of metonymy—the specter of someThing as metaphor of presence. Pollock draws on metonymic writing as an excursion into performative writing. I want to ask whether performative writing might invoke an Aokian (Aoki, 2000) notion of Metonymy—a doubling of metonymy/metaphor—for a flicker—a murmur—a spatiality of someWhere else—a moment of meaning/not meaning—why *jouissance* is untranslatable.

[3] See Derrida's (1993) *Aporias*, where he makes reference to the aporia—the impossibility—of death—and a complicated possibility of impossibility—a doubling as a "strange topography of edges" (p. 80).

homecoming—the gap—the void—the interval—the space of home/not home—a place for writing. A place for writing as a divided act. A place where the uncanny demarcations of reader/writer doublings are disturbed and disturbing. I look to Cixousian notions of *écriture féminine*[4] as a working term—as a writing that works—that works at reading otherwise—that works at spending. And I learn to listen for spectral traces that haunt the spending.

tracking signatures through the intertext

Tracking Zizek (1999) tracking Derrida with/in interstitial traces from ontology to hauntology, this paper seeks *trans*lation within chiasmatic spaces of hybridity—between writer and/as reader—disrupting and disturbing the signature—maintaining a spectral opening by contaminating the signature with multiple traces of a countersignature. I'm increasingly enticed by notions of spectrality—the specter of the reader with/in writer that haunts the work—a co-habitation—Michel de Certeau's "*One*

...the impossible logic of spectrality that forever prevents/differs/displaces the closure of the ontological edifice: the proper deconstructionist gesture is to maintain the spectral opening, to resist the temptation of its ontological closure. Again, it is easy to translate this into Lacanese: spectrality is another name for the phantasmic semblance that fills the irreducible ontological gap. (Zizek, 1999, p. 238).

and the other—the occupant and the ghost...*within the same* text."[5] SomeThing there that evokes an affinity for an author—for a work. The kind of affinity spoken of by Cixous—a mysterious affinity for the work of certain writers. And in the now of discourse—for writers that entertain in the domicile of the ghost. Cixous contends that "[w]riters carry within themselves their own disquieting strangers...."[6] I can find no meaning in

---

[4] Cixous (1990a) responds to the Lacanian question that queries what women want. I find an affinity with her notion of *écriture féminine* as writing that spends. I want to draw from a "third" discourse that works the slope of an im/possibility of spending. That takes its pulse from working out on a slope (/).

[5] For this, see de Certeau (1988, p. 346).

[6] See Hélène Cixous (1991, p. 10) for the notion of a writer's doubling habitation—a difficult navigation between the living world and the writing world.

this mysterious affinity other than a spectral presence—a presence of someThing out-of-place. And so I share my reading habit(ation)s in paratactic locations.

Uncanny. I find traces of the uncanny—the *unheimlich*—emerging throughout the discourses of psychoanalysis and deconstruction. Bennington addresses the psychoanalytic turn in Derrida's *Circumfession*—the text that courses beneath Bennington's with the intention of surprising it. Two texts signing a contract—running a course with and against the line of separation. Bennington seeks to systematize Derrida's work as/in an interactive computer program. Derrida contends that such a system must remain open and so the contract is doomed to failure. I am reading the Bennington/Derrida intertext as a performative event—an event that startles the spectacle of itself—as a pedagogical site. Could this be Zizek's notion of a provocative defeat? Is the failure of the contract the very condition for its possibility? A provocation for something else to happen. Della Pollock contends that performative writing "takes its energy from...refusal...from the moment when...apparent contradictions surge into productivity."[7]

What happens in-between signatures? Bennington addresses the complication of the signature calling up the reader's countersignature—each "counter" opening to another. If reading is translation, then every text calls for a translation that never finishes. The signature according to Bennington is "very poor security for the authenticity of writing." [8]

---

[7] And once again my reader identity is shattered in re-reading Pollock. With the flicker of a few words, Pollock (1998) refuses Derrida as she writes about performative writing as consequential and "not in the debased-Derridean sense of reveling in absence" (p. 96). Where is Pollock located? I find a "surge of productivity" in the intertext. It is in her contradictions that I begin to locate the moments for Aoki's capital "M" Metonymy—that I sense the difficulty—the im/possibility of staying at the site of a "third" discourse. The spatial punctuation of the slash "/" is a slippery place of pedagogy. If "*space is a practiced place*," as Michel de Certeau (1984) contends, it is difficult to work-out here on the slope (p. 117).

[8] See Bennington, 1993, p.153.

...this Thing that is not a thing, this thing that is invisible between its apparitions, when it reappears. This Thing meanwhile looks at us and sees us not see it even when it is there. A spectral assymmetry interrupts here all specularity. (Derrida, 1994, p. 6)

While barred from access to Derrida's text coursing beneath his own as a condition of their contract, Bennington's response seeps beneath and beyond the ends of a contract—in a new text interrupting Derrida—startling his textuality—invoking the specter of Freud in Derrida's *Circumfession*. Derrida never names Freud and yet there is a spectral presence. And here in Bennington's recent text, I am intrigued with his notion of circanalysis[9] as he locates a force of resistance—in a Derridean refusal of psychoanalysis—a laboring in the force of a "not"—*this is not psychoanalysis*—in the very utterance of refusal the thing is accorded a domicile.

I had noted several inked inscriptions in Zizek's text—a meticulous record keeping of readings of the text—there were several dated notations—inscribed as a reader's paratext in the margins. I had yet to query what it might mean to re-read—to ask what the hyphen might want—to query the domicile of the paratext—to ask who dwells there. My writing always now a responsive re-reading of an im/possible invitation "to write a paper that is not a paper." A laboring in the force of a "not"—a laboring in the domicile of a "third" ground. In the writing, a specter of the reader is always there—a specter that refuses to let the writing be still. Writing as a divided act—a chiasmatic two-way flow between writer and writer-as-reader—and it is this doubling relationship that evokes a restless writing. Re-readings destabilize positionalities which dis/appear into spaces of the void—Zizek's "the void called subject." In re-reading I would come to seek a pulse in difference—a difference that carries traces of the cinders of identities—that remain without remaining.

---

[9] See Bennington's (2000) *Interrupting Derrida* for a commentary on the complexities of Derrida's relationship with psychoanalysis.

In the space of re-reading, the identity of the writer de-stabilizes—loses points of reference. In the liminal (w)rites of passage, as a writer continues to read and re-read beyond and beneath the writing, positionality becomes unstable—and composure de-composes. Imaginaries are doubled and re-doubled—tainted and stained from ex-posures—from ex-scriptions—from detours in and out of Derridean deconstruction and Lacanian psychoanalysis—and from moments of *frisson* in the chiasmus in-between. What happens in the gaps and voids and

> The person who doesn't tremble when crossing a border doesn't know there is a border and doesn't cast doubt on their own definition. (Cixous, 1993, p. 131)

> The borderline is never a secure place, it never forms an indivisable line, and it is always on the border that the most disconcerting problems of topology get posed. Where, in fact, would a problem of topology get posed if not *on the border?* (Derrida, 1998, p. 77)

intervals between these imaginary demarcations? What happens as the "I" de-stabilizes—taking on new identities in the interval of re-reading—in the space of a re-petition? Something happens to the writer—to the reader in a pedagogy of the para-site. I struggle as a writer reading into the chiasmus[10] of psychoanalytic discourse and deconstruction—the site of resistance—the site of *entamer*—a space of biting into—as a site of pedagogy—a parasitic writing/reading relationship—one devoured by the other. And in re-reading my writing I read into the resistance of a paper that is "not" a paper—a slight shift in spatial punctuation. An invocation for "what does not arrive to arrive."[11]

---

[10] See Derrida's provocative "For the love of Lacan" in *Resistances of psychoanalysis* for a complicated reading or translation of chiasmus (1998, p.53).

[11] See Derrida's (2000) *Demeure* for his notion of a spectral law…the spectral necessity of an overflow in the opposition between reality and fiction. Derrida speaks of a *démourance*—of a false testimony that testifies as symptom—and can we not read here a rustling motion with psychoanalysis—with metaphor as symptom (p. 92).

Translating *Dichtung* as dictations, Avital Ronell contends that writing always comes from elsewhere and draws from Derrida that something compels the writing. Perhaps the specter of a reader who has been reading someWhere else. Enticed by her title *Dictations on Haunted Writing*[12] I had a difficult time burrowing into the work—until I returned to it having been someWhere else writing into readings with a polysemy of signatures. A reader shows up at the door like Kafka's traveller to the castle hoping to be let in. Is this what re-reading is about—chiasmatic movements into the text until one finds

...what haunts is also a haunt—something that doubles for a place, a familiar place. Haunting belongs to the family of *Heim*; it in fact has never been evicted from the home...the *Unheimlichkeit* that haunts our thinking, because in its remoteness there is something very close, and it is disquieting only to the extent that it is close: "They're back!" Whatever is to be called home, to a familiar dwelling, is related to *ethos*...Hauntedness allows for visitations without making itself at home. (Ronell, 1986, p. xviii)

an affinity—knowing someThing is there and never quite arriving. A curious mapping. Where? There where you are not. Until the text finds you—tethers you—wraps you around some word—that someThing that finds an affinity with you—that bites into your textuality—your working language. And in the para-sitic moment...a moving on.

As I read Ronell's comments on haunted places I recall a professor's comment about the building that houses the Faculty of Education—a comment about it being a *scary* place. Are we not speaking of a haunted house? A building that houses hauntology? How is it that the Cartesian specters of clarity and certainty came to haunt the domicile of pedagogy? A spectrality, as Zizek would say, to fill the ontological gap. And as I prepare to return to teaching each fall term, I feel as if these Cartesian specters have invaded my body—"*they're back*"—uncanny visitations—disquieting habitations that announce some kind of uncanny presence. My writing "self" re-entering the textuality of live(d) pedagogy

---

[12] Now I'm intrigued by Ronell's query in the underbelly of the text: How is it that Goethe came to cosign psychoanalysis? Ronell is tracking the excesses of signature. Ronell tracks the phantom of Goethe as Derrida tracks the specter of Marx and Freud. See Ronell (1986).

in the wake of troubling specters—shimmering in multiple disguises. I am no longer searching for a lost home in my writing but finding a *jouissance* of vacancy in homelessness. I, too, can become a lodging for a host of specters.

troubling (t)exteriorities

Michel de Certeau makes reference to a (t)exterior—*hors-texte*—as a movement of circularity between the production of text and the production of Other—the "terrain of the name"[13] as nomination sets the limits for drifting. Naming as a spatial punctuation. Can we read Derrida's shifting punctuation to create a misfire? How can we begin to trouble the brackets of (t)exteriority as/in uncanny demarcations to incite vibrant tensionality? Drawing from the Aokian notion of Metonomy as a chiasmatic "in-between" space of metaphor/metonymy, the place of

Repetition *and* first time: this is perhaps the question of the event as question of the ghost. *What is* a ghost? What is the *effectivity* or the *presence* of a specter, that is, of what seems to remain as ineffective, virtual, insubstantial as a simulacrum? Is there *there*, between the thing itself and its simulacrum, an opposition that holds up? Repetition *and* first time, but also repetition *and* last time, since the singularity of any *first time* makes of it also a *last time*. Each time it is the event itself, a first time is a last time. Altogether other. Staging for the end of history. Let us call it a *hauntology*. (Derrida, 1994, p. 10)

the slash—the place of the gap—is the space of generative possibilities in a drifting, uncertain habitation—in moments of persistent in/stability. And so I'm drawn to certain hybrid writings—to the discursive flow of "to and fro" writing—aware that chiasmatic movements are never reciprocal but lean toward. Circles colliding—only by entering another circle can you crack the movement. Metonymic writing seeks to rupture (t)exteriority. To make the brackets quiver in anticipation—and leave a trembling in the aftermath.

And I listen with a "third" ear to a complicated conversation between Trinh Minh-ha and Homi Bhabha on the notion of hybridity. The

---

[13] de Certeau (1986, p. 72). De Certeau moves into a linguistic discourse that labors in the space of the text/the text of the space.

conversation opens to a site of tensionality as hybridity is undergoing multiple re-appropriations and so begins to take on a positionality of center with a re-appropriation of power to the mainstream. Trinh and Bhabha contend that hybridity demands reopening and displacement "to keep its space alive."[14] A question of working the "re" of re-appropriation. The specter haunts the hyphen—the occupant and the ghost. A slight shift in spatial punctuation. The cadence of arrhythmia courses on—moving on—as survival...

im/perfect tenses or resonating with/in a "third" pulse

As I departed from Aoki's class in that summer of '96 I wanted more—lack drives desire and desire borrows a language and slides on the signifier. Invocations from the readings of Zizek and Lacan, Trinh and Bhabha, Derrida and Cixous and others disoriented me—dislocated me. I joined a study group on Lacan—detoured from pedagogy to human geography to Asian studies to anthropology. I was seeking a working language for interrupting the praxis of my work in schools. I wanted to read into spaces of not understanding. Where reading translates into unreadability—a curious geography that means risking your place on the map. Where ethnographic fieldwork means doing the work at home as/in homework. And I found that pedagogy was everyWhere in the spaces of language and in the languages of space and that home was not home and not not-home. And I located a working language that labored within a "third" discourse—that trembled on a "third" ground. A working language that draws from the tensions at the edges of psychoanalysis and deconstruction. A working language that spends—that un/does—that ex-scribes as it re-writes—as it moves on.

I have often been asked how my writing connects with my classroom praxis. And stories emerge in the intertext—when *m'sieur cocodrie* pops out of the three little pigs "Cajun" style—a storybook I brought back from a conference at Louisiana State University—the haunting presence of the big bad wolf as a specter in *m'sieur cocodrie*—an inky spillage

---

[14] See Trinh (1999, p. 27). Follows a series of interviews that invoke the impulse of the interval—an impulse that calls for moving on—that survives in the space of the gap. Bhabha and Trinh work with notions of liminality and repetition in ways that would render a return to center an impossibility.

that shimmers in a flicker of metonymy/metaphor. And "Cajun" resonances begin a drifting habitation in the classroom. My first grade students are engaging already in hybrid writings re-locating stories within the swamps of Louisiana. And I catch myself trying to decipher who wrote what—to separate the authorship always already so intertwined within these emergent textualities. And then we begin to ask how the wolf got such a bad rap. And *m'sieur cocodrie*? Stories leak through border crossings—we bring the im/perfect tense into our conversations. And as we begin to read into elseWhere spaces we begin to write otherwise. Complicating pedagogies.

And questions emerge in the agonizing spaces of pedagogy. When Levinas and Derrida and Critchley cannot separate out the one from the other[15]—how is it that we have come to demand individual labor from young children? And why are we asked to examine these young first words under the signifier "data"[16] for standardized evaluations–partitioned for surveillance? When I questioned the use of the word "data"—when I questioned the representative who appeared before us from the panopticon of ministry authority I was told—*"but that's what it is"*—pure essence—the violence of the law of the verb "to be"—a dangerous verb—*"but that's what it is."* This verb "to be" that demands to be interrupted. I walk out of the room. Speechless in my rage. To mark an absence? A dislocation in space to re-mark a text in pedagogy? I don't know. But now I seek to inscribe the ex-scription—to re-mark an absence as performative gesture. What is this "is" asks Irigaray—of air?[17] Is this how we bring Irigaray to a first grade

---

[15] Critchley (1999) did a dissertation on the chiasmus between Levinas and Derrida.

[16] I read this live(d) experience through Michel de Certeau's (1984) contention that data performs as camouflage: "Combatants...move forward camouflaged as facts, data, and events. They present themselves as messengers from a 'reality.'...When they advance, the terrain itself seems to advance. But in fact they fabricate the terrain, simulate it, use it as a mask, accredit themselves by it, and thus create the scene of their law" (p. 186). How can we interrupt the performativity of norms?

[17] See Luce Irigaray (1999) for a reading which takes away from Heidegger "that earth on which he so loved to walk" (p. 2). Irigaray entices him back into the world of pre-Socrates—leads him away from metaphysics as she asks "Of what [is] this *is*? Of air" (p. 5). It is in the para-texts—in the inter-texts—in the in-between spaces that one thrives on the liveliness of the gap—the performative provocation of the gap. Paratexts infuse life into the conversation through a shift in spatial punctuation.

classroom—through the air? through the spaces between the words? through the cinders of the verb "to be"? I am intrigued with Zizek's notion of a provocative defeat—I am reading it always now in my work—in the daily toil—in the labor of words—in the provocation of what is labor in the space of the gap. And how can we double back to startle the performativity? I appear before the students to assess them—and to write them—and now the specter of the writer dwells uneasily within the tenancy of the writings. I continue to struggle with the writing-of-the-other as I read my "self" in the inscriptions. What am I leaving behind in the thrift of my writing? Who is there in the text? And how can I write spaces for escaping stigmata? What draws me to the Aokian "third" discourse is the provocative performativity of ambiguity—of uncertainty—of tensionality. Where readings resist meaning—in a distancing from the master signifier—the discourse seeks to startle and to be startled—always—as a space of hybridity that moves on...

pedagogies of the yet-to-come

Deadlines as strange demarcations as near-death experiences. Marking the departure of the writer—the arrival of the reader. Fatigue so profound that it numbs—stills—one is able to release the work to the first set of readers—die in a soft abyss of death—composting in the humiliation of exposure. In the distancing of a gesture of deliverance the writer becomes a reader of a text that is now someWhere else—a text dislocated—a text that has moved on in the liminal space of re-reading—the writer dislocated but maintaining a spectral presence. The specter always already present. And a textuality spins out of one text into another—words spinning out of control—beyond a deadline—a "dead" line as cessation—an accidental death. And now deadlines and detours converge to distract. A deadline as limit—as an invocation to transgress—as the writing leaks—spills—beneath and beyond the instant of a "dead" line. The instant of my death as writer. But the specter always already restless refusing to be still—moving on—*le revenant*—as/in that which is yet-to-come. The reader, searching in the gaps that open with the death of the writer, chases after the lack that drives desire—the desire to write on—to survive.

I have come to a reading of the cessation of writing as an accidental death. And I have just acquired a doubled gesture of writing by Blanchot and Derrida. I am reading a Derridean close reading of Blanchot while I am reading Blanchot's short story *The Instant of My Death* in French and English—fragile traces of my linguistic skills in French laboring to trouble the line of demarcation. Who is writing? Where am I—a pronominal "I" that has long since lost its topographical bearings on the map of identity? Reading between the writing and the translator—*trans*lating. How many readers are always already there to take the risk of reading elseWhere in the writing? And what about the impossibility of witnessing death? In Derrida's commentary entitled *Demeure,* he queries the impossibility of witnessing one's own death: "I am the only one who can testify to my death—on the condition that I survive it."[18] My "I" is the only witness for my death as author and to witness I must live on. Derrida reading Blanchot evokes a complicated conversation between testimony and *survivance.* Who is there to testify for the witness at the ends of writing—to witness the death of the author—a death that is not a death—*that arrives without arriving*? A specter?

Metonymic writing as a double gesture evokes on-going re-writings—something happens as the reader who is always already there re-reads the writing. And drawing from the spectral presence of Hamlet—the time is always out-of-joint. Disruptions on the slope of non/linearity—as the writing ceases only when it runs up against the last deadline. And even then a productive surge as a deadline refuses to take more or to wait any longer. And the ink begins to seep beneath and beyond a closure. A textuality that spends itself in seeking.

The void that hollows out is immediately filled with the mute and anonymous rustling of the *there is* as the place left vacant by one who died is filled with the murmur of the attendants. (Peperzak, Critchley, & Bernasconi, 1996, p. 110)

---

[18] See Derrida (2000, p. 45).

dis/closures at the ends of the signature or trafficking in signatures

Derrida contends that there is nothing outside the text—*il n'y a pas de hors-texte*. And then I'm reading Gasché reading Warminski with the notion that "[a] text is possible only because it has no self of its own."[19] And from Gerard Genette's *Paratexts*—Genette is commenting on Jacques Petit's: "The Text does not exist" as a provocation "that the work and the oeuvre are always...in progress and that the cessation of this labour, like death itself, is always to some degree accidental."[20] Where are "we" then? The "we" of a doubling gesture. Are "we" not always already everyWhere and noWhere? Is this about the radicality of the death of the "we" in the promise and the terror of the incoming other? What happens as we begin to ask questions in a "third" discourse? Could this be an Aokian Metonymic moment? As we slash the tenancy of no/thing and locate the uncanny specter of thing lurking where—there in no/thing. A para-sitic situation that dwells with/in hauntology. Chiasmatic spaces to complicate what is reading. To write the reading as a double gesture. A vigilance that requires losing one's course in order to find it—to find it there where it is not.

As soon as there is the One, there is murder, wounding, traumatism. *L'Un se garde de l'autre.* The One guards against/keeps some of the other. It protects *itself* from the other, but, in the movement of this jealous violence, it comprises in itself, thus guarding it, the self-otherness or self-difference (the difference from within oneself) which makes it One. The "One differing, deferring from itself." The One as the Other. (Derrida, 1996, p. 78)

And I have learned to listen to questions that never stop asking—questions that labor in excess of their spatial punctuations. One such question emerged when I was working as a volunteer in a cooperative bookstore and helping to train a new volunteer. There in a bookstore where signatures countersigned across categorical boundaries

---

[19] See Gasché (1999) for a reading on chiasms. And see Gasché's (1987) introduction into what is called reading in Warminski's *Readings in Interpretation*. I am reading Gasché reading Warminski in reading as interpretation that unreads.

[19] See Genette (1997, p. 402).

in an almost unbearable richness of readings. When she learned that I was a teacher she asked me why she hadn't heard about the death of the author in high school. Why had "they" made it so simple? A question that has found a tenancy in my inscriptions—I carry this question with me as a haunting. If there is an ethics of hauntology as Ronell and others contend then my debt[21] at departure lingers on. I am just beginning to seek what my schooling has stripped away in the guise of thriftiness—what Foucault might mean when he says that "[t]he author is the principle of thrift in the proliferation of meaning."[22] Foucault contends that "we must locate the space left empty by the author's disappearance, follow the distribution of gaps and breaches, and watch for the openings that this disappearance uncovers."[23] It is here that the writer at the instant of death departing from the writing begins to read on...to emerge from the "dead" line to write into the aporia of a death as a moving on...to write the questions that cannot be answered—to move them on—to let them spend...

Aoki re-writes a trope for pedagogy—a trope that dwells with/in a third discourse—a trope that trembles as it is spoken—a trope that draws from the notions of Bhabha's third space and Trinh's third ground—a trope that makes it impossible to return without sounding an acoustic hybridity in the disruptive force of iterability—a trope that dissolves thematic traces and leaves us trembling in the space of gap—of interval—of void—of lack—a trope hopelessly entangled in the spectrality of Lacanese—a trope that demands a laboring reader as host(age) with/in the writing. A trope that carries on a complicated conversation with

---

21 Michel de Certeau contends that "[t]he text is born of the relationship between a departure and a debt" (1988, p. 318). And from a footnote stepping from one text to another—Emmanuel Levinas—"...nothing can dispense me from the response which I am *passively* held to. The tomb is not a refuge; it is not a pardon. The debt remains" (in Peperzak, Critchley, & Bernasconi, 1996, p. 190). See Low and Palulis (2000) for the first published version of this haunting question that emerged in a bookstore. A question that must survive—that must live on. A question that carries my debt-as-writer.

22 See Foucault's essay "What Is an Author?" in Paul Rabinow's *The Foucault Reader* (1984, p. 118). Anthropologist Elvi Whittaker alerted me to this article as we entered into the aporia—the aporetic condition—the impossibility—of writing the other as/in ethnography.

23 See Foucault in Rabinow's *The Foucault Reader* (1984, p. 105).

deconstruction. A trope that demands a complicated pedagogy.[24] *And my readings now seek these complexities—to disrupt my complicities in the hegemonic discourses of mainstream pedagogy.*

As I read in search of Aokian Metonymies as pedagogical events—textualities as doubled gestures—I find my "self" trafficking[25] through intertexts. Trafficking through a polysemy of signatures calling up countersignatures. Trafficking through the readers reading the writings—writing the readings. High volume traffic in the intertext. Trafficking in counterfeit exchanges. Trafficking as/in *trans*lation. Trafficking as/in survival—*entamer*—biting into as/in parasite to host[26]—ec-static moments.

A phantom can thus be sensitive to idiom. Welcoming to this one, allergic to that one. One does not address it in just any language. It is a law of economy, once again, a law of the *oikos*, of the transaction of signs and values, but also of some familial domesticity: haunting implies places, a habitation, and always a haunted house. (Derrida, 1996, p. 86)

---

[24] William Pinar makes reference to the concept of curriculum as a "complicated conversation" with the phenomenological "arc of intentionality," having one end in lived experience and the other end in cited readings (Pinar, 2000, p. 41).

[25] See Sabu Kohso's (1998) "Two modes of translation, or crossing over the Pacific" in R. Ganahl (Ed.) *Imported: A reading seminar* (pp.96-105). Kohso refers to "two-way trafficking" as the two-way flow in the space of translation in-between Japanese and English involving "different ways of thinking, performing, producing, and being" (p. 97). Kohso queries a meaning-making "ghost" appearing "as the 'common essence' in the act of translation"—a ghost lingering in the domicile of "strangeness" (p. 96).

[26] See Derrida's (1993) *Aporias*, where he connects politics and spectrality. And "there is no politics...without an anamnesic and thematic relation to the spirit as ghost [*revenant*], without an open hospitality to the guest as *ghost*...whom one holds, just as he holds us, hostage" (pp. 61–62). Derrida re-inscribing his work on aporia refers to a "plural logic of the aporia...paradoxical enough so that the partitioning [*partage*]...installs the haunting of the one in the other" (p. 20).

> Deconstruction...attempts to resist its own tendencies to come to
> rest...always in movement, a going beyond which remains in
> place, as the parasite is outside the door but also always already
> within, uncanniest of guests.[27] (Miller, 1979, pp. 220–221).

My teaching praxis is always working its way into the writing—spending
itself as it bites into the textuality—demanding space in tropological
demarcations—transgressing a "dead" line. I am asked to document the
mis/demeanors of my young students—it is the second week of school.
Recording the event. The phantoms have arrived. *They're back!* How to
disturb the encroaching hegemonies? I begin now to document the
location of those who request documentation. In which discourse are
they located? I find myself the writer of a documentary caught up in
(t)exteriorities. And the specter of a reader begins to disrupt the writing.
Trinh refers to a "spectral relationship"[28] between a work and its
afterlife—a re-working with/in hauntology. Another re-reading of de
Certeau and I am enticed by his notion of a "geography of haunted
itineraries."[29] And I draw on a paper ghost for survival—for moving
on—for opening someWhere else. A documentary that is not a
documentary—a paper ghost that haunts with some degrees of
separation—in near-by conversations—a paper ghost—*uncanniest of
guests*.

---

[27] See Miller (1979) for a read on "para" as an uncanny prefix where the "shimmering"
of multiple meanings invokes a refusal to stay still.

[28] See Trinh (1999) for a discussion of interview as autotranslation—generating a
spectral relationship with a life of its own—"life-as-afterlife"—to maintain a
*trans*formative process (p. 249).

[29] See de Certeau (1986) for haunted itineraries where he acknowledges "subjective
coherence," and I begin to wonder at my affinities with these shimmering spaces of
geo/graphy (p. 45).

References

Aoki, T. (2000, April). Locating living pedagogy in teacher "research": Five metonymic moments. Paper presented at the *International Teacher Research Conference*, Baton Rouge, LA.

Bennington, G. (2000). *Interrupting Derrida*. London and New York: Routledge.

Bennington, G., and Derrida, J. (1993). Derridabase. In G. Bennington and J. Derrida (Eds.), *Jacques Derrida* (G. Bennington, Trans.) (pp. 3–316). Chicago: University of Chicago Press.

Blanchot, M. (2000). *The instant of my death* (E. Rottenberg, Trans.). Stanford, CA: Stanford University Press.

Cixous, H. (1990a). *Castration or decapitation?* (A. Kuhn, Trans.). In R. Ferguson, M. Gever, T. Trinh, and C. West (Eds.), *Out there: Marginalization and contemporary culture* (pp. 345–356). Cambridge, MA: MIT Press.

Cixous, H. (1990b). *Reading with Clarise Lispector* (V. Conley, Ed. and Trans.). Minneapolis: University of Minnesota Press.

Cixous, H. (1991). *Readings: The poetics of Blanchot, Joyce, Kafka, Kleist, Lispector, and Tsvetayeva* (V. Conley, Ed. and Trans.). Minneapolis: University of Minnesota Press.

Cixous, H. (1993). *Three steps on the ladder of writing* (S. Cornell and S. Sellers, Trans.). New York: Columbia University Press.

Critchley, S. (1999). *The ethics of deconstruction: Derrida and Levinas*. Edinburgh: University of Edinburgh Press.

de Certeau, M. (1984). *The practice of everyday life* (S. Rendall, Trans.). Berkeley, CA: University of California Press.

de Certeau, M. (1986). *Heterologies: Discourse on the other* (B. Massumi, Trans.). Minneapolis and London: University of Minnesota Press.

de Certeau, M. (1988). *The writing of history* (T. Conley, Trans.). New York: Columbia University Press.

Derrida, J. (1993). *Aporias* (T. Dutoit, Trans.). Standford, CA: Standford University Press.

Derrida, J. (1994). *Specters of Marx* (P. Kamuf, Trans.). New York and London: Routledge.

Derrida, J. (1996). *Archive fever: A Freudian impression* (E. Prenowitz, Trans.). Chicago and London: University of Chicago Press.

Derrida, J. (1998). *Resistances of psychoanalysis* (P. Kamuf, P. Brault, and M. Naas, Trans.). Stanford, CA: Stanford University Press.

Derrida, J. (2000). *Demeure: Fiction and testimony* (E. Rottenberg, Trans). Stanford, CA: Stanford University Press.

Foucault, F. (1984). What is an author? In P. Rabinow (Ed.), *The Foucault Reader* (pp. 101–120). New York: Pantheon Books.

Gasché, R. (1987). Reading Chiasms: An Introduction. In A. Warminski's *Readings in interpretation: Holderlin, Hegel, Heidegger*, (pp. ix-xxvi). Minneapolis: University of Minnesota Press.

Gasché, R. (1999). *Of minimal things: Studies on the notion of relation.* Stanford, CA: Stanford University Press.

Genette, G. (1997). *Paratexts: Thresholds of interpretation* (J.E. Lewin, Trans.). Cambridge: Cambridge University Press.

Kohso, S. (1998). Two modes of translation, or a crossing over the Pacific. In R. Ganahl (Ed.), *Imported: A reading seminar*, (pp. 96-105). New York: SEMIOTEXT(E).

Irigaray, L. (1999). *The forgetting of air in Martin Heidegger* (M. B. Mader, Trans.). Austin: University of Texas Press.

Lacoue-Labarthe, P. (1989). *Typography: Mimesis, philosophy, politics* (C. Fynsk, Trans.). Stanford, CA: Stanford University Press.

Low, M., & Palulis, P. (2000). Teaching as a messy text: Metonymic moments in pedagogical practice. *Journal of Curriculum Theorizing, 16*(2), 67–79.

Miller, J. H. (1979). The critic as host. In H. Bloom, P. de Man, J. Derrida, G. Hartman, & J. H. Miller (Eds.), *Deconstruction and criticism* (pp. 217–253). New York, NY: Continuum.

Peperzak, A. T., Critchley, S., & Bernasconi, R. (Eds.). (1996). *Emmanuel Levinas: Basic philosophical writings.* Bloomington: Indiana University Press.

Pinar, W. (2000). Strange fruit: Race, sex, and an autobiographics of alterity. In P. Trifonas (Ed.), *Revolutionary pedagogies: Cultural politics, instituting education, and the discourse of theory* (pp. 30–46). New York: Routledge.

Pollock, D. (1998). Performing writing. In P. Phelan and J. Lane (Eds.), *The ends of performance* (pp. 73–103). New York and London: New York University Press.

Ronell, A. (1986). *Dictations on haunted writing.* Lincoln and London: University of Nebraska Press.

Trinh, T. M-H. (1999). *Cinema interval.* New York and London: Routledge.

Zizek, S. (1993). *Tarrying with the negative.* Durham, NC: Duke University Press.

Zizek, S. (1999). *The ticklish subject: The absent centre of political ontology.* London and New York: Verso Press.

❱ The Third Space of Ambivalent Construction

Patricia Sorensen

In Between

"Response-ability" refers not to the ability to respond but to the ability to
see the juxtaposition, the "is" and the "is not," the "said" and the "unsaid,
the "presence" and the "absence" and to move to the "third space of
ambivalent construction."[1]

Response-ability requires dwelling in the third space, on the bridge
between the dichtotomies. With equally clear vies of both sides. The aim
is not to get to either side but to grow and develop while moving in
between.

Metonomy

juxtapose
is/is not
presence/absence
said/unsaid
understood/not really
clear/mud
give/up?
yes/no

---

[1] I am referring to a phrase Ted Aoki used while teaching in the graduate summer
institute entitled "Writing Teachers' Lives" in July 2000, at the University of
Lethbridge.

maybe…
maybe not.
chaos
ambivalence
re-formulate
generate
re-create
new directions…
Metonomy

Figure 4: Patricia Sorensen, *Trestle Bridge Across the Oldman River*
(2002), charcoal on paper
Lethbridge, Alberta
Canada

❭ "High Volume Traffic in the Intertext"[1]: After Words

William F. Pinar

What is an "afterword"? Is it a space "after words"? It is, of course, "after" the "words" in this collection, and I will try, collage-style, to perform the echoes I hear as I dwell in the space "after" these "words." The words the contributors have written reverberate through me, rewriting my space, my lived space, into another...middle space, not here, nor there, but somewhere else. I remember, it was a space where I lived long ago. It was one summer in upstate New York, when I was probably 25 years old, before I became a father, before I became gay, before I became "Bill Pinar," a place/time of infinite if unnerving possibility, "lines of flight" (Deleuze and Guattari, 1987, p. 35) amidst cool sunny summer breezes off Lake Ontario. I was reading—it was not a cliché then, she will never be for me a cliché—Virginia Woolf, Quentin Bell's biography, and *To the Lighthouse*. I was rewriting the story, so that Professor Ramsay didn't blame his family for failing to reach R, so that Mrs. Ramsay didn't aggress against herself by selfless devotion to others, so that she and Lily Briscoe became lovers and the War never happened and the summer house—a middle place neither home nor away—wasn't left abandoned to the rain and the wind and the pounding sea. I was rewriting the boat-ride to the lighthouse.

That was a long time ago, but it is also a time now in the present, as I look out the window of my study this foggy, early morning in late April 2002. This book has transported me to my own "Lynch's Lane," returned to me a remote past into my intimate present, a present now restructured as an intertext, a space in-between "the tough old stars" which hover over me, tasks to do, tasks I want to do, but which, in their number and urgency, twinkle at times too brightly. This intertext is foggy and moist;

---

[1] Patricia Palulis, this volume.

it's where I can pay attention and not know, listen to whispers of a bright cool summer morning long ago, as the words in this collection echo through me and onto this page. This intertext is—might Ted Aoki agree? —a site of living pedagogy.

Where, Ted Aoki asks, are sites of living pedagogy? Where are they located? Ted suggests that we look at the spaces between representational and non-representational discourses (after words?), what Homi Bhabha calls the "Third Space of ambivalent construction," what Trinh Minh-ha calls "a hybrid place," what David Jardine calls "the site of original difficulty" (quoted phrases in Aoki, this volume). It is this site, Ted tells us, of "ambiguity, ambivalence, and uncertainty, but simultaneously a site of general possibilities and hope." After Ted, alongside Ted, in honor of Ted, the contributors to this collection articulate this site, what the editors—Erika Hasebe-Ludt and Wanda Hurren—term *intertext*. There is here "high volume traffic in the intertext" (Palulis, this volume).

What is intertext? Sannie Yuet-San Tang quotes Erika Hasebe-Ludt who tells us that the concept "implies a multiplicity of meaning present in any text....[A]ny text is the absorption and transformation of another." In this collection, these processes of absorption and transformation are everywhere evident, for me most vividly in the regular referencing of the teaching and writing of the (yes, legendary) Ted Aoki. Contributors' absorption in Aoki's work and pedagogical presence clearly effected multiple and various transformations of "possibility" and "hope."

"High traffic volume in the intertext"? Not automobile traffic, but, as Patricia Palulis notes, "trafficking in counterfeit exchanges, trafficking as/in *trans*lation—trafficking as/in sur-vival." Traffic, then, as "movement," an "import and export trade," maybe even "illegal or disreputable commercial activity," but definitely "communication...between individuals." These are "archaic" meanings, the Webster's New Collegiate Dictionary suggests. "Movement" was one of them, "messages" another. In a bottle from the sea, from an in-between space, somewhere in inner/outer space? Is that the meaning of "high" in the phrase? Lofty, as in transcendental ego, as in distantiation and bracketing? Yes, a quiet meditative space, but "intertext" would seem to be a place of loud, high-volume silence, behind and between and after the words.

For some, words are the passages to, from, and among intertext(s); Renee Norman tells us "[i]t is enough to play/the words." For Patrick Verriour the intertext is the healing/sick body. "Each morning," he tells us, "I take the same walk starting out from one seacoast and not returning home until I have glimpsed the sea again at the other end of the road."

Carl Leggo glimpses the sea, in his memory: "Always going back in my poems, knowing I have left and never left, knowing I can/always go back and never go back, the world written in the geography of our growing up." A counselor told him: "Your first year is written in your body; your life is a series of revisions." That first year was inside his mother's body, then nearby it: "I once lived in my mother's house: Perhaps I have grown bigger, perhaps I have grown smaller." Why are you so large in your absence, Mrs. Ramsay, in your presence in me?

Patricia Palulis thinks of the building that houses the Faculty of Education where she teaches, remembering a comment about it being a very *scary* place. "Are we not speaking of a haunted house?" she asks. Are we the living haunted by those who loved us, who taught us? Do we become, as Palulis quips about the Faculty of Education structure, "a building that houses hauntology?" Let's inaugurate *that* discipline. Recalling Zizek, she asks: Does a spectrality fill the ontological gap? Is this also a gap between past and present, future and past?

"Seduction by the Superficial"[2]

David Blades paints a picture of the gap. Humanity has finally died, sometime in the future. Humanity died sometime in the twentieth century, according to Pier Paulo Pasolini, who attributed our extinction not to the desire for immortality, as does Blades, but to consumer capitalism (see Greene, 1990). Maybe these are two phrases but the same thing? In Blades' reverie, "Humans simply evolved into their machines." In the margins of the historical narrative the caretaker finds, the last living human being, an Historian, has scribbled two comments: *seduced* and *Heidegger was right*. The final pages begin with the comment: *It's OK to die*. In this comment, Blades tells us, the Historian was reacting to a comment made at the start of the twenty-first century in a keynote

---

[2] David Blades, this volume.

address at a teachers' convention: "We are in danger as a species of inventing ourselves to death."

The warning not heard, our future fate was cast; the Historian knew that "every school should have embraced a curriculum of questioning since through questions children could more deeply understand their situation and Being.... Questions are thus crucial to the survival of humanness." But "in their seduction by the superficial," Blades continues, "schools silenced the provocative questions that follow from asking why." Instead, he notes, schools sanctioned a cult of the right answer, policed by standardized examinations. "As the twenty-first century began to unfold," Blades concludes,

> teachers increasingly complained about the side effects of individualization of instruction through computer integration in schools, but no teacher association went on strike over this issue....Schools could have been the agency to develop the public collectivist ethics to determine what is morally right in the evolution of a technology....But this potential was never realized. Humans, far too comfortable with their inventions, slid into the twenty-first century in an almost comatose state, missing the opportunity to discover with children the humanizing potential of asking the important questions. The final words of the Historian served as an epitaph for humankind: "Seeking immortality, we neglected to ask why."

Karen Meyer has not neglected to ask why. As Director of the University of British Columbia's Centre for the Study of Curriculum and Instruction, Meyer's labor has been the co-creation of a "third space" wherein an educational community can become self-reflexively engaged in its own educational process. Members of the community became mobilized when budget cuts (made by administrators "seduced by the superficial"?) threatened this space; they wrote letters and arranged meetings with Faculty of Education and University administrators to appeal the cuts. Community members articulated the distinctive character of their student-centered academic unit, namely that it is a site where "individual students began to (re)consider how they want *to be* in an academic environment." How to *be*? This is—is it not?—a question of ontology and ethics, precisely the question Blades' reverie on the future invokes.

Neither are David Jardine, Sharon Friesen, and Patricia Clifford seduced by the superficial. They are interested in ontology, specifically, an ontology of mathematics and mathematics education. "What if," they ask, "instead of production and consumption, the *world* of mathematics (as a *living, breathing, contested human discipline* that has been handed down to us) needs our memory, our care, our intelligence, our work...and understanding if it is to remain hale and healthy and whole?" This is a question, they note, "posed not *by us* but *to us*." Are we haunted? Because "[t]hings are their interdependencies with all things," Jardine, Friesen and Clifford observe, "to deeply understand any thing, we must understand it as *being itself* only in the midst of all its relations." This ontological meditation reveals mathematics to be "all the actual, human, bodily work which is required if it is to remain hale and healthy, if it is to continue as a living practice which we desire to pass on, in some form, to our children." After Gadamer, David, Sharon, and Patricia assert that mathematics education, i.e., the experience of mathematics, "is not something we *possess* (like some commodifiable object) but something we *endure*, something we *undergo*." Bodily and on the earth, the ontological and ethical ground.

Jeannette Scott MacArthur is not seduced by the superficial, as her meditation on ethical research makes clear. MacArthur understands that "the system tempts us to uncomplicate the world," and that this is not only an intellectual problem, but an ethical one. She rose to the occasion: "[I] chose Obligation instead of Ethics, radical hermeneutics instead of idealistic essentialism, foolishness instead of sensibility." Following John Caputo's lead she found herself "[s]tanding, not on moral *terra firma* as expected, but, like Caputo, on ground which tended to shift." Is this the "Third Space of Ambivalent Construction" drawn in Patricia Sorensen's intertext (this volume) where she asserts that "Response-ability requires dwelling in the third space, on the bridge between the dichotomies, with equally clear views of both sides"?

"[L]anguaging in Subjectivities of Performed Relations"[3]

Sannie Yuet-San Tang knows that translation is shifting ground. Inspired by Ted Aoki, Tang asks: "What is translation? Where are translation and the translator located?" She answers that they are located intertextually. "Translation takes place," she suggests, "in what I would

---

[3] Marylin Low, this volume.

call the 'diasporic space' between cultures." Patricia Palulis knows this space:

> Diaspora is a postponement of homecoming—the gap—the void—the interval—the space of home/not home—a place of occupant and the ghost...within the same text. Uncanny.

Also inspired by "scholar and sensei, Ted Aoki," Marylin Low can appreciate Tang's sense of translation. Her Japanese student has asked her: "Can we meet?...I want us to read me together." Low reflects on the student's remarkable invitation:

> An invitation to respond to a mark is returned and, in its return, I am marked. The performative words of this student, dwelling in a global(ized) site, disrupt a comfortable certainty of how I had come to *mark* her English. In life complicated by intertexts of *différance*, cries from the margins of a pedagogical place called English as a second language (ESL) could be heard—a location the student continued to agitate and contest. And she is not the only one.

Erika Hasebe-Ludt is thinking of location, about "the where" of knowing, where she, in relation to her students, colleagues, friends, and family, situates herself "in the face of other knowledge, other traditions, and other communities, and whose knowledge we draw on, whose we challenge, in order to become wiser, more informed, more inclusive, more able to effect change." Questions of where are important for her at this time due, in part, to her own "geographical re- and dis-location." She writes:

> Traveling and living away from home, moving from Europe to Canada, moving to a different place of work, living in the tensioned space of cultural and geographical displacement, my interest is to investigate how this positioning of self in relation to other cultures and locations can be/come a generative place.

Is teacher education such a generative place? Hasebe-Ludt worries (as do I), that in becoming a teacher and a teacher of teachers, "I have become part of a relentless busyness to implement a rigidly structured and disembodied curriculum that has left few openings for creative expression for both adults and children, for us to draw, paint, sing, dance, and write together differently." But her worrying, I suspect, suggests she has managed to remain apart from such "busyness" (ed. biz), living and teaching the light(ness) she thanks Carl Leggo for offering. The "gift" of Leggo's writing is that it enables explorations of "the alchemic possibilities in the spaces of the heart."

Cynthia Chambers writes from the heart, from where she remembers "ugly conversations" she wishes she could forget, but which "keep surfacing in my memory like stones on my trail down to the river." She remembers a parting exchange with a lover of four years, a memory juxtaposed with the news of his sudden and accidental death, robbing her of the opportunity to speak with him again, to speak healing words, to him, to herself. "Death," Chambers notes, "alters the landscape of memory drastically like a volcano or an avalanche." "The landscape of memory," she continues, "is filled with these bits and pieces torn from their original circumstance, now bleached and tattered." Is the heart, then, an intertext? Chambers seems to suggest as much when she suggests: "Memory is the homeland from which you are always in exile."

It is in the spaces of his heart where Patrick Verriour struggles for his life, walking each morning to glimpse healing. "When I first started this road nearly two years," he confides, "I was still in the early stages of inoperative and incurable cancer. I could barely reach the top of the first hill before turning back. In spite of my frequent protests, my wife, physicians, and nurses told me to keep on walking." In his life and career as a drama educator, Verriour worked to teach his students "to story their lives, to be playful, to be prepared for the unpredictable and unexpected, to value their intuition and to be always shifting their perspectives of themselves and others." It was a lesson, it seems, he learned as well as he taught.

"Paying Attention and Not Knowing"[4]

In the classroom, Renee Norman remembers Ted Aoki saying: "the tension is in teaching, in living, at home. If you're alive, there's tension. If you're dead, no tension." There are numerous acknowledgments of Ted's teaching in this collection, acknowledgments of relationality, generosity, of "living pedagogy."

---

[4] Antoinette Oberg, this volume.

With gratitude Renee Norman recalls the first day of class, 1994. When she enters, Aoki is already there, a physical fact yes, but metaphoric one as well:

> *I am eager to hear him speak after reading some of his writings. What draws me to Ted's work is hope and goodness and vision. He asks us, students in a narrative/curriculum course, to introduce ourselves. I speak about the profound effect his words have had on me philosophically, about the crossroads I feel I have reached in my work, and how I intuitively sense that I am in need of Ted's wisdom and poetry in order to proceed.... I feel immediate relief that this eminent scholar openly admits to movement and change, and admiration that Ted seems constantly in motion: reading, re-reading, re-learning, re-considering. The re at work, Ted would say.*

In Ted's course Norman dwelled in what Aoki characterized as "a middle place for culture, a place where people of varying backgrounds and opinions, Eastern and Western, could meet, study, discuss, share, and laugh." She attributes the creation of this middle place to Aoki's "living pedagogy":

> *Ted created an atmosphere that both evoked difference and supported it. He envisions a cultural space that is open, inclusive, and in the middle....How does one put such a philosophy into practice? Ted did this by honoring and respecting the diversity with/in the class, pulling out the varied backgrounds that people arrived with. He did it by insisting not only that we examine the new ideas of scholars from varying backgrounds, but also that we should continually question ourselves....There was no invisibility in this class...*

Also in that 1994 class Norman remembers *"the moment that remains for me most potent and memorable,"* the moment

> *when Ted told his story of being asked several years ago where his allegiance lay when war with Japan put Canadians of Japanese descent under scrutiny. I am Canadian, Ted told us he had replied, and his quiet voice rang with dignity as he related this story....When Ted spoke these words, the very last day of the course, there was a palpable listening silence in the room: a silence permeated with past mistakes, present hopes, and future visions...A silence that laid open a new kind of cultural Canada...Here was Ted's middle place for culture....I still feel the imprint of Ted Aoki....I still hear the memory singing.*

Renee Norman honors Aoki, not only with this memory, but with a poem, five lines of which sing here.

MIDDLE PLACE
(for Ted Aoki)

Dwelling with Ted
in the and
where the teacher disappears
the I's dissolve
and in their place...

What happens when the "I's" dissolve? Antoinette Oberg knows. One is released to teach in a middle place, a place between "paying attention and not knowing." The intertextual spaces in which Oberg is interested (from the Latin *inter esse*, she points out, already in the midst of) are encounters with graduate students in which they "unfold their inquiries." "There I find that paying attention and not knowing (which I have characterized as suspending expectations and delaying the desire to conceptualize) invites another layer of a student's inquiry to unfold itself." Oberg is interested in the moment when she glimpses a "congruence" between topic and method of inquiry. "At some point during my meeting with each of these students," Oberg reports, "I perceived a patterning in what had up until that moment appeared to be formless."

Not only is Antoinette "already in the midst of" an intertextual space when she encounters her graduate students. It seems they are as well. Her pedagogy of "paying attention and not knowing" enables students to appreciate that they already know how to proceed; they know how to remove obstacles and to allow "the patterning [that] already existed in their professional work to become the patterning of their inquiries." This is self-reflexive pedagogy as well, as Antoinette "seek[s] to discern the patterning of [her] own inquiry into [her] practice of paying attention and not knowing."

"Silent Scars"[5]

There are congruencies in Ingrid Johnston's account as well, if ironic and, perhaps, uncanny. She recalls her initiation into teaching in apartheid South Africa, where she taught students in an all-white segregated high school. "As their teacher," she acknowledges, "I was

---

[5] Lynn Fels, this volume.

complicit in such framing. Nothing in my own life experience had prepared me to challenge my own or my students' assumptions about whiteness as the cultural and racial norm." Now, many years later, she finds herself a teacher educator in a faculty of education where more than 90% of the student teachers are of European descent, but many of whom are preparing to teach in urban schools whose students are not. Confronting her past and engaging the present, Johnston challenges racialization: "As a white, middle-class woman who teaches student teachers, the majority of whom are also white, I feel I should be addressing and challenging the perceived norms of whiteness." And that she does, foregrounding in her curriculum classes "the historically privileged positions of power conferred by 'whiteness'."

Aristides Gazetas, too, is interested in the pedagogical politics of cultural identities, especially as these are represented in popular culture, specifically film. In his discussion of Margaretha von Trotta's film *Marianne and Juliane* (1981), "a modernized translation of the Antigone-Creon confrontation," Gazetas emphasizes "that cultural identities are locally and historically specific, and that they become available for human understanding only within certain 'language games,' 'paradigms,' and 'discursive formations'." Gazetas argues that "von Trotta's film serves as a cultural text, as part of a postmodern society, to show (quoting Derrida) that the 'condition of possibility of deconstruction is a call for justice'."

Lynn Fels performs such "a call for justice" when she demands: "Stop! Don't destroy our forests! Who are you to reap profits from our mountains?" This demand, this question, Fels asserts under "an empty sky and in the silent scars/that map our presence."

The earth grounds Fels' calls for justice: "*At the edge of the sea, in the shelter of the mountains*, issues of environmentalism, native rights, ownership, birth, and community are spelled in the embodied interactions that are our momentary presence." It is, she reminds us, "within performance we are performed." Moreover, "our performative intertext(s) invite a re-imagining of curriculum. These new interstandings lead to changes in our practices of teaching, research, curriculum development and learning as defined and sought." Indeed, as Bruce Russell's essay testifies.

Bruce Russell is concerned with the earth as well. His hope is to "widen the curricular space" in which we have historically conceived "nature" through a pedagogy of haiku. Such a pedagogy involves "an intercultural consideration of the poetic, historical, and spiritual values that lie at the heart of a Japanese aesthetic sensibility." To illustrate, he points to the use of various devices in haiku—among them, assonance, alliteration, and internal rhyme—which, coupled with a "Zen-inspired simplicity," creates a poetry aware that being "extravagant with words may risk putting an over-played description between the reader and the lived experience the poet hopes to capture and convey." For Russell, "the essence of haiku" is "immediate life experience," experience which provides a living basis for "intergenerational dialogue"—such as Aoki's pedagogical conversations with his students—and "intersecting temporalities."

Russell is thinking of "our inability to take the time to reflect upon moments of personal significance." It is important, he suggests, to guide students in the expression of emotion, but he is not thinking of reporting "the latest experience that has moved us." Rather, he refers to a "different kind of rationality involved when one attempts to interpret the importance of the understatement" reminiscent of haiku. Also referring to Aoki, Russell suggests this sensibility might mean the "opening of many middle spaces in the curriculum," in which we can explore "the influence of events in our lives."

"A Good Place to Linger"[6]

The lingering significance of the influence of events, especially intellectual events, is evident in Leah Fowler's remembrance of "a life-altering master class with Dr. Aoki in 1985." Fifteen years later, after several years on the Pacific coast, Leah finds herself back in Lethbridge, where, she notes, "Aoki once taught as a disenfranchised Japanese Canadian schoolteacher." So layered, these "narrative plains in these Alberta spaces, where I am at home and not at home" provide the palimpsest for questions that traverse the "private" and "public," for instance: "How can narrative research lead to an aesthetic and ethical inner government of a teaching self?" As a schoolteacher Leah found herself no longer able to traverse the space between the private and the public, as "the inconsistencies and paradoxes began to erode my

---

[6] Carl Leggo, this volume.

(teaching) self." As she notes, with understatement: "Our entire education system is in deep difficulty." Through her "working from within," Leah "come[s] now to teaching with more attunement, humility, and care."

Wanda Hurren recalls Cynthia Chambers' invitation to begin at home in curricular theorizing as she formulates her notion of "auto′•geo′•carto′•graphia′," a curricular collage. In this structuration of self and place, Hurren explores "ways in which curriculum might enhance what we know of our places and our selves and...how what we know of our places and selves might enhance curriculum theory and research." "Home" would seem to be the "ground level," from where she can compose "stories of place and self within the lines of [her] everyday maps of teaching, learning, living, and researching." Why collage?

> I have chosen to use collage as a textual strategy in order to indicate how these elements, self, place, and curriculum, happen in mingling ways....Collage work requires a deliberate overlapping arrangement of bits and pieces. Within collage there are no clean edges or borderlines between the bits and pieces. In my arrangement of bits and pieces of teaching and living and learning and self and place and theory and research, my desire is to create a collage that catches up the constitutive role of the mingling dance of signification.

It is a dance "under the tough old stars," as Hurren "interrupts" her "prairie winter" to read David Jardine's collection of eco-pedagogical essays by the same title. She "emerge[s] from the readings glistening with river spray. Such a moist, scholarly text. His writing is a performance of how place and self mingle in curricular theorizing." Still under the stars, perhaps, Hurren writes:

> I turn back toward town
> welcoming the same breeze
> that has blown
> over my body
> all these years

The "ground level" where Hurren works is, yes, phenomenological; it is also the ground of the earth: "Becoming aware of where our bodies touch the earth is part of this practice [of Vipassana Insight Meditation] and it is this same awareness—being mindful of where our bodies touch the earth and noting the sensations that arise—that I want to bring to the practice of curriculum." In this essay, may I say, you have.

I have myself employed collage as a curricular figuration, in the book on lynching and prison rape (Pinar, 2001). There I tried to perform the self-shattering I imagine hegemonic white masculinity must undergo to restructure itself as "moist," to borrow Hurren's adjectival characterization of Jardine's book. Now I understand more about collage, thanks to Hurren, and about performance, thanks to Lynn Fels. Fels' work "investigates curricular places of possibility, absence, and disruption realized through performance. *Performance not as a process nor as product, but as breath, intermingling, unexpected journey landscapes reeling against the sky in a sudden moment of recognition.*" Recognition and misrecognition played structuring roles in the queer politics of "race" in nineteenth-century America.

Fels notes that, etymologically, "*performance* brings us to *form* as structure and *ance* as action, as in (d)ance. Performance is, then, both form and action." Together, as in synthesis? It is performed, she continues, on "the edge of chaos, a space where possibilities seduce and life dances into being." Fels, too, has been inspired by Ted Aoki, recalling a conversation in which Aoki "inquires about the 'impossible,' that which is not yet possible to imagine into being, that which remains beyond our grasp like the force that moves the tides, unseen yet present in all our innocence and ignorance of movement." Are racial and gender justice already present, unforeseen, in our movements? Education, Fels tells us, involves "*surprise—freefalling through moments of crisis and recognition of possibility.*"

Surprise, freefalling, crisis, and recognition of possibility: do these occur as well on Lynch's Lane in Corner Brook, Newfoundland, where young Carl Leggo is cycling "all the way to Old Man Downey's house"? Surprise and astonishment, cycling toward the sea, the same sea that draws and repels as it gives Patrick Verriour a glimpse of healing. "[A]stonishment," Leggo tells us, "is a good place to begin and a good place to linger." "I seek to disclose and know again," Carl continues,

the location of my backyard,
and how this specific geographical space
represents a location for locution in the bigger world.

These are, as he notes, "alchemic transformations." Like Carl Leggo, Renee Norman knows that "place is not necessarily a physical place, but a mental and emotional and intellectual state of being that resides in the head." She too remembers Ted Aoki speaking of place, and in so doing, "he dis/placed us in many different spaces and locations and inbetweenesses of curriculum." For Norman, "curriculum is a dream." In this place:

> days pass
> filled with plans
> filled helping others
> see their dreams
> like a fiddler
> I play on
> wanting them
> to hear the music
> not the pied piper
> I want them dancing
> to their dreams
> want the caves
> that imprison them
> empty
> ...
> when at last i enter the right room
> i see wariness in my students' eyes
> they are searching too
> it's then i know
> where i am

"[I]f curriculum is a dream," Norman notes, "I am the dreamer."

"Sublime Openness"[7]

Dreams can be messy, as Marylin Low appreciates. "Reading out of education as a way of reading in," Low thinks of Ted Aoki, whose "living pedagogy began as a psychoanalytic curiosity that invited an inter-disciplinary re-reading of education and its 'difficulties' as vibrant sites of tensional anxieties—sites that are not clean and controlled as I

---

[7] Patricia Palulis, this volume.

had been taught they should be, but as sites always already incomplete, complex, and ambiguous." Like dreams, perhaps? Low continues:

> Opening to these difficulties creates the conditions for a happenstance of radical contingencies in the classroom—what Ted Aoki inscribes as metonymic moments of living pedagogy—a living pedagogy that brings under suspicion the traditional distinctive binary of teacher/learner and rewrites teaching as a messy text.

Messy is not simple or plain. "Resisting the desire for plain language," Low continues, "I...was at once both startled and affirmed by Doug Aoki's claim that this 'translation of complex material into plain language is actually a refusal to teach.'" The father taught the son well, did he not?

Is appreciation of complexity also openness? Patricia Palulis recalls Zizek's characterization of the hole in the flag as a moment of sublime openness. In such a moment, what Palulis terms "an Aokian moment," we might remain "mindful of our location in the language of pedagogy—for just as language courses through us, we are located in discourse—a doubling movement." Is this "doubling movement" possible when we enter the gap, dwelling in the intertext? "Drawing from the Aokian notion of Metonymy as a chiasmatic 'in-between' space of metaphor/metonymy," Palulis writes, "the place of the slash—the place of the gap—is the space of generative possibilities in a drifting, uncertain habitation—in moments of persistent in/stability." Is this the "drifting" and "uncertain habitation" of the boat-ride, as the Ramsays make their way through the bright blue sea toward the lighthouse? "What happens as we begin to ask questions in a third discourse?" Palulis asks. "Could this be an Aokian Metonymic moment?" Are these the moments made parenthetical, intertextual, in this collection in the poetic and visual pieces (by Constance Blomgren, Kathy Nolan, Tasha Henry, Michelle Bertie-Holthe, and Patricia Sorensen) punctuating this collection?

"Aoki re-writes a trope for pedagogy," Palulis acknowledges, "a trope that dwells with/in a third discourse—a trope that trembles even as it speaks." She continues:

> As I read in search of Aokian Metonymies in pedagogy —textualities as doubled gestures—I find my "self" trafficking through intertexts—trafficking through a polysemy of signature and countersignatures—through the readers reading-the-writings—writing-the-readings—high volume traffic in the

intertext—trafficking in counterfeit exchanges trafficking as/in *trans*lation—trafficking as/in sur-vival—*entamer*—biting into as/in para-site to host—ec-static moments.

Ecstatic moments of "sublime openness." These are the locations of living pedagogy, are they not?

In my rewriting of the boat-ride to the lighthouse, Mrs. Ramsay is there, umbrella open to protect her face from the bright crisp sun on the sea. Professor Ramsay, Cam, and James, yes, they are still there, but Andrew is too (not killed in the Great War), and Prue as well. There are sandwiches and drink, blue brightness all round. Father and son are reconciled. But Mrs. Ramsay doesn't notice; her eyes are fastened onto the hill below the summer house where her beloved Lily Briscoe sits, looking intently at her canvas: "It was blurred." "With a sudden intensity," we are told, "as if she saw it clear for a second, she drew a line there, in the center. It was done; it was finished. Yes, she thought, laying down her brush in extreme fatigue, I have had my vision" (Woolf, 1927/1955, p. 310). Thanks to Erika Hasebe-Ludt and Wanda Hurren and those you brought to this book/intertext, now, thanks too to our "line in the centre"—the living pedagogy of Tetsuo Aoki—we too have had our visions. May they reverberate—as "after-words"—in ourselves and our students.

References

Bell, Q. (1972). *Virginia Woof: A biography.* New York: Harcourt Brace Jovanovich, Inc.

Deleuze, G., and Guattari, F. (1987). *A thousand plateaus: Capitalism and schizophrenia* (B. Massumi, Trans. and Foreword). Minneapolis: University of Minnesota Press.

Greene, N. (1990). *Pier Paolo Pasolini: Cinema as heresy.* Princeton: Princeton University Press.

Pinar, W. F. (2001). *The gender of racial politics and violence in America: Lynching, prison rape, and the crisis of masculinity.* New York: Peter Lang.

Woolf, V. (1955/1927). *To the lighthouse.* New York: Harcourt, Brace & Company.

❭ Contributors

Ted T. Aoki taught in Alberta public schools for nineteen years, receiving both his bachelor's degree in social studies education and his master's degree from the University of Alberta and completing his doctoral degree in curriculum studies at the University of Oregon. In addition to achieving assistant, associate, full and emeritus professorships at the University of Alberta, he holds honorary degrees from the University of British Columbia, the University of Lethbridge, and the University of Western Ontario. He has been honored by the Canadian Education Association as well as the American Educational Research Association. In 1994 he was named a Kappa Delta Pi Laureate.

Karen Meyer is interested in re-imagining academic community, particularly around graduate studies. She is exploring pedagogical spaces and alternative ways of engaging in academic contexts; the asking of ourselves, How do we want to be in the academy? And, What is our relationship and contribution within local and global communities? Karen is Director of the Centre for Curriculum and Instruction in the Faculty of Education at the University of British Columbia.

Sannie Yuet-San Tang is completing her Ph.D. in Nursing at the University of British Columbia, Canada. Her dissertation research looks into the "discourse of culture" in health care, and how the "text" reproduces the political economy of health care in a neo-colonial and neo-liberal state such as Canada.

Constance Blomgren currently teaches at Matthew Halton Community School in Pincher Creek, Alberta. She has taught from the elementary to adult level. Her scholarly interests include hermeneutics, semiotics, and photography and her master's thesis was a qualitative exploration of the significance of family photographs. Initiated with the class that formed the focus for this piece, black and white portrait photographs of students forms a new area of artistic and scholarly interest for her.

David W. Jardine is Professor of Education in the Faculty of Education, University of Calgary. He is the author of three books, *Speaking with a Boneless Tongue* (1992), *To Dwell with a Boundless Heart* (1998), and *Under the Tough Old Stars* (2000) as well as numerous articles on curriculum, hermeneutics, and classroom practice. He is a co-author with Patricia Clifford and Sharon Friesen of the forthcoming book *Re-Imagining "The Basics" of Teaching and Learning*. He lives with his family in Bragg Creek, a small community in the foothills of the Rocky Mountains west of Calgary, Alberta.

Patricia Clifford and Sharon Friesen are co-founders of the *Galileo Educational Network Association*, which helps teachers and students explore the generative possibilities of teaching and learning in technologically enabled environments. Between them they have over fifty years of classroom teaching experience. They recently won the Prime Minister's Award for Teaching Excellence and have published several articles in journals such as *Harvard Educational Review*.

Jeanette Scott MacArthur is a drama educator whose experience includes a number of years of teaching in public schools in British Columbia as well as in the Teacher Education Program at the University of British Columbia.

Marylin Low's interests include languages and literacies in a global era, assessment and the post-colonial subject, and messy texts of living pedagogy. Her earlier pedagogic experiences involved international students from Japan. She currently works in remote and linguistically/culturally diverse areas of the Pacific region with elementary teachers in literacy and assessment.

Kathy Nolan is an Assistant Professor in Mathematics and Science Education at the University of Regina. Her research interests include teacher education, math and science epistemology, and critical and narrative research methodologies. Her contribution in this book is drawn from her doctoral dissertation entitled *Shadowed by Light, Knowing by Heart: Preservice Teachers' Images of Knowing (in) Math and Science.*

Patrick Verriour is currently on medical leave from the University of British Columbia, where he has taught drama in education in the Department of Language and Literacy Education since 1978. His research and writings are concerned with the imagination, and the interconnections people make in their lives through dramatic play and story.

Bruce David Russell was raised in New Brunswick and teaches in the Vancouver school district. He is currently pursuing doctoral studies ("Intertextuality and Inner-City Education") under Ted Aoki's guidance at the University of British Columbia's Centre for the Study of Curriculum and Instruction.

Cynthia Chambers lives in Lethbridge, Alberta, where she teaches curriculum studies at the University. She writes creative non-fiction as curriculum inquiry. Her work weaves memory, collective history and theory into social critique; telling the truth, as she understands it in the moment of the living, the teaching and the writing.

Wanda Hurren lives by "the lake" in Regina, Saskatchewan, and is Associate Professor in the Faculty of Education at the University of Regina. Her research and writing focus on issues of curriculum, identity, spatial practices, and epistemology. She is the author of *Line Dancing: An Atlas of Geography Curriculum and Poetic Possibilities* (2000).

Antoinette Oberg is Associate Professor and Graduate Advisor in the Department of Curriculum and Instruction at the University of Victoria. Her research focuses on her practices related to students' experiences of inquiry. The keystone of these practices is acknowledging that students arrive already situated in their inquiries.

Carl Leggo is a poet and Associate Professor in the Department of Language and Literacy Education at the University of British Columbia where he teaches courses in writing, curriculum, and narrative research. He lives joyfully with his wife, daughter, and son in Steveston near the Fraser River.

Erika Hasebe-Ludt was born and raised in Germany, studied at the Freie Universität Berlin, and taught with the Vancouver School District and at Simon Fraser University. She researches and teaches in the area of teacher education at the University of Lethbridge, Alberta. Her interests focus on interdisciplinary intercultural issues in curriculum, literacy, and life/writing. She lives by the coulees in Lethbridge and by the harbor in Vancouver, with her family.

Leah Fowler teaches undergraduate pre-service teachers and graduate students at the University of Lethbridge. Her research focuses on difficulty in teaching and narrative research methods in curriculum studies and language arts. Her new book (manuscript submitted for publication) is called *A Curriculum of Difficulty: Stories and Narrative Analysis in Educational Research.*

Lynn Fels is currently coordinating editor of *Educational Insights* for the Centre for the Study of Curriculum and Instruction, Faculty of Education, University of British Columbia. Her work investigates performance as a journey-landscape of inquiry and pedagogical exploration. Keenly involved in performing arts education, she spends free moments planting tulips in her Vancouver garden.

Aristides Gazetas received his PhD in Educational Studies from the University of British Columbia in 1997. Since then he has written two books on film narratives, *Imagining Selves: The Politics of Representation*, and *An Introduction to World Cinema*, both published in 2000. He taught Art History and Film Studies at the University of British Columbia for over fifteen years. He resides in Richmond, BC, with his wife. They now are proud grandparents of two grandchildren.

Tasha Henry teaches Creative Writing and Drama to secondary school students in Toronto, Ontario. She is currently a candidate in the Master's of Education Graduate Program at York University. Her research interests involve looking at the relationship between ethics, pedagogy and the literary imagination. Tasha is also a published poet who maintains that writing is one of her necessary survival tools.

David Blades is an Associate Professor of Science Education at the University of Victoria, BC. An award-winning scholar and teacher, his research focuses on the philosophy of science and technology education with an emphasis on the implications of ethics, cultural diversity, and interdisciplinary/international approaches for school science education program development.

Ingrid Johnston is an Associate Professor in the Department of Secondary Education at the University of Alberta. Her research interests are in the area of postcolonial literary theory, curriculum studies, teacher education, and issues of cultural difference.

Michelle Bertie-Holthe is pursuing her graduate studies in education at the University of Lethbridge. She has taught secondary English in classrooms in Southern Alberta. Her research interests are in the area of autobiographical inquiry, difference, and marginalization.

Renee Norman is a poet and writer who teaches language/literacy, curriculum, gender, autobiography, and drama courses at the University of British Columbia. She is the recipient of the 2000 Distinguished Dissertation Award from the Canadian Association for Curriculum Studies. Her poems, stories, and articles have been published in many literary and academic journals and in newspapers. Her book *House of Mirrors: Performing Autobiograph(icall)y in Language/Education* was published by Peter Lang in 2001.

Patricia Palulis is a teacher in the Vancouver School District and has recently completed her PhD in the Centre for the Study of Curriculum and Instruction at the University of British Columbia. She has taught in England, Japan, and Libya and in the Canadian Arctic and is interested in language and spatiality.

Patricia Sorensen has worked with children, teachers, and parents as a speech-language pathologist for sixteen years. She also has two wonderful school-aged children. She recently returned to university to work on a Ph.D. in neuroscience where she explores the neurological underpinnings of fetal alcohol syndrome.

William F. Pinar is appointed to the College of Education and to Women's and Gender studies at Louisiana State University, where he serves as the St. Bernard Parish Alumni Endowed Professor. He has also served as the Frank Talbott Professor at the University of Virginia and the A. Lindsay O'Connor Professor of American Institutions at Colgate University.

Studies in the Postmodern Theory of Education

General Editors
Joe L. Kincheloe & Shirley R. Steinberg

Counterpoints publishes the most compelling and imaginative books being written in education today. Grounded on the theoretical advances in criticalism, feminism, and postmodernism in the last two decades of the twentieth century, Counterpoints engages the meaning of these innovations in various forms of educational expression. Committed to the proposition that theoretical literature should be accessible to a variety of audiences, the series insists that its authors avoid esoteric and jargonistic languages that transform educational scholarship into an elite discourse for the initiated. Scholarly work matters only to the degree it affects consciousness and practice at multiple sites. Counterpoints' editorial policy is based on these principles and the ability of scholars to break new ground, to open new conversations, to go where educators have never gone before.

For additional information about this series or for the submission of manuscripts, please contact:

Joe L. Kincheloe & Shirley R. Steinberg
c/o Peter Lang Publishing, Inc.
275 Seventh Avenue, 28th floor
New York, New York 10001

To order other books in this series, please contact our Customer Service Department:

(800) 770-LANG (within the U.S.)
(212) 647-7706 (outside the U.S.)
(212) 647-7707 FAX

Or browse online by series:
www.peterlangusa.com